PIER REVIEW

A ROAD TRIP IN SEARCH OF THE GREAT BRITISH SEASIDE

JON BOUNDS AND DANNY SMITH

PIER REVIEW

Copyright © Jon Bound

All rights reserved.

No part of this book m̶a̶y̶ ̶b̶e̶ ̶r̶e̶p̶r̶o̶d̶u̶c̶e̶d̶ ̶i̶n̶ ̶a̶n̶y̶ ̶f̶o̶r̶m̶ nor transmitted
nor translated into a m̶a̶c̶h̶i̶n̶e̶ ̶l̶a̶n̶g̶u̶a̶g̶e̶,̶ ̶w̶i̶t̶h̶o̶u̶t̶ ̶t̶h̶e̶ ̶w̶r̶i̶t̶t̶e̶n̶ ̶p̶e̶r̶m̶i̶s̶s̶i̶o̶n̶
of the publishers.

Jon Bounds and Danny Smith have asserted their right to be identified as
the authors of this work in accordance with sections 77 and 78 of the
Copyright, Designs and Patents Act 1988.

Condition of Sale
This book is sold subject to the condition that it shall not, by way of
trade or otherwise, be lent, resold, hired out or otherwise circulated in
any form of binding or cover other than that in which it is published and
without a similar condition including this condition being imposed on the
subsequent purchaser.

Summersdale Publishers Ltd
46 West Street
Chichester
West Sussex
PO19 1RP
UK

www.summersdale.com

Printed and bound by CPI Group (UK) Ltd, Croydon, CR0 4YY

Paperback ISBN: 978-1-84953-811-4
Hardback ISBN: 978-1-84953-941-8

Substantial discounts on bulk quantities of Summersdale books are
available to corporations, professional associations and other organisations.
For details contact Nicky Douglas by telephone: +44 (0) 1243 756902,
fax: +44 (0) 1243 786300 or email: nicky@summersdale.com.

CONTENTS

AUTHORS' NOTE

We've always loved the seaside – and the tantalising glimpses of a better life you get when you're only there for a couple of days or weeks.

Like most good things, this started with us drunk and laughing at a silly pun. Neither of us had cared much about piers before, but the more we thought about them, piers became an integral part of the memories we wanted to explore. Each beach would be a cultural Madagascar evolving its own unique pier species. And we would get to eat a lot of chips.

So we press-ganged an acquaintance into doing the driving. We told him he would get a free, albeit working, holiday and then we tried to figure out what it would cost us. We hadn't even got the petrol money, but luckily someone had recently rebranded 'begging' as 'crowdfunding'; a plan was born. We promised updates, postcards and all sorts of rewards to those who slipped us a few quid for the camping, kiss-me-quick hats and penny arcades. We had to promise to write a book too.

We even had plans to make up sticks of rock with the words of Danny's mum when he told her what we were doing: 'You're wasting your life.'

We are, still, but don't let that spoil our postcard from the Great British seaside.

Hi-de-Hi!

Jon and Danny

ROUTE MAP

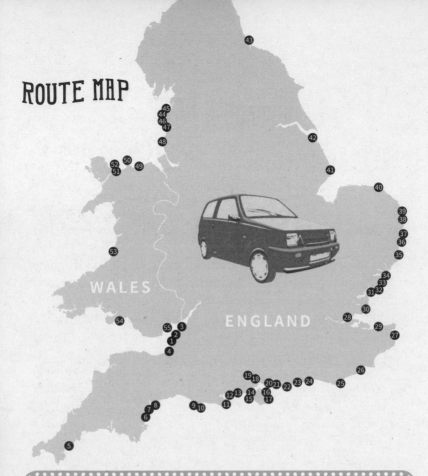

WALES

ENGLAND

1. Weston-super-Mare, Grand
2. Weston-super-Mare, Birnbeck
3. Clevedon
4. Burnham-on-Sea
5. Falmouth, Prince of Wales
6. Paignton
7. Torquay, Princess
8. Teignmouth
9. Weymouth, Commercial & Pleasure
10. Weymouth, Bandstand
11. Swanage
12. Bournemouth
13. Boscombe
14. Yarmouth, Isle of Wight
15. Totland Bay, Isle of Wight
16. Ryde, Isle of Wight
17. Sandown, Isle of Wight
18. Hythe
19. Southampton, Royal

20. Southsea, Clarence
21. Southsea, South Parade
22. Bognor Regis
23. Worthing
24. Brighton, Palace
25. Eastbourne
26. Hastings
27. Deal
28. Gravesend, Town
29. Herne Bay
30. Southend-on-Sea
31. Clacton-on-Sea
32. Walton-on-the-Naze
33. Harwich, Ha'penny
34. Felixstowe
35. Southwold
36. Lowestoft, South
37. Lowestoft, Claremont
38. Great Yarmouth, Britannia

39. Great Yarmouth, Wellington
40. Cromer
41. Skegness
42. Cleethorpes
43. Saltburn
44. Blackpool, Central
45. Blackpool, North
46. Blackpool, South
47. St Annes
48. Southport
49. Colwyn Bay, Victoria
50. Llandudno
51. Bangor, Garth
52. Beaumaris
53. Aberystwyth, Royal
54. Mumbles
55. Penarth

CHAPTER ONE

ALL QUIET ON THE WESTON FRONT

'WAKE UP WAKE UP WAKE UP'
  'WAKE UP'
  'WAKE UP'
  'WAKE'
  'BLOODY'
  'UP'

I've been texting 'WAKE UP' for an hour. I have, by now, packed. I've also put the fire on because it's September and I get the feeling that this might be the last time, maybe until next summer, that I will be warm. The television is giving me an Amber Wind Warning and I am in the process of deciding whether to find out what one of those actually is when Jon calls. He sounds delicate, like he is putting a brave face on. I've got to go back to his house to help pack the car. He tells me he'll be a few minutes, so I figure I've got an hour.

Okay, I'm up.

Back at Jon's and he still hasn't packed, so he's doing it now. This involves him grumpily banging round his house in surly confusion while me and his girlfriend answer obvious questions.

'Will I need a towel?' shouts Jon from upstairs. Apparently there are no questions too stupid, but there are naive, hangover-induced ones which can flummox you with their simplicity.

'Do you want to use mine?'

'Will the campsites have them?' comes the answer.

'Would you use a communal towel left in a public shower room even if they existed?'

You can hear him thinking for a beat.

'So do I need one?' says Jon.

'YES,' both me and his girlfriend shout in near unison. I decide to make myself busy and pack the car, something that will be my job for the next two weeks. I'm good at packing cars: I expect it's from years of playing Tetris.

———————

I've not driven half a mile when I get a voicemail from my other half to tell me I've forgotten my iPod. Too late, we're on the road. This reminds me that despite thinking hard about which towel to bring I didn't pick one up.

Midge, our designated driver, doesn't feel comfortable enough driving my car on the motorway straight away, so it's me who will drive to our first pier. My car, as the cheapest travel option, will take on the 2,000-mile trip. It's a ten-ish-year-old Renault Clio which hasn't exactly been badly maintained but I know nothing of cars, so leave it to its yearly service.

Midge is waiting outside his house when we get there, economically packed. We get his kit into the car easily and head straight to the nearest petrol station. This is the real start to our journey. We break into the float for the trip with 50 quids' worth of unleaded. We've budgeted about £250 for fuel, based on the very roughest of estimates.

Immediately we hit a problem: none of us knows where the M5 is. Or, I know one way to it, but we're already on the road and

I'm pretty sure it's in the other direction. The satnav we're to rely on so much during this adventure is useless for such short-term decision-making so I take charge and head into town, hoping to see a sign.

Ganesha is 'Lord of New Beginnings, Remover of Obstacles, and a Patron of Letters, Writing and The Arts' and it's only fitting, when the journey begins, to pay tribute on a makeshift shrine at a petrol station in Sheldon. As Ganesha is fond of offerings of red sweets, I put down some cherry throat sweets and Big Red chewing gum. I say a quick prayer while Midge, who we picked up with a small rucksack ten minutes earlier, looks on with confused disgust. My belief system is either a complex mess or devastatingly simple depending on my mood or willingness to explain.

'What's that for?' he asks.

I explain about Ganesha and how he's the perfect totem for the beginning of the journey.

'But you're not Hindu,' Midge points out.

'I don't have to be: I'm just using it to focus our intentions and, hopefully, use our will to affect our reality. The simplest definition of magic there is,' I explain.

'That's bollocks,' says Midge.

'Oh, it's that too.'

Ritualistically, and with the affectation I've come to expect, Danny is fiddling with an image of the Hindu god of travellers. We'll need luck, but I'm not sure there are any gods we can appease at this stage. For what is the god, or who is the saint, of the pointless?

––––––––––

Weston-super-Mare is the only place to start the journey. The whole way down the motorway my memory is jogged by certain vistas and road angles, including the moment the motorway splits and winds around a sheer drop to the right. I remember it because without fail this would be the point where my mother would freak out because she's scared of heights, and my dad would plaintively explain that short of taking a 20-mile diversion this was the only way they could go. Looking back I'm sure there was the hint of a smile on my dad's face.

––––––––––

Weston-super-Mare is the spiritual home of the Birmingham worker. It's often – disparagingly, one would assume – called 'Birmingham-on-Sea'. It is the nearest seaside resort to our hometown and was the place we felt compelled to visit first.

Every pointless escapade must have rules – in fact, rules are even more important when the objective isn't. Danny's idea of visiting every pier in the country, which he told me about one late night in our local, didn't have any more structure than that. We resolved to do it, without doing anything rash like doing anything about it.

Around a year later the plan was resurrected. The more we thought about it, the more piers cropped up in culture: we'd seen them in adverts and pop videos, heard of fires and anniversaries on the news. Many were nearly 200 years old and felt hugely connected to our own past.

This time we went as far as searching for piers on the Internet, and discovered the National Piers Society, who publish a list of 'surviving piers'. That list became our target and our godhead, once we'd rationalised it down to something we thought roughly manageable. The process went like this: there are only two piers in Scotland, they're miles away, so let's not do Scotland. Okay, England and Wales then. Does the Isle of Man count? Well, it has its own parliament so maybe not. The Isle of Wight counts, though. That left 55 'surviving' (a word we didn't care enough about to fully appreciate its definition) 'piers' (ditto), which were all seemingly within reach – but only by car if we were going to do it in one go.

This led us to search for a driver. If Danny wasn't driving – and he can't – I wasn't driving either, which led us to being rebuffed by most of the people we could usually nudge into supporting us, which in turn led me to tossing my keys to a man whose real name I'd only learned because I needed to put it on the car insurance and with whom I'd probably never spent more than a few hours in my life. Danny didn't and still doesn't know Midge's real name, but anyone who trusts us gains our trust in return.

———

Midge is always there. Any meet-up, party, hootenanny, social, mixer or get-together, Midge'll turn up. Crucially, Midge is unemployed and has got nothing better to do. I consider him one of Birmingham's spirit loci, a permanent feature in the landscape. He is a small and wiry man who is almost impossible to age except for his references to 'before your time'. We get him good and drunk and ask him in front of a crowd if he'll be up for it.

———

Midge's involvement also adds a rule. We've got to get him back to sign on. Two weeks is our absolute limit.

———

The traffic is minimal but I would be hard pushed to name the amount of time it takes to get from Birmingham to Weston-super-Mare because I am far too excited. It's long enough for Jon to shake his hangover anyway.

When I was ten I was put in the car with some friends of my mum. They were driving down to Weston for the day and I was going so I could keep their eldest son company because we 'got on'. We didn't get on. It's just that I was the only person in class that didn't pick on him despite his habit of sticking his fingers up his bum and making people smell them. I later found out he became a police officer. We drove for two hours, which in kid time is ten squillion billion hours, and when we got there the pier was closed. Everything was closed. We sat in the car for a bit, had a walk on the beach, ignored the smell coming from Trevor's fingers, and drove the ten squillion billion hours home. I mention all this because when Jon parks in the car park, and we get to the front, I get the same feeling because, again, pretty much the entire front is closed. Everything except the pier. I look at Jon – if you squint, Jon looks like a cross between Philip Seymour Hoffman and Paddington Bear.

'The tide's out,' I say, scanning the vista.

'The tide's always out in Weston,' Jon says darkly.

———

I pull into a shopping-centre car park in Weston-super-Mare, get out of the driver's seat and, as theatrically as I can manage after two hours' driving with a hangover, toss the keys to Midge with 'that's me done, anyone for a pint?' In truth I do expect to drive, or at least share the driving, as we go – it would be unfair not to – but I'm in serious need of a drink and this is a way of announcing that intention without seeming desperate. From the car park, I don't know where the pier is, none of us do. I have been to Weston before, quite a few times, but don't recall ever having seen the seafront.

The shopping-centre exit deposits us on a patch of grass, ringed by shrubs and benches in the best regenerative style, with no clear route to our first pier. Grand Pier has been regenerated too, but not to the extent of putting signs up on this side of the grass. Regeneration always has a habit of wanting to keep you in its landscaped bosom. The developer–council partnerships don't extend to partnerships with the rest of a town, especially if it's been paid for from a different pot of money.

We wander around the town, taking in what look like more seafront-y streets based on the types of shops and the names of pubs. The surroundings become more beaten and ripe for generation, re- or otherwise, and we strike local colour. Opposite a near-brutalist college building is a piece of what must be civic-sanctioned graffiti. In modern stencil style it depicts what I eventually twig to be famous sons of Weston. John Cleese – although the front-on orthographic projection of his silly walk gives his face a Terry Jones quality I'm sure he wouldn't like – is easy to place. Jeffrey Archer is a little more difficult. Even the most 'localistic' of citizens must have thought it odd to celebrate the Lord High Perjurer but, no, he's there, smugly peering over the harbour wall. The others I can't place, but these two beacons of the middle class are auspicious icons for the start of the trip: one funny but with age not as nice as I'd thought; the other nice but with age not as honest as… well, just not honest.

————————

Originally opened in 1904, Grand Pier is the newest pier on the list and has been open less than a year after the second devastating fire in its 107-year history. The first fire happened in 1930 and cost the subsequent owners £60,000. The second fire came as recently as 2008 after what officials concluded was probably an electrical fault. This fire happened just after a million-pound refurb and a further £39m was then needed to turn it into the glistening white structure that now juts out from the curve of Weston's beach. There's a covered walkway in the middle of the promenade with a gently undulating, patterned roof that was probably described as 'an echo of the sea's dynamic waveform' by a very expensive architect. Halfway up is a hut that sells beer in plastic pint glasses to refresh the dads whose three-hour driving stint shouldn't have to wait the full length of the pier to be rewarded.

Describing itself as the 'ultimate indoor theme park', it is a surprise to arrive at the arcade complex to the sound of David Essex telling us to hold him close and not let him go. Surely the soundtrack to the 'ultimate indoor theme park' is frantic European techno? Or 15-ft robot Vengaboys playing Jive Bunny covers on an endless loop? If we'd been further on in our trip, we wouldn't have been surprised at hearing David Essex, because David, as we would find out, haunts the south coast like a varnished cockney ghost.

WESTON-SUPER-MARE Grand

Opened: 1904 (Architect: P. Munroe; Angus Meek for 2010 rebuild)

Length at start: 1,300 ft (396 m), extended temporarily by 1,500 ft (457 m) in 1907

Length now: 1,300 ft (396 m)

Burn baby burn? Twice, once in 1930, and again in 2008.

The last of the so-called 'Grand Piers' to be built, it was extended in 1907 to dock steamers at the sea end, but the currents proved too strong and the extension was demolished. Still supported by 360 original cast-iron piles from 1904 along with 71 new steel piles added in 2010.

The Grand Pier is a proper pier, one you'd imagine if I said the word to you out of the blue, with arcades, shops and candyfloss. The shops are very keen to tell you all about the rebuilding by letting you purchase books and DVDs. I flick through a book that tells me proudly that a scene from *The Remains of the Day* was filmed on the pier, and of the many, many fires and many, many owners in its history. It does seem a little like the wrapping has yet to be taken off – for a building that's designed to be so open to the elements, it's not got a mark on it. Like the shopping area, it's a little too clean – antiseptic even – a bit corporate. We're searching for a bar, for something to do as much as anything. The eating area is service-stationesque and dry. It occurs to us that we need to work out what we'll be doing when we get to these piers. Walking their length and reaching the end of each is already off the agenda, for here only corporate clients get to do that.

The massive multistorey arcade looks like London's Trocadero. Or how the Trocadero used to look, not how it looks now, which is like a post-apocalyptic bartering hall. Weston Pier has several floors of exciting, but closed-looking, rides and huge arcade machines. Hidden about them are still the tuppenny sliders and ratty eighties fruit machines. I'm not sure if they ran out of attractions or kept some of the old ones for the nans. We note the 4D cinema and postulate that perhaps a pedant pointed out that time is also a measurable dimension. We walk past the Laser Maze, the dodgems, the go-kart track and Crystal Maze (which is just a hall of mirrors rebranded for the 'meh' generation). The Psychedelic Experience, from what I can make out, is a series of darkened rooms with black lights and decorations you crawl around while wearing paper glasses with light-polarising lenses. It's branded as a 'sixties experience', suggesting the only notable thing about the decade that brought us civil rights, youth culture and leaps in technology was mind-bending drug use. I swipe a pair of the gaudy paper glasses.

───────

Captain Jack's bar is in darkness, the doors from the arcade are locked, the dark wood looks cold, the shadows gloomy. We approach it from the outside – the 'stunning outside terrace'. A woman with a pushchair struggles with the door but gains entry. Danny inches in, shuffling against the wind, leaning forward, letting his open shirt billow around his T-shirt like a cape. But an unlocked door is not an invitation to the Captain's table. There is no more life in the saloon than in the fibreglass Johnny Depp that guards it. Naming a family bar after a Disney character, even one that's a notorious alcoholic, is an odd move. Not that this Jack is in any way official. Like the insurance-pimping meerkats in the claw games, this is culture appropriated, not licensed. Better surely, would be a Merchant Ivory-themed tearoom.

Oddly appropriated too. The rebuild happened in 2010, years after the first *Pirates of the Caribbean* film, so it can't have been at its most ubiquitous, and piracy doesn't seem to be a very Weston thing in any event. It's not a grand naval town or port; it doesn't even have the history of smuggling that the Cornish coast can claim. It seems part of the fourth film in the franchise was filmed not too far away, about 150 miles down the road in St Ives. So it's possible that after exhausting the heady, arty delights of the mini Tate they have there, the faux-pirate band could have sought a more boisterous tavern up the A30.

───────

Holding onto Midge's shirt so he isn't carried off in the wind, we walk back towards land, trying to ignore the frantic sound of the Walls-ice-cream-branded flags snapping backwards and forwards in the wind.

Jon wants what's known in the drinking game as an 'evener', that is a drink during a hangover to get you back on an even keel. Personally, I try never to drink before 3.30 p.m. because, well, a man's got to have rules. But on holiday all rules are suspended so I am eager for the first official pint of the trip.

The sea is always out at Weston and the pubs are always shut, it seems. After several failed attempts to get into a clearly open tourist information office we chance walking into the town. The further from the front you go, the more Weston transforms into an average working-class market town; a shopping centre, bored-looking youths and vomit shadows in the fire escapes. We detour back towards the front and finally settle for the Wetherspoon's because if we can't open a set of doors that haven't stopped several old people from getting into the tourist information centre, I don't fancy our chances in town.

———

Johnny Depp may indeed have stumbled, Keith Richards-like, into the very same Wetherspoon's pub we do now. The nautical stylings and cheap burger offers may have attracted him. It may have been, as it is with us, that all of the more interesting and independent-looking places were shut at 3 p.m. on a Monday. We have scouted and baulked at venue after venue until, eventually, the consistency of a chain has triumphed over the desire to see the town properly. Standing at the bar there's a sort of decision to be made. We have our pier budget, but we've been unable to decide quite what this covers. We've had plenty of time to think about it, but we've been lazy and often a bit drunk when we were planning. We're discussing this, still working out our new, more intense relationships while ordering, and the barman struggles to focus on what we're after (lagers and a coke for the driver).

———

The Cabot Court Hotel is large and has many levels, mostly decked out in the uniform Wetherspoon's decor: new wood stained old, coffee-house beige and framed history on the walls that only the most socially awkward or stood-up will ever read. One level is themed quite convincingly as below deck on the most relaxed ship ever, even going to the trouble of having two large window-shaped screens showing the wake of what one would presume is a large boat. I decide we should sit outside and perhaps enjoy the last of the sun. As soon as we step outside the gale takes a quarter of my pint, turns it into lager vapour and distributes it over a spluttering, near-blind Midge. We head inside laughing at our soaked friend.

———

While it's not exactly the interior of the *Black Pearl*, there are maps and moody lighting – enough to convince you that it might be the skinny one from *The Office* sitting in an unlit alcove talking to a girl in jeggings.

We're starting to appropriate culture too. David Essex's big hit 'Hold Me Close' was playing as we entered the Grand Pier and it's an instant hit with us. It's one of those songs that it's impossible not to 'do the accent' for when singing, which enhances its comedy potential and makes it acceptable for men to indulge each other with. Danny starts first, a wavering cockney attempt at the title line, which soon overwhelms sentient thought. Which means it's started: leave a group of males together for an extended period of time and conversation will soon be drowned in a mess of stock phrases and in-jokes. Less than four hours into the trip was a little sooner than I expected, but I guess that the planning stages brought us together and exhausted the 'getting-to-know-you shit' that might have held this point off.

I don't know Midge well, but just how well I've come to know Danny Smith is still a little unnerving. Like Midge, I first met him at a meeting in a city-centre pub for – and yes, this is a bit nerdish – bloggers. That is, people who defined themselves by the fact they wrote blogs on the Internet. Midge I liked, still like a lot, and see in a fair number of social situations. But Danny and I have become much closer than that.

The reason for this is something to do with shared backgrounds; most of the people who live near us, and most of those in our social circle, are not 'local'. Graduate careers and easy mobility (geographical if not social) do mean that you end up spending a lot of time with people where the common ground is culture and the now. The past is more difficult to work with. The lack of a race memory of where you live means that experience gets homogenised. No matter how much you have in common, place will create a deeper bond. We're both a little obsessed with a 'local businessman' (his words and, officially, those of the police too) from the seventies and may surely be the only people in their early thirties to have read his poorly written and boastful autobiography.

We also have class in common, both being educated working-class kids now a little uncomfortable both in our middle-class surroundings and with our history, and that has to be part of the roots of this project. Working-class people of our age from Birmingham didn't go to the seaside for summer holidays. We were born at the boom of the package holiday, and if you're not from the Midlands you can't understand just how alien the coast seems to us. We have a foot in both the future and the past: and piers seem to have that too.

Danny knows things about me that almost no one else does, including many of my trigger points for self-destruction. I've just got to trust him, myself and Midge as well. Our driver, too, will have learned much that's unpalatable about me by the time we reach the last pier.

———

Weston-super-Mare has two piers. The creeping spectre of our own poor planning shows its ghoulish humdrum face when we realise that we have no idea where the other pier is. Our mobile devices, those slick slabs of plastic and magic that all three of us expend furtive glances and spare minutes on, are rendered near useless. It seems that out of the major cities in England, mobile phone coverage is as rare as Tory tears. After a few minutes of screen-tapping frustration without any signal, Jon exhales angrily and mutters 'I have no idea how these animals live' as he heads to the bar to ask the less-than-cognisant bar staff for directions.

Assured it's 'that way', we head off. We asked for the list of all the working piers in England and Wales from the National Piers Society; it never occurred to us that it could be wrong. We neither had the arrogance nor the motivation to check and so took the list as gospel. This, in a sense, is probably the only logical way of doing it. There has to be an official list from another party or else we could have got lost in an ever-decreasing spiral of details and semantics around what constitutes *working* or what is a *pier*.

Birnbeck Pier was closed to the public nearly 20 years ago, roughly 130 years after it had opened in 1867. It was originally used and abandoned as a jetty to visiting steamers and pleasure boats because of the notoriously varied tidal waters of the Bristol Channel. At the moment it's a gothic sketch in iron and barbed wire that we can't get near. Of all the piers we are never to get on, this one haunts me the most. Its old, weather-worn, wooden buildings and Victorian ironwork tell of ghost stories and *Boy's Own* adventures.

In 2006 the Manchester developers Urban Splash bought the pier and held competitions to decide how they should redevelop it. Everything from luxury apartments to an aquarium were suggested, but the £4m price proved too costly and the pier was sold privately in 2010. The future of Birnbeck Pier is often speculated upon locally, but I think the romance and danger of the rusting iron struts and lonely, distant island framed by a low setting sun will almost certainly be ripped away and a focus-grouped concrete 'complex' will be put in its place.

WESTON-SUPER-MARE Birnbeck

Opened: 1867 (Architect: Eugenius Birch)

Length at start: 1,150 ft (350 m)

Length now: 1,040 ft (317 m)

Burn baby burn? A few sparks in the long-gone arcade, and part of the pier collapsed during a storm in 1903.

Now closed, it was home to the Weston-super-Mare Lifeboat Station until 2013. In 1891 Weston's second ever telephone was installed here, six months after the first one was installed in the town. In the sixties, the Beatles staged an early publicity shoot around the pier, posing in Victorian bathing costumes.

Our next pier is our first non-pier, no nearer to being open than most of the shops on the sand-battered prom. As we strike out vaguely north, assisted by sporadic GPS, I'm most disappointed that a shop called The Rock Shop Newsagents is shuttered. Not only does the name promise proper seaside delights, and newspapers, it announces itself 'Home of the Steve Yabsley Outside Broadcasts'. I don't have much of a clue what those might entail. It could be the newsagent with a megaphone, or it could be some endearingly terrible hospital radio DJ who does his request show live from there on a Saturday morning.

When I get back home, weeks later, I look at a picture of it. In the picture the shop is open: postcards on a spinning stand, a hatch through which to serve ice cream, various windows full of seaside ephemera. I also find out all about Steve Yabsley, including that the show is an 'annual Saturday spectacular'. Nothing like defining yourself by a seasonal event, which is very seaside indeed, I suppose. I also spend as much time as I can stand listening to Steve's output. It is exactly how I suspected it would be, which makes our decision later in the trip to listen to as much local radio as possible for local colour even more baffling.

Turns out that there's an easy route and a hard route to Birnbeck Pier. The easy way is to take the road. Instead, we hoist our trouser bottoms and cross a kind of path circling an inlet, the sea breeze smoothing water across the concrete. If it were dangerous it would be roped off, we reason. The same with the uneven causeway that's at the end of it. The rock pools contain the usual mix of potential sea creatures and discarded wrappers. When we get there, our trust in Britain's paranoid health-and-safety culture allows us to get up close to and even underneath the fading structure. It's not much more than a framework, and the island that it reaches and then forks off – which, if I were being critical, might make it more of a bridge – may be all that's holding it up and out.

And that's it. We don't have a ritual to perform, so we head back to the car and, after Midge complains greatly about the biting point and the handbrake, to the real nearest pier to Birmingham.

––––––––––––

Logically, the next pier would have been first, but Weston-super-Mare is where we needed to start, not where we should have started. If logic or reason were part of the trip then it would have already never happened four or five times over. So we get in the car and drive the 20-mile diversion back to Clevedon.

As we park on a coast road, the sun is slowly fading and the junction between land and water is looking more English and peaceful than I've ever seen. My seaside has always been the commercial seaside; this is not, it's just quiet. Nice.

And it's closed.

We arrive at the toll gate at 5.50 p.m. and are just working out how to pay when the realisation that closing time is 5.30 p.m. pops a crimp in our visit. There's nothing we can do but gaze through the wrought-iron gates. The gates look darker than they should due to a thick coat of green paint, and the pier looks older and more fragile than it should due to the growing end-of-season dark.

Although we had been assured that piers rarely close for the season any more, they do, apparently, close for the day. Clevedon Pier towers above the beach, jutting out from the slope of a hill. It's designed simply, with a walkway and a small seating pavilion at the end. It was opened in 1869 and lasted, despite minor upsets, until the seventies when it was closed after stress testing collapsed some of the boards. Then began a long scrabble for funding. The combined efforts of local councils, a preservation society, and grants from English Heritage led to its reopening in 1989. It's now the only Grade I listed pier in the country.

It's nice to be by the coast: in Birmingham the canal is the closest we really get to nautical. In a country of ports, smugglers, pirates and market towns, the Midlands are exceptional in their isolation from the sea. We have no real affection for the canals, despite every few years the council trying to rebrand them as exciting redevelopment potential or inner-city resorts. If you believe the hype, the canal system in Birmingham is a cross between a corporate, open-air gym and a cosmopolitan, cafe-culture paradise. But people in Birmingham rarely think about the canals. To us they're a quirk of our industrial past, and everybody half suspects they're full of dead rats, shopping trolleys and near-sentient fungal diseases.

In Birmingham we're divorced from nature almost completely. Most of us are third-generation inhabitants of dark factories, as far from the sea as the population of gulls that live on the rooftops near our high streets and in our concrete school playgrounds. Jon actually asked me once in which direction the sun set. Perhaps even more shamefully, I only knew because I remembered it from John Wayne films as a kid.

The water at Clevedon is coffee-brown with weak, white foam, and the Bristol Channel is at its roughest as the tide comes in. I leave Jon in a reverie and Midge to mooch as I walk out onto one of the concrete jetties. If you walk out far enough it feels like being completely surrounded by the sea. The sea is so big it doesn't fit into a human brain. When faced with it, I find it's hard not to believe in the existence of a higher power, because I'm in the presence of one. A big expanse so complicated, nuanced and ancient that not only do you not matter, it's unlikely that your existence is even registered. I love it.

CLEVEDON

Opened: 1869 (Architect: Hans Price)

Length at start: 1,024 ft (312 m)

Length now: 1,024 ft (312 m)

Burn baby burn? No, but it did collapse during stress testing in 1970

The only surviving Grade I listed pier. Described by Sir John Betjeman as 'the most beautiful pier in England', and constructed with rails from one of Brunel's railways. Also the setting for the video of One Direction's 'You & I' single.

Getting down onto the beach, I'm feeling a desire to feel some sort of loss. I swing my legs off the side of a concrete jetty and stare out into the water. This is the first time I've looked out properly as all focus at Weston was on the town and finding our way. Here the channel is where the action is; the tide is encroaching and breaking gently onto the slope. Others such as us are taking the wind, including an international array of flags across the beach road. I watch a cute couple enjoy the emptiness: she's taken her shoes off to slip into the surf and he's dotingly taking her photograph.

Clevedon has little else to offer. I have at least heard of Burnham-on-Sea and Midge is keen to get there. He's not going to push, but I can sense the desire to make it to wherever we're going as soon as we can.

———

Midge negotiates the coastal road while me and Jon pretend he doesn't smell of stale, vaporised lager.

———

If you're a back-seat non-driver like the supine Mr Smith, reclining in a nest of bags, supplies and cardboard, then the tension of travelling as a passenger is relieved. For me every crunch of gear, every slip of hand on steering wheel, every audible 'what?' at the satnav is a tiny shard of wince. Midge is still getting used to the car and on unfamiliar roads, but I can hear the engine and it's not revving how I would assume it should for the speeds we're doing. Worse is that the indicators don't click off sharply once you're round a corner. It's worth controlling it manually or else you look like you're swapping two lanes, or parking, or are a fool. I try to mention it casually, but to no obvious effect. The tick-tick breeds frustration. I distract myself, and the car, with music: in this case, Fleetwood Mac.

It works until we have a little scrape as we park in the dusky back streets of Burnham-on-Sea, but the worry about the surroundings and leaving all our kit in the car is more pressing. Eventually I make a resigned pact with myself – I'm going to have to leave stuff in worse places, for longer, so I need to trust my luck. If anything can go wrong, it will. Trust fate to shit on you and you'll never be disappointed.

We're going to learn all sorts of facts about piers and Burnham-on-Sea is, I'm told by Danny, 'the shortest'; in essence, it's nothing but an amusement arcade on stilts. We're in need of amusement, so that's okay.

———————

Burnham-on-Sea is very proud of its status as the shortest pier in Britain and is indeed laughably small. With an Edwardian pavilion roof, it sits defiantly on the empty seafront. It's basically an elaborate hut on stout concrete stilts. We venture inside to drift amongst the arcade, which appears not to have been updated since the seventies; browns and creams swirl into the carpet. 'Also Sprach Zarathustra' (the theme from Kubrick's *2001: A Space Odyssey*) plays wryly and grandiosely from one of the ticket machines at the back as we walk in. I beat Jon at a rifle game but there's nothing worth swapping the tickets for. The prizes veer from novelty tat and bouncing fun balls to strange, grocery items like catering packs of gravy or jam.

BURNHAM-ON-SEA

Opened: 1914 (Architect: unknown, but possibly inspired by Isambard Kingdom Brunel – or so some claim)

Length at start: 117 ft (36 m)

Length now: 117 ft (36 m)

Burn baby burn? Concrete doesn't burn.

Shortest pier in England according to the people of Burnham. The Burnham-On-Sea.com website says 'Weymouth's Bandstand Pier is shorter... but only because most of it was deliberately blown up by the council in 1986, and that's clearly cheating!' It was the first concrete structure of its kind in Europe.

Most games in an arcade aren't really much fun, either being simple games of chance or ones where the time needed to gain the knowledge and skill is never rewarded. As long as you know what you're getting into, it's fine, but not everyone does. The worst kind for me is the 'skill with prizes' scam – you win tickets which can be redeemed later for prizes. If one is of an iconic bent, the neon-lit 'Redemption Areas' provide great metaphor about a higher power. I'm not thinking this right now, but there's something in the hundreds of tiny steps needed to gain a much-postponed reward. What I do think right now is that it would take something like ten years of constant prize bingo to get near the 1,450 tickets required to win a box of PG Tips. I'm also trying to take a furtive photograph of the box and, after doing so, slink embarrassed to the exit.

It's about 7 p.m. now, and I manage to manoeuvre our party into a small hotel bar which advertises Banks's ales outside. Banks's is a brewery local to us, so I comment on how unusual it is to find here. I'm not too sure it is, but it's enough to sell it to Dan.

———

It's pleasant enough in a mock-Tudor way. The kind of place that uses a Windows Publisher template for its menus, and you can play pool as long as you don't mind stepping over the dog. And it's nice to be at the seaside, even if the seaside is a couple of streets away. Going to the toilet, as I walk past the hotel reception, the staff look up with puppy-dog hope and I almost check in out of pity.

———

Midge is still keen to press on. He wants to get to his mate's place, where we've been invited to pitch camp halfway to the next pier, as soon as possible. He has reasons: driving in the dark across the top of Exmoor won't be pleasant and it won't be polite to arrive too late at a working man's house. But I'm already deeply uncomfortable about stopping at the house (or indeed in the garden) of someone I don't know, so want to spend as little time as possible there.

The bar itself is functional, worn monogrammed carpet betraying past pretension and regulars crowding the serving area, but the staff are friendly enough and we settle down, overlooked by current TV favourite *Come Dine with Me*. I drink quickly and order another while Danny quizzes Midge about just where we're stopping.

'So, where do you know this guy from?'

'He used to let us sleep on the floor of his pub.'

'...'

'I used to follow this band – Strap-on Jack – and they played at the pub in this village we're going to. The landlord was great.'

'And it's him we're stopping with?'

'I got in contact again with him on Facebook not long ago; I don't know him that well really.'

I'm now even more nervous. Not genuinely scared – in truth, I'm just imagining being terribly uncomfortable, a weak tie to a weak tie. No bond at all.

'He says it's going to be windy, so we can stop on his bus.'

When someone abandons the satnav you expect to be on the home stretch, but it's night, miles from anywhere, and Midge seems to be navigating by The Force alone. I find the best thing you can do in the back seat is shut up and let the adults worry about things, but Midge is swearing softly under his breath and I can't help but offer my opinion occasionally.

Heading to the village we listen to more of *Rumours*, perhaps a peculiar choice given Midge's punk credentials, Danny's rock stylings and my studied mod-ness. We'd discussed the idea that music might be a problem, but the Mac's masterpiece finds agreement. I'm fascinated by the group dynamic of Fleetwood Mac; Lyndsey Buckingham wrote songs about how he didn't love a woman and then that same woman (Stevie Nicks) sang them.

I'm also interested in how time changes people, and use myself as the closest example. My 18- or 20-year-old self – lost in the throws of a mod revival, and still worshipping The Smiths – would have despised anyone who expressed a preference for such soft, countrified, rock; but in my late thirties I hear it differently. Has the world changed or have I changed?

It's now dark, headlights have to be flicked regularly from full-beam to dipped and back again, Midge mutters about a hill and a pub and a left turn. Despite not driving quickly, he's taking turns very late. Eventually he makes a decision and turns up a gravel path, which soon becomes a grass one.

We come to a halt, hemmed in by a wire fence and brambles. Midge gets out to check we're in the right place. A glance at Danny suggests he doesn't think we are. Neither do I.

A figure is silhouetted in the doorway, but it's no one with whom Midge has even a passing acquaintance. A torch flashes. We hear the answer to an unheard question:

'See, what you want to do is... get the fuck off my garden.'

CHAPTER TWO

THE MAGNIFICENT DEVON

We later find out that Midge's directions were taken from his memory of the route based on Google Street View. Eventually we are met at a different driveway by a bald and sternly amicable man named John, who welcomes us into his house. Like all houses built before a certain time it is a charming haphazard affair, with rooms that have grown out of others organically as and when they were needed, as opposed to modern two-up two-down affairs built with set squares and formulae. The kitchen smells strongly of weed. Nick is an ex-landlord and somewhat of a local legend for health-and-safety-nightmare gigs in the pub he still lives near, the White Horse Inn.

As he ushers us into the living room he offers us beer and sits in a chair that seems to make his boots look like the three-inch-heeled bastard stompers they once were. After some chit-chat with Midge, with whom he shares that same impossible-to-age punk quality, he stays quiet and lets his brother do the talking.

His brother, John, is a pleasant middle-aged gentleman who remains quite perplexed at the purpose of our quest. 'Why?' is the first reaction of everyone save a special few. It seems that some people are naturally suspicious of anyone doing anything out of the ordinary but as soon as it has a context they understand; their minds are put to rest.

Telling people about the trip always causes one or more of four reactions:

1. Complete and utter indifference, as if you couldn't have told them anything more mundane.

2. Confusion followed by a series of questions and then normally reaction 1 or 3.

3. Completely getting it and being on board.

4. Reciting as many piers from memory to check we're actually going to them and then eventually making some up for no other reason than to fuck with us.

John is a two, then a four.

We spend the next half hour playing pier bingo and keeping an eye on a football match I mentally refuse to make a note of because all football is rubbish.

Now this could be seen as quite remiss of me, but I'm willing to bet that Jon has noted which football match it is and is able to deduce something clever about John by which team he is supporting. This is one of the ways that, as alike as we are, me and Jon differ.

I have always been disinterested in football and over the years have even come to resent it. Not being a football fan has made me somewhat of a pariah in male circles – most men use football as the balm to ease the stress of speaking to new men. As an observer of this phenomenon I have a theory that this is something to do with having a shared experience, language and culture, and instantly being able to work out your place within a hierarchy by exposing which team you support and always having something to talk about. If you're not a fan, men really don't know what to do with you.

Most of my early teenage years were awkward. The eldest in a new generation, I was too old to play with the kids on the swings of the numerous pub playgrounds where our family convened, and the men of the family didn't really know what to say to a long-haired proto-goth who spent his time reading and drawing. So I ended up sitting with the women. This explains why during my late teens and most of my twenties I always felt more comfortable talking to women: men are generally dull and frankly most of them smell bad.

But ten or so years of bar work has given me a fair bluffing game when it comes to football, so after some polite chat and much-needed bottles of beer we retire to the bus to spend the night. The bus itself sleeps a comfy five and has its own kitchenette, plus lovely electricity for us to juice up our various electronic devices.

We drink beer and listen to Jon play us the best of the singing bloody milkman or some shit, then go to bed.

I can't sleep. I'm on a bunk in a converted coach and, directly above me, the skylight is mottled with black. In it I see a picture of a bull terrier. The dog isn't breathing heavily, but one of my companions is. Not snoring exactly, but a rhythmic exhale, enough to break any cocoon of wakelessness I can conjure. I get up and sit in the diner area, and read the book I've brought with me: *English Journey*, a travelogue by J. B. Priestley from the thirties where he traces a fairly random route around the country and simply records what he sees.

What he sees is a country in a state of social flux. The upheaval of the Great War had left many in desperate need of support. The book is supposed to have inspired Orwell's *Road to Wigan Pier*, and even to have helped to win Labour the 1945 General Election, but reading it today you're left with a feeling that not much has improved. Jobs have changed from the traditional to the transitional, and from the make to the make-do, but there's still the same powerlessness of anyone but the rich. Priestley spends a lot of time meeting not the manual worker, but the commercial traveller: the supposedly white-collar worker who is no better off or any more free than the most put-upon factory fodder. So who is free?

We are, at least temporarily.

From the garden dead end I had to direct Midge's reversing with a torch, although that didn't stop him veering dangerously towards the undergrowth. We eventually got back to the main road where he pulled up and called his mate.

'I'm by a red phone box...'

I sleep fitfully unless in perfect darkness and quiet. I'm also starting to feel my age and make at least three trips to the toilet overnight. The toilet in this case is England's green and pleasant land, behind the bus.

'The bus is wired up so you've got power,' John has told us, 'but the toilet isn't plumbed in, so if you need to piss just use the bushes.'

If you've spent much time on coaches over the years, then the mechanisms that you're not allowed to touch become fascinating. The trepidation of a blackout wee in the country, in the cold and the damp, every step a potential slip on wet grass, is tempered by the joy of being able to open the door with the driver's lever. It swings with a satisfying smoothness. Now I'm back in my bunk, and Priestley is visiting the Daimler factory in Coventry. He postulates the conversion of one of the new breed of motorised coaches to a touring motorhome. It seems a good idea, big enough to live in. In a caravan everything is something else; the sofa is a bed is a cupboard, things fold down and out, you pull open the microwave and are surprised it's not also a wet room.

We have a generous light breakfast with John, who manages to be just as chirpy and friendly in the morning as he'd been the night before, which is more than we can manage, so we set off.

From anywhere Falmouth is out of the way, but on a trip where you're following the coastline it's really bloody out of the way. It's fair to say that Midge has been publicly decrying this to anyone who would listen. Ever since we saw the route, his hope has been that Falmouth Pier would blow into the sea. Me and Jon have explained that even if Falmouth Pier had been blown up by weirdly pier-specific terrorists, we would still have to visit it because it's on the list. But I think towards the end his animosity towards it is fuelled by his generally grumpy nature rather than a desire to dodge the task.

While we are on the motorway it begins to rain. Big fat fists of rain slam against the car, reducing the windscreen to a kid's runny painting of the landscape, and the beating against the roof drowns out the stereo. I think it is quite pleasant, romantic even. It's only when I see Jon's white face and Midge's equally colourless knuckles on the steering wheel while they tell me how dangerous it is that I know anything of the sort. The gods are testing our resolve and we pass, like the Ghostbusters swallowed into the mini-earthquake before they go into Dana's apartment building. I decide to keep that to myself; neither Jon nor Midge seem in the mood for pop-culture references. So I sit back and watch the giant white windmills slowly turn.

Midge still isn't quite there with the car. I can feel the engine uncomfortably lurching and, while I need to trust his judgement, I can barely see ten yards of road ahead. In a break in the waterfall, sun sharding from behind a cloud, the landscape looks magnificent and so English. Hills bounce fat trees across the horizon, the hedges and lanes give the vista the impression of a circuit board controlling life itself. I can see an obelisk and suddenly feel deeply connected to the earth, to the past, to a pointless idea of pastoral Englishness.

It's easy, if you've seen enough films, to imagine Arthur and Lancelot materialising out of the mist. It's easy, if you've half-digested as much literature as I have, to imagine them tilting at the overbearing wind turbines which change colour as you flit in and out of the autumn light. And it's easy, if you're a romantic sort, to start to imagine Pier Review as a sort of quest.

I've quizzed Danny about who's who – in the literary sense – on our trip before. I turn my head round to him and his nest.

'Which of us is Sancho Panza? Is it you?'

'The stupidly loyal servant? It's not me. Nor is it you.'

'Okay, what about *Hitchhiker's*?'

'We haven't got the room.'

'No, the book: who's who?'

'I'm Ford, you're Arthur.'

I'd expected him to want to be Zaphod, but Ford Prefect – reckless, drinking gonzo travel writer – fits, sure. Arthur Dent? Well, there are parallels, right down to the poorly drawn love interest.

'So, Midge is Marvin.'

If the climate of England hasn't changed much in the last couple of thousand years then King Arthur must have been freezing. Maybe the Holy Grail was the Dark Ages' equivalent of a two-bar electric fire.

Falmouth appears not out of a mist but out of this past Englishness, as we drive through a heavily wooded area cut by a brook. I'm just contemplating how Robin and Little John fit into our story when we hit a municipal car park.

I've become responsible for car parking. Midge asks if each place is okay, and I have to check terms and fill the meters. At home I enjoy my abilities to park cheaply and conveniently; it's one dad skill I can master despite my sheer lack of practicality. But after spending time guessing navigation around the dark of Burnham yesterday, I'm pretty much just going to hit the signposts and hope that the driver starts doing more of the decision bits of the drive.

Dan tells me that there's a Kurt Vonnegut quote: 'No matter how good the travel writer, they never tell you about the car parking.' So the Kurt Vonnegut Car Park Rating Scheme is born, each pier to be given a mark out of ten for parking ease and cost. When I later try to find the quote, no reference to it seems to exist anywhere.[*] Too late. We resolve to print the legend and the scores continue. Falmouth gets poor marks; it's a long way to the pier and not cheap. Coasting into the town we passed a sign, not from god but just as transformative – 'Marks & Spencer welcomes you to Falmouth' – and the polished timbers of the new development we follow look like they've been installed to show off organic produce. We skirt past a famous man's chip shop and into the lobby-cum-gift shop of the Maritime Museum. We don't go in; we can't afford it.

———

Unfolding myself out of the car at Falmouth is a slow and sore affair but excitement at being outside the car and in the bright weather means I am able to do so without too much complaining. The streets of Falmouth are cobbled near the front where the boutique gift shops and the normal high street are making the transition from middle-class tourist season to welcoming the students for September. The pier itself, as if to add insult to Midge's injured driving hands, is unspectacular, nothing more than a concrete jetty into a clear, green-tinged sea. The harbour is busy, with a large army-grey ship dwarfing everything around it. It looks, to my mind, like when a child plays with different scale toys. A busker plays classical guitar moods, knowing his audience will prefer those to pop singalongs or a 30-minute version of 'All Along the Watchtower'.

———

[*] It turns out to not be Vonnegut but J. G. Ballard. Ballard said, 'No travel writer I have ever known has written about the importance of parking.'

It's not immediately obvious where the town is. The eye is drawn to an expanse of gunmetal grey, a ship we can't adequately describe to each other. Perhaps if we'd been around some educational establishment dedicated to the sea we would know if its purpose was transport or war. We follow the line of the harbour and guess that the flow of uniformed men is them knowing where the action is. The fleet's in town and they've got shore leave.

Frank, Gene and the other one are in our way as we look into a charity-shop window at nautical-themed books. Having failed at buying postcards yesterday, I leaf through a box of old ones in the Oxfam but they're frighteningly expensive. There's something very M&S about the town, a sort of solid and reassuring atmosphere with overtones that you might not find exactly 'with it'. We pass a giant haberdasher's, which isn't only proud to show the Cornish desire for independence from the UK but seems to want to break from Europe too. Cornwall evidently thinks it can take a seat at the big table.

Any table will do us. The pier is flat and uninteresting; little more than an extended walkway between Millets and Superdrug, the street lamps continue as if it's nothing but a pavement for the sea. We walk it and stare across the boats, but there's nothing there that isn't better expressed in the town itself.

FALMOUTH Prince of Wales

Opened: 1905 (Architect: W. H. Tressider)

Length at start: 510 ft (155 m)

Length now: 510 ft (155 m)

Burn baby burn? Nope, but was taken over by American forces during what they would call 'doublya doublya two'.

The foundation stone was laid by the future George V, who was Prince of Wales at the time.

With both a gift shop selling cards and a post office, we know we can't put it off any longer. We pick up a wodge of postcards and go into the post office, doing the maths in the queue.

'May I help you?'

Already, after only a day, me and Jon are a little creased around the edges.

'Please may I have 385 second-class stamps,' says Jon.

She blinks. '385?'

'Yes, please.'

And with that she goes to count them out. Jon looks in his wallet and asks me 'Will this be enough?' holding up a tenner. Quick maths not being a strong point, I nearly answer yes, but the cashier says 'that's £138.60.'

When we were setting up our website for donations to fund the trip we were deciding what relatively low-cost things we could offer to people giving us different amounts. For the fifty-quid tier I had had an idea.

'How about for fifty quid we offer to write them a postcard from each of the piers?'

'I don't know, that could be a huge hassle,' said Jon.

'Don't worry, no one will give us that much anyway.'

But people did. Nine people did. Thankfully we talked two of them out of having the postcards, but that still means on that first morning, in a traditional pub with a jukebox set to 'dad rock', we have to handwrite the first 28 of 385 postcards.

We take the nearest option, the Prince of Wales pub right opposite the pier. Daytime drinking is something I enjoy even more than the classic night out. It's relaxed, there's no pressure to find the trendiest spot or the best band, nothing to keep looking over one's shoulder for. You just slowly become detached from the world and more connected to your companions. Stella Artois, breakfast of champions.

Note that at this point I didn't pick Stella out of a vast selection of ales because I like it; it doesn't taste nice. It just tastes of something, which the other lager options don't. For all the town's 'not just any' organic pretence, the pub doesn't seem overwhelmed with imported or local treats. It seems to be the other type of M&S, the comfortable beige. In Weston we got posters of kitsch flashbacks – The Three Degrees, The Wurzels. Here, the handwritten whiteboard above the urinals promises Edison Lighthouse, so obscure that it's more quiz question than smirk-inducing. I remember their hit and suspect they may be local.

We pass a brick kiln chimney and a sign for a ploughing match as we head through much Englishness into Devon.

Paignton is two and a half hours away from Falmouth. Not that it bothers me much, having made my own little nest in the back seat. There is an art to back-seat travel, a Zen, a state of near-ignorant bliss that must be held onto by, ultimately, letting go. Being in the back seat you're powerless. Free of driving and navigating duties, you couldn't affect the journey even if you wanted to. The front seats can't hear you even if you had an opinion, so you might as well just leave them to it. Years of bus travel and a childhood escaping into books from my siblings on long journeys also means I have no problem reading while moving. Also, it helps that I have a peculiar quirk of my physiology which means that I fall asleep on any car journey longer than ten minutes. So the really long journeys, for me, are naps punctuated by listening to Radio 6 and writing postcards, and on more than one occasion, both at the same time.

We are existing in an eternal present of potential disruption and disaster. I'm not a good traveller. I'm not fatalistic about what might happen to us – at least not yet – but I worry. I get nervous. What if the car breaks down? None of us has any mechanical knowledge. But public transport wouldn't have been better for me. Sit on a train, is it the right train? Is it working? Have I got the right ticket? What if it doesn't stop at the right place? What if it breaks down, what if... I can't relax. Not until all decisions have been taken from me, which is sort of why I can cope a lot more easily with the regimented 'watch-the-screens' nature of travel by air. I mean, they're actively trying to make sure you don't get on the wrong plane, and the consequences of a breakdown require less thinking than having to spend the night on Crewe Station.

I have always found the idea of the 'English Riviera' comical, the sort of gentle self-mocking humour that we British would pride ourselves on if we weren't so gently self-mocking. But looking out at the white buildings in the distance, sprinkled on the cliffs and framed by a sailor-blue sky, I can see it. Just. Paignton front isn't big or littered with shops. The buildings facing the sea are almost exclusively hotels punctuated by a few pubs and, because it's the end of the season, they are pleasingly empty.

People are on holiday in Paignton. Not many, and no one glamorous, but there is definitely still a holiday atmosphere. The esplanade is punctuated with shelters that betray pragmatism in the face of more recent PR sheen – the palm trees, the 'your trip, your way' slogan. Paignton, the shelters say, is in England and, as such, at some point the wind will lash rain horizontally at you, the pensioner. You, they say, will be grateful for the glass lovingly etched with obscenities, the hard and overly polished bench, the proximity of the litter bins. You will be grateful as it's free and you can stare out to sea for free. You may sit, until it's time for tea back at the guest house.

But the shelters also face inwards, offering a view of a scrubby patch of grass and flat hotels. I take a snap of an old couple huddling in the shelter from across the lawn. They look content. Happy, almost. They look okay with the past and okay with the present. I'd like to reach that stage one day.

PAIGNTON

Opened: 1879 (Architect: George Soudon Bridgman)

Length at start: 780 ft (238 m)

Length now: 740 ft (226 m)

Burn baby burn? In 1919 the pier head and buildings, including a billiard room, were destroyed in a fire and never replaced.

1880 saw a full-cast performance of *HMS Pinafore* by the D'Oyly Carte in the pavilion: it was retitled *HMS Pinafore on the Water* for the occasion, although that seems a bit of a tautology.

The pier is mostly arcade, a sight even I will become slightly bored by. The arcades today are the same as those of my youth. Of course the 'wild west shoot-out' still exists but it's bookended by handgun video-game machines where you have to foil zombie bank robberies or kill every bad guy by shooting them specifically in the crotch. One-armed bandits have now become 'fruities' and, despite the themes, they all have the same pattern of lights and sporadic belts of annoying music. The grabbing games and other derivatives of old bunko carny games never change. They may be reskinned or filled with whatever passing fad is sneezed up into the public consciousness, but they're still just a rigged weak crane grabbing at a meerkat that's too heavy to be carried by it.

I pop back into the arcade and spend my two tuppenny pieces on a *Star Trek* coin waterfall machine. It's original *Star Trek*. Kirk and Spock stare across the heavily patterned carpet, their minimal, utopian space future further away from here than anywhere. Yet it's somehow very apt.

Devon is a long way from Cornwall, but things are going to become easier. I can see Torquay from Paignton Pier, and I spend a lot of time looking through the structure: across the railings at the future and through the decking planks to the deep past. These are the directions you can look without being depressed by the unloved mini-go-karts, the unfired guns on the shooting range or the unbounced trampolines. Those on holiday in Paignton just now are not bouncers, shooters or goers. Slightly symbolically, a tatty raven sits atop a deserted stall.

We dutifully reach the end of the pier, stare into the distance and leave. As we head back to the car I catch the eye of an old man as he peeks from under his anorak to lick an ice cream. He smiles, genuinely happy as the toggles whip around in the wind and he shuffles closer to his wife in a matching anorak who he's sharing the ice cream with.

When I said I could see Torquay from Paignton I wasn't just guessing that the next outcrop of civilisation on the coast was our next destination. Torquay is almost close enough to smell, if it weren't that most seaside towns smell the same, and I know the place very well. I can recognise the front quite easily: it's empty of interest almost all along the way; a sea wall plaited with white painted railings and well-kept but uninteresting lawn fringing.

I've been to Torquay, I calculate, more than 30 times. Many of them I can't remember or they have slipped into each other the way memories do, but the indiscrete indiscretions and excursions do form a good map of the town. I know where to go to get drunk, to bet on football and horses, to take romantic early-evening strolls. And to park, in theory. However, each turn of advice I give Midge results in nothing more than a loop back around to the stone-walled front.

————————

Torquay is a six-minute trip up the road and we're in good spirits because we've broken the back of the travelling that day, so me and Jon get stuck into the crème de cassis from a care package of out-of-date booze given to us by someone who knows us too well. It tastes like cough medicine with an aftertaste of coffee, and seems to be impairing Jon's instructions to Midge because, despite his claim of having been to Torquay 'loads of times', he is leading us in several circles up and down some near-vertical steep hills.

'Try this one,' shouts Jon, and Midge dutifully swerves the car and the contents of the back seat, now a finely tuned organisational mess, shift on top of me for the third time.

'No, this one.' Again the road offers no parking. I hear a little humph from Midge as he decides to ignore Jon entirely and we head over to the opposite side of the front and follow the parking signs.

The prom here is featureless, as is the bulk of the town, its hotels and guest houses, its utilitarian shops and wide ordinary streets wedged over sturdy cliffs. The cliffs are stark, look man-made and divide the stay from the play. They provide blind corners and one-way systems, and we eventually give up and park in a costly council space across the marina from the pier.

Torquay seems pleasant, but small, more of a harbour village than a town, one that has enjoyed close to 120 years of tourism but always maintained the haughty standards of the Victorians and, later, the emerging, aspirational, middle-class Edwardians. The Pavilion Shopping Centre is a great example of this. Stark and defiantly white, it's an almost unbearable fiddly mixture of classical forms and lines, with pillars and plinths, and art nouveau metalwork. Every available surface is decorated with pineapples, trees, cherub faces and natural forms. It's a building built for the serious business of whimsy and to complement the empty pier.

Torquay's Princess Pier is wide and flat, the end connected to a curving wall built out from the bank of the natural harbour to create a marina that is filled with various yachts and other forms of marine propulsion so far out of my realm of experience that the whole thing might as well be a unicorn stable.

'That's not a pier,' I say to no one in particular.

TORQUAY Princess

Opened: 1894

Length at start: 780 ft (238 m)

Length now: 780 ft (238 m)

Burn baby burn? In April 1974, fire gutted the pier-head building 'The Islander', which was demolished to deck level.

Agatha Christie often roller-skated down it as a child, then very little happened. Not even a single murder. Apart from those of fish.

'That's not a pier,' Dan says.

'It isn't the pier, Dan, it's the harbour wall – the pier is down the road.'

Like Weston, I know the place but haven't been on the pier. But there's not much to know; the only pleasures available on this outcrop are fishing and sitting. Almost everything else is 'prohibited', as the well-worn signs tell us: including roller skating, as previously practised by the young Agatha Christie. All those perfect murders in her head and a little bit of roller skating was probably the biggest transgression she made. It's an empty place, far from the notional centre of town. We don't spend too long there and are quickly hunting for somewhere to take a rest and a drink.

We're not stopping here overnight; there's another pier in Devon to take in and we're going to go as far as possible into the night before making camp, literally. In a tent. This is something I'm trepidatious about. Camping to me means music festivals, fire, drink and drugs. On holiday, beds are holiday camp or hotel. But we have to do this as cheaply as possible: the budget has room in it for the essential seaside B & B experience and we're trying to wangle a night at the holiday camp of our youths, but camping or mates' floors are all we can expect on the rest of the trip.

The hotels of Torquay are something I know very well indeed. Until a few years ago, I spent every Easter weekend in one of the town's multitude of mid-sized three-stars. A combined football team and social club outing with little imagination put in to the destination – and, to be fair, a main interest in getting away en masse to have fun rather than explore new places – means I've been here year after year.

If you've not stayed in one, I should point out that they're more boarding house scaled up than Grand Hotel scaled down. The carpets are heavy and dark, surfaces glossed, doors either heavy and banging or suspiciously light. Where sunlight streaks into the rooms, it illuminates a flurry of dust. All the bedspreads are furry, and the breakfast fruit is heavy and slightly fizzy with fermentation. They are mostly family-run and the staff are stretched just that little bit too thin to keep everything on track. The same guy who is overly familiar with your hung-over breakfast will be helping you prepare tomorrow's headache way after midnight in the hotel bar.

We often took over the whole place, even overflowing a few people into next door, so we didn't experience the quiet, forlorn afternoons that you might think you'd get in places like these. You've seen *Fawlty Towers* and the big takeaway is not the farce inside but the sepulchral dampness to every outside scene. I've not sat in stifling, shared TV lounges, nor been thrust into uncomfortable mealtimes with strangers.

'I suppose you're wondering what gathered us all here,' says Midge to the waitress in Bar Mambo. To say she doesn't hear him is to be kind to them both, but Danny picks up the thread and fills her in. I'm not sure either of my compadres has any real designs on her; she's attractive if nondescript, much like the seafront we can see from the bar's balcony.

We exchange the usual banter about who's drinking what. The barmaid mimics our accents, wrongly, so Midge tells her about the project and she completely blanks him, not even recognising that he's spoken. Midge waits a few more seconds and goes to sit on the patio. I opt for a different tack.

'Your pier is rubbish.'

'Sorry?'

She was asking for clarification, not forgiveness, so I tell her about what we're doing.

'Oh, it's not MY pier,' she says dismissively. She does this a lot when talking about Torquay. There's a little movement of her shoulder as if she is shrugging off any responsibility for the place. Originally from Highbury in London, she moved to the coast to escape what she called 'a very abusive relationship'. She leans on the word 'very' and it hangs in the air for a few seconds.

'What's the main difference between London and here?' I ask, trying to move the subject on. It is kind of sweet how long she thinks about it, like I've asked her something she obviously thinks about herself a lot anyway.

'I think it's the morals.'

'What about them?'

'For example, friends back home would never start going out with an ex of yours once you finish with them. But here they see nothing wrong with it.'

I go to ask if this has happened to her recently but the expression on her face makes the question redundant.

'There's less people down here, it's bound to get a bit incestuous,' I offer.

'They're all like that.' Quickly, with a shade of bitterness.

'By the way, you were wrong about our accents. The one that you did is a Black Country accent, it's different to a Brummie's.'

At this point I want to change the subject. 'People from the Black Country speeak loik thees, yaam alroit babs?' I say, drawing out my speech and mangling the vowels like our attic-monster cousins to the north. She laughs, I smile.

'How is that different to how you were speaking before?' At least she is laughing.

———

There's inevitably something of nostalgia to the place for me. I can see roughly the place in which I once drank myself stupid before breaking my collarbone, and I can see the spot up the high street where my dad was more excited than I think I've ever seen him to spot Don Partridge, 'King of the Buskers', busking. Don, I was told, had a top-five hit with a song called 'Rosie'. I don't think the version my dad sang had the correct version of the lyrics, but I'm happy to have it circling in my head anyway.

As we pass the penny arcade, I do a double-take as I am sure I see keyboard raconteur Rick Wakeman going the other way. That completes the feeling of things past.

———

I notice that we've lost Jon. Looking around, I see him standing in front of one of the few gift shops on Torquay's front.

'What's the matter, mate?' I ask when I get over there, trying to follow his gaze into the window of tat.

'Is that even allowed?' he nods towards the figures, admittedly not really seen in the melting pot that is Birmingham.

'Oh yes, Jon, you're allowed to have them now, but they're just called "gollys".'

'So they're not golly...'

'Nope, just "gollys" now, Jon,' I interrupt. 'Keeps the jam company happy.'

We drag ourselves away from the shop. Luckily it isn't open or I believe one of us would be in possession of half a dozen gollys in various poses, and perhaps a bone china Daniel O'Donnell teapot.

The road to Teignmouth from Torquay is mostly coastal and, at one point around the strangely named Labrador Bay, the road throws you from the top of a hill, the foliage breaks, and the view punches you in the eye. A reddening sun is low and fat in the sky, as the sea breaks underneath and begins to take on some of those red tones. I wonder if you ever get desensitised to the beauty of a view like that. Can it become so mundane it would barely be worth breaking your stride for? And if you never do become desensitised – if such an appreciation is hardwired, then what is the evolutionary point? Why has this seemingly useless trait been passed on?

———

Not far up the road, Teignmouth Grand Pier is well kept. It's faced by an impressive columned building and guarded by a couple of concrete and magnolia toilet blocks. The whole place has a spic Edwardian vibe. Our second pint on the astroturfed balcony over the marina at Torquay has put us a little behind and the buildings on the pier here are closed, as are those toilet blocks.

TEIGNMOUTH

Opened: 1867 (Architect: J. W. Wilson)

Length at start: 700 ft (213 m)

Length now: 625 ft (190 m)

Burn baby burn? Some years after fire destroyed the Castle Pavilion, it was turned into a go-kart track in the sixties.

Not too long after the opening, Arthur Ryde Denby bought the pier and planned to relocate it to Paignton. However, because of structural problems, a new pier was built at Paignton instead and Teignmouth was restored. Joseph Wilson, who designed Teignmouth Pier, also designed another one at Westward Ho! but it had to be demolished after only two years.

Teignmouth is a pretty seaside town, but the pier is closed and the locals are wary of us. We walk under the pier, as it seems the only other appropriate thing to do. 'If you can't go on it, you go under it' is immediately the rule.

———

I attempt to take an arty photo of the stilts cross-hatching the horizon, but am distracted by a sound of splashing. The tide may be lapping quietly, but the noise is Danny having a piss up against the sea wall as deep inside the heart of the pier as he can. I join him. It's a long ride to the campsite and we've already started drinking our booze float.

Dan rang to confirm our pitch while we were back in Torquay. It's at some isolated place about as far as we can possibly reach tonight. Apparently there's a bar, which means we now want to get there as soon as possible.

———

We have decided that this one is as 'done' as we are going to get it. Anyway, we have no idea where the campsite is and it is looking like we won't arrive until dark, so we head off. The only hope of navigating to the campsite is by satnav, although I sense the relationship between Midge and the machine is on rocky ground. It's the little clues you pick up on that give it away, like Midge telling it to 'fuck off' whenever it speaks, or him referring to it as 'that fucking thing' whenever it is mentioned. I check the postcode on our spreadsheet and Jon puts it in. We don't notice our mistake until much later.

The journey is buoyed by our drunken hubris. Me and Jon take it in turns to play music at each other, trying to make each song better than the last, a kind of music-geek Top Trumps.

There's something in our make-up that's never more delighted than when we show people something they don't know – educating them, I suppose. We're plugging our phones alternately into an aux jack, the scratch and pop between selections reverberating through the car, and we're slowly turning them up and up like DJs towards the end of the night.

I cut a swathe through maudlin indie of the nineties, Danny has some obscure Australian hip-hop from his trips working there. It's okay, but I will each song to finish once we've had verse and chorus – music as information. Most songs are too long. Only 'Won't Get Fooled Again' by The Who is too short and I'm saving that for Brighton.

There don't seem to be any rules to the game we are playing. I suppose a new esoteric song beats an older one, but all can be trumped by Fleetwood Mac's 'The Chain'. A song that's made even Midge's moderately light foot bear down on the accelerator just a tad, followed by whoops from us, his pissed cargo. But encouraging someone who, the day before, admitted that he doesn't see too well in the night to hurtle down country roads isn't our only mistake. The thing about a satnav is that it insulates you from the journey. By taking the responsibility for navigation, it turns the outside to background, severing your link to direction and reducing the driving to a video game. We don't know we are going in the wrong direction. It isn't our job to know; it is the confident-sounding robot's sitting on the dashboard.

———

Louder and louder, and shorter, and more plug-removal pops, and we're getting close to our camp and Midge is visibly ready to stop.

———

When that little robot tells us 'you have reached your destination' in the middle of a village nowhere near a campsite, we scratch our heads. We check the postcode again. In fact, Midge, checking the postcode again, realises our mistake. The danger of having one drunk dyslexic shout the postcode to another drunk dyslexic in the dark is obvious *now*, but late o'clock in a truly random village in the south-west of England is no time for recriminations.

———

No recriminations. Danny is very dyslexic. He read the address out to me. I programmed it in. I had to have remedial spelling lessons at school but have spent most of my working life dealing with words. I do have problems with tables, syllables and forms – which has led Danny to diagnose me as dyslexic too. Which means I can't blame him and he can't blame me.

Midge can't blame either of us. Not only would it be politically incorrect, he's also sort of our employee (unless the Job Centre are reading this). It's tense. We carefully, with the poise and deliberation only drunks can command, reprogram the route and there are no sighs of relief as it tells us there's more than an hour to go. We turn, Midge huffs and puffs. We go up another private road, a steep gradient. There's a smell that may be the countryside, or it may be the engine. I pray for cowshit.

———————

One piece of luck is that I'd spoken to someone from the campsite on the phone that day and, despite the booking office closing at 7 p.m, they were very relaxed about us arriving late, pitching our tent and paying in the morning.

———————

It's pretty much pitch black apart from spots of artificial light in the middle distance as we finally take a sand-splattered side road and dune-ish hillocks guide us to the entrance. There's only one other tent pitched. We drive the shortest distance past required for modesty and park up on the slope by a bramble-strewn hedge. Nothing has gone wrong in the last hour, but we've not been talking, music switched to the implication-free radio. The only respite from the studied silence has been a strained plea for a stop, any stop, for a piss.

Danny isn't in a great mood. He's not really looked at the tent we've got as yet and isn't quite sure how to put it up. He and Midge start to spread the canvas out and look puzzled at the various lengths of metal. I can't really help – my camping experience is limited to falling back stoned into the cheap Argos dome tents at music festivals, whereas this is proper scout stuff. I decide that discretion is the better part of pitching camp and stand back, looking helpful and eager.

———————

For those that have never camped (a shockingly large number, I'm finding out) there are certain conditions that make putting up a tent difficult. Sobriety, or lack thereof. The wind doesn't help either – essentially you are trying to nail a large sail into the ground. Putting a tent up in the rain is miserable but not difficult, but putting a tent up at the top of a hill in the tail end of Hurricane Jeffrey without paragliding into a caravan is an exercise in soul-crushing frustration. Having seen the tent before also helps, but as I only borrowed the tent for the trip too much time is spent with a torch in my mouth trying to decide which three of the 14 poles are slightly larger than the others.

There's a rough wind pulsing the groundsheet and a drizzle forming in the air. If I look away from the static caravans and away from the two tents, my view is empty of life. Scrubby fields fall away to the sea; the air is salty and wet. I feel I want to be alone and start rummaging through my brain for words to comfort me. I pull out Auden's 'Roman Wall Blues' and recite it to the happy campers. It's a sad poem of loss and longing that will pull us closer together. W. H. was the Morrissey of his day, still ill after all these years.

Soft ground is a bonus, but one you don't get at a caravan site. Site owners tend to level out a field with hard rocks and shale before covering it with soft dirt. The upshot is me pushing the pegs into the ground with the palm of my hands, now bruised and bleeding from bending the metal things once they sank a couple of useless inches.

Putting a tent up becomes the work of seconds when everybody knows what they're doing. My only help was Midge, who had pissed off in a grump because of the extra hours our satnav mistake had cost us, and Jon, a man so insulated from this sort of thing that he had to be told to bring a towel and whose idea of helping is to recite poetry while I bite down on the pegs in my mouth. I later find out I have chipped one of my teeth.

———————

I finish a desolate piece of Auden and I'm about to follow up with A. E. Housman when I gather that the clanging of poles and tent pegs is more urgent than perhaps is needed.

———————

Having abandoned my plan to put the tent up how it is supposed to be in favour of trying to fashion something out of the jumble of pegs, poles and sheets that we can maybe sleep in, I finish with not so much of a 'taa daa' but a 'fuck it'. A full stop to the stream-of-consciousness swearing I now realise I have been projecting from the top of this hill in Weymouth. Only part of me feels bad as we step over the child's bike of a neighbour's tent in search of the bar.

———————

Two men in jeans lean across the counter, bantering amiably with each other and the steward. They don't react to our presence, but the barmaid's cheerfully blowsy as she pours a couple of pints for me and tears off a packet of Bacon Fries. The bar itself is compact, but there is bench seating and stools for around 50 people here at least. Apart from the guys bantering amiably under the telly, we're the only customers. We sit next to each other facing into the room, and I notice posters for and photos of misshapen cabaret acts we could see if we only lived right here.

In the corner a scratch-chinned, blond guy is packing amps, keyboards and wires into flight cases. His calf-length jacket catches the light from the fruit machine. I recognise him from somewhere. From earlier.

CHAPTER THREE

BOURNEMOUTH STRIKES AGAIN

I awake stupidly early and outside the tent there's dew starting to settle. The air is freezing cold. I'm alone in the field and I piss up against the bushes behind the tent. As far as I can see there is grass, foliage, trees. And, if I were to spin around, the sea. I won't spin, though, as I'll wet the tent.

It's a little too gloomy to see clearly, about four o'clock I think. The night has passed the darkest point but not yet turned to morning. If I'd not been to sleep at all yet this would be tired-headache time, but I'm clear, fresh even. Connected to the land. Enjoying the stillness. I can feel the rough grass through the thin soles of my pumps. I didn't notice the amount of wood and bush when we arrived last night. This bit of Dorset isn't even farmed much it seems. We're left to nature.

Over the brow of the small incline, there's a guy walking across the next field. A healthy stride, but he's walking from memory rather than purpose. He spots me and adjusts his path slightly to pass me more closely. As he turns I see that he's carrying a bag and has something – a walking stick, most likely – in his hand or on his belt. He's wearing odd clothing for a rambler: no North Face jacket but more a tunic or knee-length coat. Odd is normal round these parts.

He looks tired but hails me brightly when he's within hailing distance.

'Sir, could you tell me where I am?'

'This place is called Pebble Bank.'

'Am I near the port at Weymouth?'

'It's a bit of a trek, but it's the first town you'll come across.'

'Good, I am to meet a ship from France. At first light.' There are ferries there, I think.

'...'

'Do you have water, that I might drink?'

I don't, we don't. We do have some crème de cassis I've been tentatively swigging from during the day, so I offer him a nip. It's tart. He glugs and the parts of his expression that peek through his blond beard growth show it doesn't go down well.

'I thank you, stranger. I must away.'

'...'

'There is a dark force across this land.'

He turns, his stick glints in the half-light, and snags on a guy rope. The porch bit of the tent crumples in, but I wave him away. It doesn't matter. I crawl back in and doze again.

———

The light in a tent is different. You can tell not only how bright the day is outside but also the mood, just by how the quality of light makes the hairs on your arms look. A couple of minutes later I realise Midge has been watching me lying on my back while waving my arms in front of me like I'm doing slow-motion, clumsy t'ai chi.

'Shut up.'

'I'm cold.'

'What are you, some kind of poof?'

'Leave him alone – put a jumper on, love.'

'Yeah, you poof, put a jumper on.'

The family opposite have woken up and the father has made the classic mistake of thinking that the tent is soundproof. Well, either that or he thinks that homophobic abuse is a perfectly good way to address your 11-year-old boy in public. I'm mentally patting my pockets for my knife to slash the tyres of the car he clearly likes more than his child, when I hear them clump the doors shut and drive off.

Getting out of the tent is a bit of a hassle. The front half, which is supposed to be a porch area, has collapsed and the rain in the night has soaked through to everything, including the inner tent, because the flysheet is touching it. This fact may not mean anything to you, but if one of my old scout leaders is reading this they may come find me to take a couple of badges away. The day is as overcast as I had worked it out to be in the tent, but the earplugs I habitually sleep in had deadened how close we were to the coast. From the front of our tent, on the top of this hill, you can look out to where the grey clouds and the mist coming off the sea meet.

———————

First night in a tent wasn't too smooth for me, but I'm up early and go to the shower block with Dan. It's reminiscent of a swimming-pool changing room and, similarly, it doesn't seem possible to get dry afterwards.

———————

Me and Jon set out to find the bathroom facilities, hoping that they're open this early, and I remind him to grab his towel. Campsite bathrooms are remarkably civilised now, with tiled rooms with big mirrors and stalls for showering. Mercifully, the toilet stalls are empty of the usual Morning Dad moving his bowels shamelessly with whistling gusto.

'I thought they'd be grubbier,' says Jon, impressed as he lays out several bottles of expensive-looking toiletries, creams and pots of powder. My old wash kit is stained with dirt from a couple of continents and greasepaint, containing mostly old sticks of eyeliner, plasters and a tub of tiger balm oil. I quickly shower and dress, leaving Jon to ritually cleanse his self.

Heading back to the tent I see Midge, who I automatically point towards the toilets. Luckily, he seems equally reluctant to talk in the mornings. I take the tent down, mostly by stuffing the wet components in the bag and resolving to let stupid Future Me deal with them. I hate that smug prick, swanning around in the future. Fuck you, ME, now you've a wet, rotting tent to worry about.

Then I set to repacking the car, the second job I correctly guess will become mine exclusively during the trip. I sit in the car and wait for warmth to happen. Camping can be miserable, especially when you lie down listing all the horrible things that you have to do that day. The only way to combat that is to throw yourself into the next job as soon as you can, just get it done and enjoy the gap until you think of the next thing. It sounds obvious, but it took me 30 years to work that out. Also, as I look out into the grey, turbulent sea this morning, I realise that some parts of my life would have been a whole lot better if I'd been able to transpose that thinking to everyday life.

As we arrived last night after the reception closed, we can't leave this morning until we pay. Midge pulls up in front of the door and I get out to see if the reception is open now. It isn't, and I get back in the car with little intention of waiting another half an hour peering through the condensation.

'Let's just post the money through the letter box. I mean, we could even just do a bunk if we wanted.'

'We can't do that.'

'I don't really want to do a runner; we'll leave a note.'

I dig a brown paper bag out of my bag and scribble my name, number and the amount of money on it. We don't have quite the right change, but an extra 50 pence or so is a cheap price to pay to be on our way. The ink from my pen doesn't dry quickly and the 'Thanks' has already smeared by the time I stuff it through the metal flap.

Nobody chases us out. We head to Weymouth, happy knowing that there are two piers in the town, so we could potentially be three piers up before noon.

We reach Weymouth itself in a matter of minutes, though finding a car park isn't so easy. It's stopped raining, but the air is heavy and the sky a flat sheet of light grey. Trailing through the close back streets towards the seafront, I catch sight of a tatty newsagent where there may be cheap postcards to be had, but will have to wait to visit on the way back.

Weymouth on a grey wet morning is as miserable as it sounds, so when we look out onto the seafront and see the complete lack of piers, it is hard not to take stock of the situation. Why do I care? Why am I standing in the cold with a slight hangover, looking for an architectural feature that I haven't given more than two thoughts about before this trip? I was never a big fan of piers before this and, after two days of looking for them, I am beginning to hate them.

The pier entrance is across an expanse of tarmac with dips and pits of water. The bottoms of my jeans, already ratty, are damp and flick against my heels as our steps quicken. At the side of this wasteland car park, a metal arch announces the 'Pleasure Pier' across little more than a pavement along the front.

'Both of those things are a lie,' says Danny.

But, when we cross the expanse of depression, past the toll gate for the ferry, there is a pier of sorts.

WEYMOUTH Commercial & Pleasure

Opened: a structure on the same site was there since 1812 but, as we now know it, 1933

Length at start: 900 ft (274 m)

Length now: 1,300 ft (396 m)

Burn baby burn? The pavilion theatre, built in 1908, burnt down in 1954 (when it was known as The Ritz) and was rebuilt as the current Weymouth Pavilion.

A cargo stage was added in 1877 to facilitate the landing of Channel Island potatoes. Land reclamation alongside the pier, and the failure of planned Olympics-related refurbishment, have left this pier a dull concrete outcrop. The opening ceremony was carried out by the Prince of Wales, soon to become King Edward VIII. No information survives as to whether it was a factor in the abdication.

We follow the edge of the car park on a metal path away from the front and we reach a large bus stop painted council cream. There's a cafe up on the second floor of some building or other but the sign is so cheap and weather-worn that I can't tell if the cafe will open later this morning or 40 years ago. The only signs of life are dispirited teenage graffiti and an arcane sign that tells us NO FEATHERING, which I can only presume is a fishing thing, not a teenage sex thing. The area smells of salt and piss and, despite the relief of Redcliff Point appearing in the distance through the haze, we quickly check this pier as 'done' and start the long walk through the car park back to the front.

Little more than a thrust of concrete into the thick sea, the pier is two levels of flaking despair. The centre is taken up with a moulded building, each entry into it blocked with gloss blue paint bubbling off warped wood. There are people here fishing, but they're not happy. We are, or at least I am. This is the sort of dankness that I thought we might find, one of the downsides of the seaside – it's an interesting depression. This is pier as functional item and the function is no longer required.

There's a concrete (of course) viewing platform of sorts, but it's fenced off. The concrete blocks that steady the wire mesh don't hold it tight. We could get up there if we wanted and I can sort of feel Danny's mind mulling the idea. I say nothing.

People are starting to arrive in cars to wait for the next boat as we head away. I overhear a guy in a heavy hi-vis coat suggest that the next crossing will be delayed. It dawns on me that not every part of the trip can be driven by our spreadsheet – we're due to get over to the Isle of Wight this evening. I'm not sure I'd be able to be calm if the ferry were cancelled. I know that something will go wrong. I know that we've built in contingency days, I know we've not booked any of the campsites as such, but it'll still come as a dull drop to the stomach when something is seriously 'up'. Add to that the fact that tonight we're stopping at a mate's house, and I don't want to mess him around.

———————

After World War One, Fred Barrington, Swift Vincent and others made large-scale sand sculptures on the beach at Weymouth, taking advantage of sand which is reputedly closer to silt than actual sand. Even though upon investigation it just feels like, well, sand really. The tradition of sand sculptures still lives on and we walk past a pretty impressive version of the Mad Hatter's tea party, presumably inspired by the recent Tim Burton movie version of Lewis Carroll's classic *Alice in Wonderland* story. I am torn between respect for the artist (and the massive amount of time and skill it would have taken him to create it) and the urge to jump down and attack the thing with a golf club. Even the imagined satisfaction of seeing all that hard work crumble keeps me a little warmer as we walk to the next pier.

———————

There is – according to the list – another pier here. It could scarcely be worse, and it isn't. It's okay, it's nice, with a nautical art-deco look about it and a clock atop it, reminiscent of every 'Clock Garage' from Castle Bromwich to Spondon. It's called the Pier Bandstand but doesn't look much like it hosts fat men in starched jackets pursing their lips every Sunday. It doesn't look much more than a cafe-cum-arcade that overhangs the beach a little.

WEYMOUTH Bandstand

Opened: 1939 (Architect: V. J. Venning)
Length at start: 200 ft (61 m)
Length now: 48 ft (15 m)

Burn baby burn? The seaward end was dynamited by two schoolgirls – as competition winners – in 1986, leaving only the bandstand and making it the shortest pier in the UK.

Only a third of the 2,400 audience seats were under cover of the two cantilever roofs, which could often put a dampener on performances.

Pier Bandstand, Weymouth hasn't been a proper pier since 1986 when two schoolgirls, winners of a national competition, pressed a button that set off a small amount of explosives and destroyed the crumbling seaward end that had become too costly to maintain. Although, with the mood I am in, it would have saved them the price of the explosives if they had given me half an hour and a nine iron.

All that stands there now is a tacky-looking arcade and a Chinese restaurant, half fenced off by the sort of giant metal fence panels that serve no real purpose because a child can push them down.

***

The wind is drying the air, but drawing up the particularly fine sand. We trace our route back to the car and I stop to buy as many postcards as I conceivably can – they are dreadful, poorly cartooned in pencil rather than ink, card fraying at the edges due to a lack of lamination and low sales turnover. The jokes are similarly stuck in the hateful seventies, one of them centred around a homosexual man at an army recruitment office. Don't ask, and I won't tell you how queasy it makes me feel. I buy six of each; they are cheap.

There were plans, which never materialised, to turn the two so-called piers at Weymouth into two actual piers as part of the whole seafront being remodelled for the London 2012 Olympics. I don't know why money should flow so far down to the coast just for some sailing event, but if we were trying to push for sand modelling to be introduced as an Olympic sport, I'd be all for it – so long as nicknames like Swift Vincent catch on.

The drive to Swanage is silent, punctuated only by the six or seven songs that 6 Music play and the intrusive bossiness of the satnav. The joy of reaching a new pier is already being tarnished by repetition and disappointment, and is being taken over by the joy of unfolding my back and legs from a car that, despite our best efforts, is beginning to smell of socks, of damp and of men.

Near a place called Worgret Heath, foot-high letters painted on a trailer at the side of the road read 'NO GIANT WIND TURBINES HERE'. We've seen plenty. They change colour as you pass them for no other reason than the differing of the light. The relentless swoosh and cut of the air drums the heartbeat of the landscape. They are powerful. They are beautiful.

I'm aware that some don't like them, but I've never really seen the reason why – sustainable power generation does seem to be gaining a foothold in the south. There are solar panels everywhere. If you don't like them you don't like them, but the campaigners always say 'NOT HERE', implying that they'd be fine if they were on the other side of the hill or in the next town. Not here, near Weymouth, on the road to Swanage. Not with our history here on the Jurassic Coast. Not where we take our rowing boats out to the secret cove for a picnic.

———————

Walking down the hill, I remember something.

'We should get something to eat after this one.' As I say this, I see Midge visibly sags with relief.

Jon hesitates. 'Three or four more piers today and I don't want to be late meeting Dean.'

'You guys haven't eaten since we started,' says Midge.

'That's not true.' Jon doesn't sound too sure.

I start thumbing through my notebook. To be honest, it could be true; I fried my hunger glands long ago with cheap speed and cider, and I now rely on cues from the people around me to remind me to eat. But if the people around you are a body-conscious mod and a tiny punk too polite to mention that we promised to sort out his food arrangements, it could just be possible that Midge was right.

'Ha, that's a lie!' I pound my notebook with satisfaction. 'We had toast for breakfast.'

'That was yesterday...' Midge's eyes narrow, checking if I'm joking.

A couple of pages in my notebook pop unstuck.

'Oh, okay, let's get some food, food is important,' I say.

Jon just shrugs, his bin-liner coat shining despite the cloudy sky.

To get on to Swanage Pier you have to purchase a strolling ticket from a nice old gentleman in a booth. He carefully rips off the ticket from a large roll with his stiff fingers and pushes them over the counter before you have a chance to ask for them. I give him a pound coin and he stares at it like it's the Gordian Knot. I instantly feel bad for being so flash. But then I remember not to be fooled. The Swanage Pier Trust may look like charming, arthritic volunteers but they are in fact hardcore. In 1993 they took ownership of the pier, which had been in disrepair for 27 years, and promptly raised the £1m needed to renovate the elaborate split-level structure, even bringing the paddle ferries back to the bay.

Swanage knows its place in history: Punch and Judy, taking the waters, Leslie Ash having a Kodak moment, shipwrecks. Danny snogs the mannequins in the museum and touches things I'm not sure you should touch. He pokes a model frogman and reads the frogman's *Beezer* comic. He spends too long on the 'what the butler saw', turning the handle one battered print after another. I have a go, too. It feels like we've now got to the roots of the summer. I am most intrigued to see a young Keith Richards strobe past along with the topless exotic dancers.

It's fitting, as this is by far the most *Carry On* pier we've seen – deliberately playing up how it would feature on a famous McGill postcard, luxuriating in the history of a Two Ronnies film (fittingly enough, the 1982 TV Special *By the Sea*).

SWANAGE

Opened: 1896

Length at start: 643 ft (196 m)

Length now: 643 ft (196 m)

Burn baby burn? No, but breached in 1939 as a war precaution and damaged during strong weather in 2013.

An earlier pier existed nearby, which was used to load locally quarried stone onto waiting boats. The current version has a museum stuffed full of 'saucy' Donald McGill postcards and 'What the Butler Saw' machines. The pier has over 100,000 visitors a year, which in 1982 included both of the Two Ronnies.

The pier is pleasant, with much white ironwork around its edges. Brass plates underfoot contain messages, sometimes personal, sometimes quirky and amusing. Occasionally someone has put flowers between the slats next to the plaques. Anglers dot the edges, only discernible from the men just standing there by the equipment they scarcely touch.

A paddle steamer boards and leaves while we are on the pier, much to our amusement. Swanage is the first split-level pier that we have seen and we are dwelling longer than usual because the atmosphere has a jolliness to it that we haven't really experienced yet on the trip.

————————

Further up the pier a fisherman's mobile rings. There's blood smeared across a memorial bench, cast sparklingly in light reflected off the white cliffs. The boards, the lumpy iron railings, the hand-painted signs for boats to catch, all seem lit for and shot in an old grade of film – bright reds and slightly off-whites dominate.

————————

'What are you doing?' I straighten up and turn to face Midge with as much nonchalance as I can force.

'Nothing.' I scrunch up my face and shake my head to illustrate how much nothing it is I am doing.

'Yes you are, you're stuffing something between the boards. I saw you at the last pier as well. What is it?' Midge presses with a smile on his face.

I've always had the impression that Midge's continued friendship with me has always come from his certain knowledge that, however odd or different he is from the general populace, it comforts him to know there's always someone weirder.

'It's salt.' It was bound to come out sooner or later. 'I'm trying to make a protective salt ring around the country. It's a magick thing.' Midge walks over and looks down.

'And you can do that with sachets of salt from KFC?'

'It's symbolic.'

'It's bollocks,' he says with a laugh.

We ask a passing tweed cap to take our photo, faces through the holes, as a young family with fat wife and all.

Looking around Swanage town we are overwhelmed with the food choices. I suggest the Wimpy we walk past. Wimpy was the English burger bar that existed in this country before McDonald's. I honestly thought they had all closed and can't think of a better metaphor for a dying English culture than eating in a now nearly defunct chain hamburger shop.

'I'm not eating in a fucking Wimpy,' Midge says flatly. Granted, he hasn't eaten much in the last three days and is probably looking forward to an actual meal.

'Come on, it's perfect, look,' I say, gesturing to the menu of food that all looks terrible.

'Definitely not, no.' Midge storms away.

Jon shrugs, his apathy for food balancing almost neatly with his love of obscure British brands.

Wimpy made it from America to England 20 years before McDonald's and quickly spread to India, Japan, Ireland, New Zealand and South Africa. It was the only game in town as far as chain restaurants or American-style dining was concerned. From my youth I remember a mascot that consisted of a hamburger dressed as a Beefeater (and I half remember a

Spectrum computer game starring the squat tower warden). Even back then Wimpy had been erroneously marginalised as an English knock-off of McDonald's glamorous authenticity. Since then, you still see them around the country, cowering in service stations like beaten dogs or looking confused on some backwater high street, sticking out like a pensioner wearing their slippers to the post office. The most English thing about Wimpy is not the table service that they seem to have a child-like stubbornness in keeping, but their tenacity to stick around, refusing to believe in defeat because of their once brief but almost worldwide dominance.

We head into town, make a circuit of the eateries, and choose to eat dry fish and chips. Due to some complicated system we manage to confuse the waitress enough for her to bring cans of cider we haven't ordered. We obviously look like the cider-before-lunchtime types. We eat quietly, drinking ginger beer, aware perhaps that we've snagged the best table in the restaurant. There are regulars, old guys and gals on permanent vacation, or those who quickly gain a routine while on holiday, who want the table. It's the one with the sea view. We have our heads down, writing. The table is fairly silent. I exchange a few Internet messages and think of the people I'm missing. Of people back in Birmingham essentially. Heinz sauces will do that to me. I squeeze some red out over my chips and feel guilty.

Nothing is as English as Heinz ketchup in the sauce game, except perhaps HP. The HP bottle really is iconic – the round-cornered square, the unusual colour and the name that has nothing to do with the taste. It's from a time before modern marketing, much like large parts of Swanage.

I went to school within smelling distance of the HP factory in Birmingham. On a day when the wind blew from Aston Cross towards the park, you could feel the tang of molasses in your nostrils. I used to swear I could tell whether it was original, fruity or curry flavour production that day. The illuminated HP sign shone like the chip-shop equivalent of the bat signal, except this one shone across the M6 as opposed to the rooftops of Gotham City; it meant you were home. We won't see it when we complete our trip, as it's been taken away. The factory closed and production moved to a cheaper facility in Holland, despite Heinz saying that they'd do no such thing when they took over the local company that had been making HP sauce for decades. The demolished site is now being rebuilt as a modern factory, with the usual mixed-use plans for a hotel alongside. Like many a modern building, it seemed to go up too quickly to have a lasting impact; construction without toil seems so temporary. The HP sign is in the storage warehouse of the local museum, the brand's association with a place now historical and intangible.

'Jon, have you noticed we're getting stared at?' I say loudly, hoping the other patrons get the hint.

'It's probably the jacket,' says Jon, once again referring to the thin bin-liner bomber jacket he's wearing. Despite its complete lack of practical value he hasn't taken it off since we left Birmingham. 'It was designed by Paul Weller for Liam Gallagher's fashion label, thus making it the most mod piece of clothing ever created.'

'Both Paul Weller and Liam Gallagher are fucking pricks, though, Jon. You're wearing a prick's coat.'

Jon looks hurt briefly then shrugs. Midge shoots me a look and I'm suddenly aware of the numerous pairs of eyes on me from the other people in the chippy, mostly elderly with either raised bushy eyebrows or jowl-wobbling heads. I try to look sorry but then shrug as well.

_____

I haven't bought Heinz products since that day; there's no orchestrated campaign, I just feel uneasy. Little choices that we can all make, little remembrances of things past. Forget the fossils in the museum opposite, forget King Arthur, forget the 'Ralph Coates museum' that I can't believe exists but am sure I saw a sign for. The reminders of history are all around us. And reminders of the present too. There's a piece of Banksy graffiti near where we get back into the piermobile. The sauce signal is calling us onward.

_____

Bournemouth is so good they named it once, but you probably have to repeat it a couple of times if they haven't got a hearing aid in. Driving into it, the place looks like a very modern student town with a one-way system that is conspiring with our satnav to give Midge an aneurysm. Bournemouth has had a reputation as a retirement resort and home of the invalid since the 1840s when a physician, Augustus Bozzi Granville, included it in a book called *The Spas of England*. Granville is also credited as the first person to perform a medical autopsy on an Egyptian mummy.

Despite its reputation, Bournemouth has always been forward-thinking. It was one of the first towns to have a telephone: reportedly the telephone number was '3'. It was also the first local authority to introduce CCTV (in 1985, one year after Orwell's prediction) supposedly to stop small crime and vandalism. However, considering that most of the council's income still comes from parking fines (the local clamping vans have an almost supernatural alacrity), it's not a big leap to suggest a connection. In spite of this, or perhaps because of it, when we find a car park we are almost immediately approached by a lady wanting to give us her car parking ticket, which still has an hour or two left on it. It seems a very English thing to do, appealing to the pagan, anti-establishment streak we've had passed down since the Saxons. Punk (the political attitude, not the fashion trend) could only really have taken root in Britain, tapping into our genetic memory of centuries spent under the rule of some invading force.

It was a precaution against the latest invasion threat that Bournemouth Pier, along with most others on the southern coast, was part-demolished in 1940. But piers are nothing if not survivors and the German threat wasn't able to finish what storms, erosion and an infestation of Teredo worm had started during the previous 84 years. Bournemouth Pier reopened in 1946 and has been given two major refurbishments since, the latest costing £1.7m in 1979.

BOURNEMOUTH

Opened: 1861 (Architect: George Rennie, then Eugenius Birch for the 1880 iron version)

Length at start: 1,000 ft (305 m)

Length now: 750 ft (229 m)

Burn baby burn? No, but wormrot, bad weather, and anti-invasion breaching by the Royal Engineers in 1940 have all damaged it at some point or other.

A much smaller jetty existed for five years before the George Rennie pier replaced it in 1861. A 1949 British Pathé film shows girls playing the 'new sport' of sea cricket (essentially cricket in the sea) with spectators watching from the pier. Continuing as a home for odd sports, it now has a zip wire, 'PierZip', connecting the pier head with the beach – reportedly the first in the world.

Bournemouth Pier also costs 6op to step onto, but this will be a brisk walk rather than a stroll through the arcade and across a seriously sturdy structure. Blue panelling acts as a windbreak, with benches and cut-throughs. Midge walks on ahead, as is becoming the norm on each pier. He's consciously giving us space to do the things he says he doesn't understand. He is, as I know and have seen, perfectly capable of doing anything we're doing, but he has decided that we're 'the artists' and he is the hired help. He's not only practical, but thinks deeply about life and how people get through it. He's also not immune to what he refers to as 'that psychogeography stuff', liking Will Self every bit as much as I do and happy to spend time in the mindspace where place and emotion collide. I think he's enjoying the trip, but we've yet to really fall into 'comfortability'. I'm not yet able to be comically nasty to him. With Danny, I can be, but we're taking a break from each other here – we are separated by the windbreak and swap over as we walk towards the theatre that blocks any view ahead to the sea. When we do walk around the theatre to the end of the pier it's a little featureless, a glass-fronted terrace for dull meals and a perfunctory coin-operated carousel. We could be anywhere.

Bournemouth seems to have been regenerated at just the wrong time: the late eighties and early nineties, a decade of mirrored glass and the sort of modernism that flirts with post- without ever being sure what the artistic movement was about. It leads to tubes of no use, metal coated in plastic, bright-but-dull red and blue. The pier and its plaza are cut off from the pavilion and gardens by a raised ring road, and the only building that you can really see on shore is a glass lump.

We watch the surfers. There's wind, but not enough for them to get much of a ride. Cue conversation about surfing: Danny will mention having a go in Australia and the film *Point Break*; Midge will admire the determination and hippyish outlook on life amongst surfers. The closest I'll get to surfing is various hair products. Still, it's a colourful and decidedly rooted activity. They can only surf with the correct conditions, right equipment and experience. They will be back; this is a commitment.

What looks from a distance like it might perhaps be another local bit of colour – a charming local craft market – turns out to be stalls of the sort of tat to be found at car boot sales up and down the country. Danny buys a leather wrist-bangle; it's too rough to be called a bracelet and it's not shiny.

'We should find a coffee shop or something,' says Jon, checking his phone for local Wi-Fi hotspots.

'By "something" do you mean "a pub"?'

'I know your 3.30 thing, but we could find a pub, yeah,' says Jon a little defensively.

'There's a holiday clause in that particular rule anyway; we could find a pub, I suppose.'

'We've got a ferry to catch later,' says Midge, 'shouldn't we just push on?' He knows that his isn't really a deciding vote and he is too tired to put up that much of a fight.

'Anyway, I've got a couple of phone calls to make. It'd be good to be in one spot to make them,' I say, deciding it.

I'm starting to feel a little cut off from the world outside the Clio, and the blandness of the surroundings isn't helping. My usual connection is the web, but the lack of electricity and the patchy phone signal mean that we haven't really been able to use it. I really fancy sitting in an airy, independent coffee shop, able to linger with my laptop, but searching the town reveals nothing quickly so we head into a pub, The Brasshouse.

It's cavernous and dark, and the air is thick with chain-food grease and fun music. It's a place for people to wait for coaches, surrounded by luggage, after the hotels chuck them out but before the holiday is officially over. The place is full of tired, irritable bonhomie and everything has the furry texture I associate with impatience. There's no one here who doesn't wish it was yesterday or tomorrow. It's the long, dark pub lunch of the soul. With chips and peas.

We find a table near to a plug socket and use the beer mats to clean off the peanut crumbs and sticky splashes of syrupy pop or lager. I plug the laptop into the wall and chain-charge my mobile too. There's no Wi-Fi, and deep within the windowless hole, little signal for 3G either. I quickly give up and offer to get some drinks. Midge is dozing, wanting nothing but to shut his eyes. Danny wants cider.

I stand at the bar for about five minutes; there are no staff serving. The indentured youth in their white shirts are tasked with moving burgers and chops, not liquids. The pub is a chain, with neat blackboards announcing the same food you can get in any town in the UK, not locally caught fresh fish or anything we might associate with the seaside. No shellfish, no winkles to be eaten with pins, no reference to anything apart from the price. They offer fish and chips, but they aren't in the slightest bit bothered to advertise which sort they've caught. In an indignant huff I retreat to the table, then go to the toilet, but my conditioned thirst drags me back and I'm able to get us some yellow fizzy. It's not nice.

Danny is on the phone to Pontins; we're intending to stay at their Southport camp for a night but that's not proving easy. In my youth I remember people joining our holiday party for a night, but booking less than a week on the phone or via the website is impossible. Playing our 'we're writers' card might be the only way in, but trying number after number to reach the press office doesn't seem to be working. They say they'll ring him back. They don't. People he's spoken to are unheard of in the office.

Finally he says: 'Of course, we'll let you read everything we write before publishing.' A beat. He mouths 'like fuck'.

I don't think it's going well and my mood is being dragged lower to match everyone else's here.

———————

I'm not a big player of computer games, but due to my addictive nature I did once accidentally play Pokémon on an old colour-screen Game Boy for 50 hours straight. And it has kind of influenced my thinking somewhat. In the world of Pokémon every new town or city you reach will have a Poké centre, in which you can recharge yourself and rest your battle-weary pets. Pubs have long since taken on this role for me. They're a place in real life where, no matter where you are, you can go to regroup, a neutral safe space out of the constant babbling stream of life. Unfortunately Midge, our own little pocket monster, is taking this a little far by actually sleeping. After three days in a car we look like rough sleepers anyway. Midge is helping no one by falling asleep. Of all the behaviours tolerated in a pub, falling asleep is rarely welcomed, so every so often I nudge him with my foot, an act that a casual observer would call a 'kick'. Of course, if there were any staff watching I'm not sure how a homeless fella with long hair kicking his sleeping mate would have looked much better.

We silently and unconsciously spread out our bathroom trips knowing that, these being the first decent comfortable toilets in a while, we may need some time. Sitting down, I study the spreadsheet for a bit.

———————

I am a huge fan of the band Blur. At their height of thought they created a melancholic Englishness that balanced the nostalgic with a soft personal blanket. 'This Is a Low' is their hymn to the shipping forecast, a radio institution loved for its hypnotic and hypnagogic shopping list of coastal locations. It cuts a blade through that yearning for a past you've never experienced; it helps to connect you with the world – to share the ennui. It'll be okay, we all feel like this. That's what makes times like this bearable, that others feel the same.

––––––––––

'Errrrrrm, guys...' I begin, back in the car and looking over the top of my laptop.

'That doesn't sound good,' says Jon, looking round from the front seat.

'What?' shouts Midge.

The music is loud in the front because there are no speakers in the back. Both Jon and Midge go to turn the music down, their fingers touch, both hands recoil slightly and Jon finally turns it down.

'Well, remember the spreadsheet? The one with all the piers and dates on it?' I begin. I have no idea how they're going to take this.

'Yeah.'

'Well, all the nights where we sleep somewhere are highlighted red.'

'Okay,' says Jon.

We both know he's only glanced in passing at the schedule.

'Well... I forgot one.'

'What?'

'I missed one, I'm looking at it here, I forgot one.'

'What does that mean?' shouts Midge, clearly struggling to listen to me, the satnav and concentrate on the road.

'Well, we're going to be away an extra night. Instead of getting home Friday it'll be Saturday. Twelve days is now the quickest we can do this.'

Jon shrugs, Midge says nothing.

'Well, we've got two weeks,' says Jon, 'is that okay for you, Midge?'

'I've got nowhere I'm supposed to be. As long as I'm back for Monday for the dole I'm all right,' says Midge.

'Well, that's all right then,' I say, as I highlight that particular row red and add an extra day of piers to my life.

A short trip up the coast, and barely out of town as such, we park right on the seafront next to Boscombe Pier. Sand is being blown into intricate concentric curves along the camber of the fresh, black road. This end of town is quiet and low-rise, and we're nestled in the crook of heathery cliff and beach. There's a glass-fronted bistro opposite us and there's a comfortingly middle-class smell of garlic. It's really unlikely that we'll get to eat or drink anywhere nice on this trip, and that's for a few reasons. One is that we're attempting to revisit our past and these sorts of places just didn't exist when we were younger. Another is that we have very little money for sustenance. But the real reason is that none of us will admit to wanting to be comfortable. We're working-class heroes, at least on the surface, and I'm not sure any of us will want to be the one to break cover first. To request hummus rather than ironic candyfloss. I am tempted, though.

I've not been making many notes in the car itself, relying on either the sameness or the shock to preserve the right memories from the bits in between stops. In the eight minutes from the municipal car park in Bournemouth to the panini belt of Boscombe's beach we pass through St Swithun's Roundabout, whereupon a flood of related memories pour down through the gap in the roof next to the radio aerial, like the rain sometimes does. Not memories about the supposed saint himself, or the weather-related superstition, more the Billy Bragg song 'St Swithin's Day' and Dubstar's cover version. Billy Bragg, known as the Bard of Barking, isn't someone who should really fit the coastal theme of the book but at his most personal his songs do speak of the clear water before overcommercialisation. This song in particular is political only in the most self-political way – it is a song of loss and memory, which is fitting for us. I've seen Billy do it live recently, and he makes reference to the film of the book – David Nicholls' *One Day* – that's supposedly based upon the song. The film *One Day* doesn't have the song 'St Swithin's Day' on its soundtrack because of the 'blatant wank reference'. Even the most sensitive of yearnings eventually leads your hands to 'make love' to a memory.

At this point I've become quite a dab hand at writing the countless postcards in the car. I am never able to remember the addresses, though. Even after writing a lot of them I still have to pull up the addresses on a tiny spreadsheet from my phone, a process that makes me inexplicably cross each time I do it. So I don't notice the sun as it creeps out from behind diminishing clouds, nor the suburbs slowly fading away into rolling countryside. This is probably why Boscombe is my favourite pier, the magical transformation from dull modern pier in a city by the sea to beautifully minimal modernist pier on a beach with blazing sunshine highlighting the difference between the two.

BOSCOMBE

Opened: 1889 (Architect: Archibald Smith, additions by John Burton in 1960)

Length at start: 600 ft (183 m)

Length now: 750 ft (229 m)

Burn baby burn? No, but was breached for defence purposes during World War Two.

The first pile was driven into the seabed by Lady Shelley, daughter-in-law of Percy Bysshe Shelley. The skeleton of a 65-ft whale that had been washed up on a nearby beach in 1887 was displayed on the pier for several years, and often used as a slide by local children. The pier 'resembles an enlarged bus shelter', according to pier expert Cyril Bainbridge, author of *Pavilions on the Sea*.

Boscombe Pier seems to be intended to be a memory of itself. It's got a fine line in modernist lettering, and it's minimalist in its descriptions: Ices, Stores, Diner, Take Away. And in a typeface suspended from the swooping shade – a light Helvetica, I suspect – are the simple words 'Boscombe Pier'. Even the postcards here are well designed, if not cheap enough for us to buy any. Everything is in keeping with the birth of the modern era, the taste of a new generation. Have you ever been to an art-deco Harvester before?

Designer bod Wayne Hemingway describes Boscombe Pier as 'one of the coolest piers in the country'. What I like about that is the inherent hedging of his bets in that statement, in case someone else might chime in and point out a slightly cooler pier to Wayne and he doesn't want to be caught out. Let's face it, no one but a very special type of fan or a certain type of idiot is going to visit enough piers to be able to contradict that statement. And being that very special type of idiot, I can confirm that Boscombe is in fact one of the coolest in the country. It's no wonder that Wayne, sort of, picked it.

Revived in the sixties by the borough's architect John Burton in the modernist style and shored up with concrete, it is indeed impressive – from the sweeping roof, looking like the wings of a fifties spaceship, to the black-and-white tiling of the entrance, even extending to the font used for the 'REEFSIDE ICES'. Both me and Jon, as design whores and font freaks, enjoy this greatly and, with no sense that it might be weird, stand taking photographs of the font, much to the confusion of the shopkeepers.

––––––––––

There's nothing on the pier as such, just benches and the ability to look away. Sky is blue, sea is green. I ponder again why we give so much meaning to the sea. Dirt is just where you are; the water is a huge blob of romance. Here, as the sun sets, there are loving couples of all ages. The older ones are sweet. Love is free and can't be taken away, only thrown away. The ultimate working-class commodity.

Though we stood together by the edge of the platform, we were not moved by them.

Honest.

––––––––––

Boscombe Pier is pretty desolate. It once hosted a theatre and roller rink. Now it is just a concrete platform jutting out to sea, bisected by a windowed windbreak in the middle, but it is nice. It could be the weather or the genuine vibe of love for the place. You can feel the pride of the little seaside town focused on this modernist quirk of our culture and it feels nice to share it.

CHAPTER FOUR

WIGHT HERE, WIGHT NOW

For such a small island, the Isle of Wight has an inordinate number of ferry services. The first that we come to leaves from Lymington. The process is surprisingly low-key. It's like a traffic jam or festival car park: you arrive at the port and really have no indication of whether people are waiting to board or just parking up. There's something inherently light and disorganised about the whole process.

Without really knowing what to do, we stop driving and I drag Danny along for moral support to what I think must be the ticket office. It's stark and tiled. Jacketed smiles sit behind protective glass. There's an expanse of white grid flooring and a confusing lack of queuing or activity. I hesitantly negotiate some sort of open return ticket. It costs a lot – £60 or more.

We get back in the car and in a couple of minutes a guy in a hi-vis jacket starts beckoning us forward. Up a clanking ramp, and then into exactly the right place on the deck. We have to stay in the car until some light goes on or some door closes.

For those of us in our working-class thirties the ferry was usually the first way we'd leave home soil, maybe on the sort of short trip we're taking now: to France or one of the British Isles. All of the journeys work in the same way: wonder at the engineering solution of packing the cars and people so tightly, then wonder at the shape-cut doors and the way your body feels a different weight. And boredom.

Ferries are slow, almost glacially so. Almost immediately we head to the canteen and buy cans of lager. A nagging part of my psyche wants to be wearing Union Flag boxer shorts and throw some plastic furniture around. I quell this class group memory and sit down to enjoy a particularly interesting item in the free magazine about the garlic farm on the island.

I know almost nothing about the Isle of Wight. I honestly couldn't have pointed to it on a well-labelled map before I started planning the route. I was sure that there was an island off Britain that was a weirdo tax haven but that was more likely to be the Isle of Man, and I knew a friend of mine had worked there for a summer (his verdict: 'fucking boring as shit'). I also know Dean lives on the island. I've never met Dean but Jon seems confident in how well he knows him and has said there is a place for us to stay, a fact I appreciate even after only one night spent under canvas.

For Danny and me the boredom comes straight away, sitting opposite each other at a window table. Midge's comes either before that, as he continues away from us to the upper deck, or when he returns to sit and talk.

We exhaust the entertainment options quickly. Like any space where the public are regularly trapped without distraction – life's waiting rooms – someone will eventually come up with a plan to shovel media at them. Posters become leaflets become advertorial magazines become rotating plasma screens. Content has to be rootless and free of time – because it costs, costs to update – so it becomes nothing so much as a mulch.

Midge is bored, restless, and under-breaths 'fuck off' at a crying child, but in our direction. I ignore it.

We compare the blue of the cans to the blue-green of the sea and make notes. We've been rumbling along for at least 20 minutes and don't really seem to have left the mainland. Scrubby outcrops are still sauntering by as I contemplate the isle ahead.

———————

The slowness of the ferry and the bright sunshine are sapping any momentum we have built up today, as are the cans of booze me and Jon put away on the crawl over the water. The deadline of 'no driving in the dark' hangs over us. We have four piers to hit before meeting Dean and it gets dark about an hour after we dock.

———————

There's a pier in Yarmouth, and it's less than ten yards from where we get off the ferry. Midge heaves the car into a bay and we waste no time at all ticking it off the list.

On our spreadsheet, which we can now only see intermittently because it's on the Internet rather than on a piece of paper in the glovebox, Danny has put an 'info' column. He had sat and looked for information on each pier: adding postal addresses, contact details and, in one or two cases, entrance fees. It had never occurred to me that you might have to pay to go onto a pier. They were, I thought, nothing more than palaces of consumerism – arcades, food – so that entry fees would have been as odd as having an entry fee to the supermarket or the pub.

Yarmouth Pier has an entry fee of 30p, but no real way of enforcing it. No gate, no volunteer, just a cast-iron tub in which to slip your coins. I dig through my shrapnel and start putting in our contribution. For some reason the idea of paying to get onto what is evidently little more than a boardwalk turns Midge off. He wanders off over the crumbling tarmac and down the side of the pier towards the beach. We press on. To nothing much.

YARMOUTH, Isle of Wight

Opened: 1876 (Architects: Denham and Jenvey)

Length at start: 685 ft (209 m)

Length now: 609 ft (186 m)

Burn baby burn? No, but has been hit by drifting boats a couple of times.

Originally built to dock steamers from the English mainland, which is 'amusingly' known as the North Island by locals, it provided a base for all sorts of transport. In the nineteenth century it was quicker to travel by steamer from Yarmouth to Cowes than to go by carriage. The Isle of Wight road system has improved. A bit.

It's 'still the longest timber pier in England open to the public', which doesn't sound like much but, given that the constant attacks by gribble worm mean that the timbers always need replacing, that's some achievement. Housewives' favourite Alan Titchmarsh has led the most recent battle to keep the structure safe.

There's no glamour to Yarmouth Pier. It's the longest wooden pier in England, but even to people who have a vested interest in piers that's quite a dull fact.

To me Yarmouth Pier is notable because it's the first pier that Midge chooses not to go on to.

'Why would he not come onto the pier?' I ask Jon, nudging him.

'Why would he?'

'Well, he's going to every pier anyway. He might as well be able to tell people that he's been on every pier in England and Wales.'

'Not everyone is... like us,' says Jon with a strange mix of shame and pride.

With the sun low in the sky and a view that is truly strange to an Englishman – one where land can be sighted over a huge stretch of water – Yarmouth Pier lends itself to quiet reflection. But we have other piers to visit.

I think perhaps that the Isle of Wight's tourist season lasts a little longer than that of the mainland. It's getting on in the day but still warm; we lean over the railings and look out over the water past the now-loading ferry. Dan tries to explain how to tell how long it is until sunset. He stretches out a thumb to the horizon.

'So the sun sets in the... er...' I'm guessing, as this is one thing that never sticks in my head. There's no way I can naturally remember left and right or east and west, so every time my hands have to do a little weighing-scales dance before I work it out. '... west.'

'Right.'

Dan explains something learnt at a far-off scout camp, involving the distance of the sun above the horizon. I understand it for just as long as he's saying the words. My eyes are drawn downwards to the boards. Each is punched with a dedication. Letters painted white and gouged out with a stencil font we're sure is a standard. It's not the first time we've seen this. Piers are trying many ways to pay for their upkeep and this one is trying them all. There's a 'Lottery Funded' sign, the toll and these names: they're part memorial, part about belonging to a community. Some are obviously commemorating lives lived, but there's a sense of people wanting to belong to the area and perhaps to the pier – including a 'Pier Preservation Group', which makes me think of Ray Davies and whether we're getting sucked into that 'strawberry jam, vaudeville and variety' world. A false nostalgia.

This is a most genteel form of graffiti, a sanctioned and celebrated act of tagging. A kind of territorial pissing for the philanthropic classes. I've only ever written my name with a marker pen on public property once, and the fear of being caught (by the driver of the number 11 bus) meant I never became a graffiti artist. We are, by making this trip, making a sort of mark around the country, at each place an invisible blue plaque erected upon history.

We have to trust the satnav as we drive to Totland Bay, because it seems that on the Isle of Wight they removed all the road signs to confuse the Germans, but never got round to putting them back. We pull in. There's a small beach with public toilets, a parking bay with three spaces and a ruined pier. A couple sit in their car staring out to sea while a dog climbs over them looking for the thing that restless dogs look for but never find.

TOTLAND BAY, Isle of Wight

Opened: 1880 (Architects: S. H. and S. W. Yockney)

Length at start: 450 ft (137 m)

Length now: 450 ft (137 m)

Burn baby burn? There was a fire in the amusement arcade in 1978, and weather damage finished it off.

It was bought and used by artist Derek Barran as a studio from 1999 until 2008. Derek says 'I'm told that a lot of local people were created on this pier, so it's clearly had its moments. We've had some pretty good parties here ourselves.' It's now closed after failing to meet the guide price in an auction.

From over here the view of England – the whole country which we are attempting to drive around, along with Wales – lends humility to the decision we've made. The decision I have made to get away. While you can quite clearly see the coastline and some of the activity on it, you have no real idea where it begins or ends on the left or on the right. The sun sets slowly and, in the browning light, the rust stalactites tearing themselves from the structure look ancient and organic. Totland Bay Pier is boarded, scorched and crumbling, but a beautiful site and sight. The sky only flecked with cloud, I can feel the outdoors press hot against my cheeks.

We slip down to the pebble beach, where Danny sits on a wooden strut and I search for flat stones. I've never been particularly good at skimming stones, but I play ducks and drakes all the same.

We linger much more than perhaps the structure itself deserves, long enough for people to park up, walk away and then return, having walked a series of nice-looking dogs along the seafront. We're quiet and happy as we leave in the last of the light and drive across the island to Ryde.

It occurs to me that the term 'dogging' may have come from the cover that its participants use. Remote public spots where you can wank someone off through the window of a Ford Mondeo are also essentially where people go and walk their dog (or conduct drug deals). There is something very British about dogging; with its arcane system of rules and signals, the sheer organisation coupled with crippling furtive exhibitionism is something only us repressed Brits could do, polite even in our perversion.

The couple we see are not dogging, as far as I'm aware, but I do consider telling Midge to flash the lights three times just to see if the old woman might present her naked arse to the passenger-side window. They're simply enjoying the view, though, which is stunning. The sun setting over the sea in a clear sky gives everything a weird overexposed photograph quality. Jon, lost in his own thoughts, is clearly stunned and even Midge ceases his endless mooching to watch the sun set. I try and climb the pier but only succeed in hanging off one of the struts shouting at Jon to take a photograph. Before the sun sets completely I look up to see the ramshackle pier completely silhouetted against a red sky and then even I stop. The image burned into my memory. Looking down I see someone has set aside a near-perfect, heart-shaped pebble on a low post. I know a talisman when I see it, and it stays in my pocket for the rest of the journey.

The phone signal is patchy and I've had a missed call from Dean – in whose house we're being put up tonight. He lives close to Ryde and its pier, so we're adjusting plans to see the last pier on the island (at Sandown) in the morning. All in all, they're better in the light.

Everything about the island is obviously quaint; the place is in some ways a preserved microcosm of the larger island over the sea. We pass warning signs about red squirrels, and joke about them attacking us. We also pass a sign for Animal Farm. I look from Danny to Midge and can easily tell one from the other.

We park on a surprisingly industrial road alongside the seafront. It's now dark and in the gloaming what lights there are are not welcoming. The front is not busy, the pubs are empty and the pier stretches out over the black reflective water into the dark. Ryde Pier is a long one, so long that it has a real – ex-London – tube train that runs up it. We head into the station, which seems to have managed to take on the utilitarian appearance of travel links everywhere. Posters behind scuffed plastic, yellow tubed light, it feels like we're heading back home on the last train from some outer suburb.

There's a train on the platform as we arrive, and I finally pick up a call from Dean. He's in a pub just over the road. While I'm saying hello and that we'll join him in a short while, Midge and Dan leap onto the train. I'm a little confused as to where we buy tickets, looking around and talking to Dean. The doors close with me still on the wrong side of them, and I feel that hairy, sinking feeling in my gut. I've missed the train. I'm alone. They look at me through the window with a mixture of pity and banterish glee.

And then the train pulls off away from the pier.

In the wrong direction.

I wave cheerily.

But I'm alone.

The train carriage is decorated like a thirties tube and is populated by people who seem bemused by our predicament. The ticket collector turns out to be completely sympathetic and doesn't ask us for a fare.

RYDE, Isle of Wight

Opened: 1814 (Architect: John Kent)

Length at start: 1,740 ft (530 m)

Length now: 2,305 ft (703 m)

Burn baby burn? No fires, but in 2012 a car collided with the railings of the pier causing £10,000 worth of damage.

The oldest seaside pier in England: April 2013 was the 200th anniversary of the laying of the pier's foundation stone. The following month, a small section of the three-metre-long gangway at the pier's main berth collapsed into the sea.

The now-demolished Concert Pavilion features in Philip Norman's book, *Babycham Night: A Boyhood At The End Of The Pier*. His family ran the venue in the fifties, when it was known as the Seagull Ballroom.

Looking around the platform I see that there isn't another train up to the end of the pier for about 20 minutes and I don't fancy the wait, so I start to walk. Once around the front of the pier you can walk up alongside the train track, safe from electrocution only by your good sense and a crossed-wire mesh. The pier isn't only dark; it's damp and industrial. There's nothing to see and not just because of the gathering gloom. The pier is almost entirely featureless, forcing itself out into the channel to a dock of some kind. There's no one else here, nothing to see, nothing to think about. I abandon the pier and head to the pub, nearly taking a side-swipe from an incoming bus.

This pier is work, not play. The road is work too, a surprisingly complex dual carriageway, not the quaint beauty of the other towns we've seen on the island. I text to say where I am going:

'Hola trainspotters, am in pub on front: The Marine Bar. See you soon xx'

I do feel a little bad for not spending more time on the pier, but a half-hour walk in thin drizzle to, well, nothing isn't what this trip is about. We've already not made it on to, or to the end of, some of the piers as a result of fire, dismantlement or our own tardiness – so being in the pub next door isn't a problem. In fact, in my more self-aware moments, I think that 'in the pub next door' is somewhat my station in life. I'm often the first to want to leave any gathering, feeling that I've seen enough, that I'd rather escape the pressure of the herd. I've lost count of the number of support bands I've missed at gigs because of being in the pub next door. I've arrived late, left early, and nipped out. All to be where I'm comfortable instead of where there are too many people and too many decisions. I've often thought that if I was at the Last Supper I'd have missed the bread and wine bit, because I'd have said 'fancy a pint?' to Matthew or Judas and been downstairs in the public bar.

Dean is in the public bar of the Marine Bar and Diner, a glossily painted and cream-wall-and-brown sofa type of a place. Only the photos of scooter boys and mods tastefully framed on the wall give it any personality at all.

Dean is easy to spot. He's the only one in there. Ryde is off-season.

I've travelled quite a bit, and while travelling there is a certain feeling you can grow about the inevitable fuck-ups you make, a special sanguine attitude that you develop. I see this immediately form on Midge's face. To his credit the shrug is almost audible as we both start laughing at the situation.

We exit the train at the next station and a quick look at the timetable tells us that the next one back is in half an hour. We caught the right train at the right platform, just going in the wrong direction. The station is a smaller version of most of the train stations found inside or just outside cities all over Britain; pretty much unchanged from Victorian times, with filigree ironwork painted a bright racing green. On the opposite platform a couple take a break from their bickering to eye us suspiciously. I spend my time with my eyes closed listening to the satisfying 'chink chink' of Midge pacing around, enjoying the only chance to stop and wait I've had in three days.

'Jon's at the pub with Dean. If you get off at the stop where we got on you can go meet them,' I tell Midge as we get on the train.

'Where are you going?'

'I'm staying on and going to the end of the pier like we intended.'

'Then so am I.'

Ryde Pier has nothing at the end of it but a bland and dirty docking station for the Wightlink catamaran and is as grubby and utilitarian as a suburban bus stop, without even a fruit machine for entertainment. There is little to look at and with another half-hour to wait for the return train we elect to walk the 2,305 ft (I checked) back down the adjacent walkway. The way is plain, apart from a streetlight every 50 yards or so and even they do little to mitigate the crushing black you get out at sea at night.

Halfway down we look at a perfectly round moon doubled on a flat sea. As above, so below. Magick mostly works on the principle that smaller, simpler versions of things can stand for the things themselves. So by being in a certain frame of mind and by manipulating these symbols you can affect the larger world.

I've never been one to take a lot of photographs, but when I point out the reflected moon to Midge I understand his want to get his camera out.

'It's amazing,' Midge says, bending down to his viewfinder.

'It's magick,' I whisper to no one.

It's good to see Dean again, and to have some time alone with him before the others catch up. He's a very old friend who moved over here a few years ago, extending an open invitation to come to stay whenever – and now I'm taking full advantage by dragging two unwashed strangers with me. We chat about family and mutual friends, and I try to explain what I'm doing. Dean is keen to reminisce and tell me about some of the things he's been doing and about the island. Seeing Melvyn Hayes walking past the shop where he works is the highlight.

My madness and my friends – who turn up after we've had about two pints – are easily accepted. A real friend does that. You have shared histories: in this case Dean's been my football manager, employer, business partner and drummer. That's enough to be getting along with. He's been a formative influence on me – helping to plant the idea that you can do odd things and still live in the real world.

———————

Dean turns out to be a friendly, ruddy-faced man who has the considered opinion of a guy who has been around. I instantly like him. I get the impression that Dean has not only been around the block a few times but has been around some other blocks and a motorway or two as well. He's not really clear about why he moved to the Isle of Wight in the first place, but I imagine the story would be an entire book of its own. Because of the family I have, and the jobs that I've done, I have been around most types of scurrilous, dangerous and corrupt people that a working-class background can produce. I find that the people who have seen, done and lived the most have a certain silence, a way of talking without saying anything, a confidence that comes from the lack of bragging that belies a man who would rather demur and watch than crow and boast. As genial as these people are, make no mistake, they are the scary ones.

There is an amount of this vibe I get from Dean, a no doubt nice guy, evidenced by not only the fact he was willing to support our venture and put up a mate with two strangers, but also by the way he was so happy to do so. We stayed up late into the night at his place, drinking cider from cans, discussing our leftist leanings, and shouting at *Newsnight*. Pausing only briefly to appreciate being indoors.

———

On BBC Four is a programme showing swathes of a black-and-white British Pathé film about a young woman in Italy and her holiday romance. She swooshes through the piazzas of Rome, enchanted by the air, the sun and the freshness of discovery. She smiles and I have an almost uncontrollable desire to talk about how I've decided my smile has changed. I've appropriated the smile of a friend of mine, I think. I shape my lips before I let my bottom one drop to reveal my teeth. Danny recognises the signs and changes subject midstream.

Dean talks some more about life on the Isle of Wight. It's very insular apparently – very hard for outsiders to get work. He was lucky enough to be helped by an old mate who he works for selling and installing window blinds. He also tells me about the trouble he's had managing a football team – young lads of 16 and 17 – every game is against a team from or on the mainland and there are continual fights. He's giving it up.

———

Dean had to be up before us so he retired first, leaving us to find the spare room with one bed and two airbeds. Jon, of course, bagsied the bed.

———

I'm roused from sleep by a shout. It's about 4 a.m.

'Help!'

I stumble over Danny and Midge, who are sleeping on the floor, and hurry towards the cry. We're in a secluded part of a quiet island. This isn't the childish scream of a teenage drunk.

'Help me! God.'

I pull on my pumps and open the front door, carefully pulling it to but not closed.

'Help!'

It's coming from the other side of the house. I jog through the garden past the bins. I can hear something moving in the scrubby bushes. But when I get there: nothing.

I dodge through the gap down a narrow path of sorts – lit only by the light from the upstairs apartment – and finally come out on to pebbles and can see the sea. I'm alone. It's a special kind of dark where you can see every star in the sky, not something you ever will do in Birmingham. Cities pollute even the night.

I run over the beach, and I fall over something.

———————

Dreaming. Blue and yellow shapes float. A shout. A sudden pain in my side, a scream and a weight hitting the floor. Not altogether awake, I look around, not quite working out where I am. To my left is Jon, face down, half-groaning, half-laughing. Serves him right.

———————

I'm roused from sleep by a shout. It's about 8 a.m.

'Jon, I'm off to work.' Dean had said he started early, but I'd assumed that I'd be up by the time he went. I put my trousers on, and have a cup of tea with him as I think about leaving the house.

'It's been good to see you,' he says. 'You should come back soon.'

'I will, mate. Thanks a load for this, it's been good to sleep in a bed after last night.'

'You have a long way to go. I hope you find what you're looking for.'

'I just hope we make it.'

'Help yourself to anything you need, and make sure you check out my private beach before you go – it's round the side of the house and down the path. Each apartment here gets a stretch of beachfront. You're not allowed to own the beach on the mainland, but you are here.'

'I will. I'll go down before we leave.'

And with that we hug, and he leaves me to it.

The private beach intrigues. While it's not exactly next to the house, the idea of having a bit of the waves that is yours alone is something I'm thinking I'd like one day.

I go for a shower, waking Danny and Midge as I pick up my wash bag. I get to the bathroom to find I've not brought my shower gel or shampoo with me, so I use some of Dean's. Rifling through my bag after I'm dressed, I can't find them in there at all, and I realise I've left them in the shower block at the Weymouth campsite. I'm pissed off. They were expensive items, but it could be worse. I stuff my remaining toiletries and my towel into my shoulder bag, leave it by the sofa and make tea for the boys. I want to hurry them up and make the place clean and tidy enough to leave.

Midge is sitting watching breakfast television. I suddenly hugely fancy the female half of the presenting team. Danny complains the milk is off, and I don't fancy anything.

———————

Dean has gone by the time we get up and Midge is silent in the mornings. He exudes a 'don't fuck with me' vibe, finely honed, I suspect, from years of being a man of below-average height in the swirling crowd of a punk pogo pit. We leave Midge to his ablutions as we head to the 'private beach'. Following a route that may or may not have been through other people's gardens we arrive at a small shingle beach. Over the water I can faintly make out the coast of England, the weird sail of Portsmouth's

Spinnaker Tower jutting up over a largely flat skyline. At once I feel very far from home yet am reminded that the world is a very small place.

We've had to walk across a lawn pregnant with dew – my feet are soaking. Again we look at the mainland and plan our trip back to it. Turns out that we can't get the ferry from Ryde on the ticket I'd bought, so we have to go back across the island to Lymington. Sort of fitting, but it will mean maybe being an hour or so later to Brighton tonight.

'Jon, is this yours?' I hold up a holdall. The bag wasn't with the rest of our stuff but left in the corner of the living room.

'All my stuff is in the car,' he says, although god knows how he would know that because I have just packed his stuff while he was in the bathroom.

'Are you sure?'

'Yeah, it's probably Dean's gym bag or something.'

Outside, Midge is checking today's route on a tiny map covered in gaffer tape he brought with him.

'Is this yours, mate?' I shout down to the car, holding the bag up for him to see.

'Nah, all my stuff's in the car.'

I know all his stuff is in the car because I had to repack it to get Jon's in, but it was worth checking. I go back inside.

'Are you sure it's not yours, Jon?' Jon looks again and looks at me with an 'I'm not a child, mom' stare. I leave Dean's gym bag where I found it and begin the process of folding myself into my nest.

I do a last sweep of the flat. Dean lives in about a quarter of a beautiful, old Edwardian house. I find a bag and ask Danny if it's his. He says no and so does Midge. It's got a towel on top so it must be Dean's gym bag. I place it carefully back where it came from and make sure the electric sockets are all off. After one last confirmation that we've got everything, we reverse off the gravel drive.

———————

With only a slight chill to the breeze reminding you it's not the bright summertime, we head towards Sandown Pier, the most obvious pleasure pier on the Isle of Wight. We park a couple of roads away from the sea to escape what I presume is mounting parking costs, judging from Jon's frowning face whenever money is mentioned. But the sun is already stark in a clear sky and as we walk down the road to the seafront we are greeted by a flat, azure sea. The memory, even now, is bright and saturated like a cartoon.

'Are my glasses straight?' I look at Jon after ten minutes of trying to adjust them.

'Yep, it's your ears that are fucking wonky, you ugly bastard.' The severity and shock of the abuse is of course directly proportional to the level of friendship.

———————

Whether it's the sun, the early morning or the fact we're nudging ever further south, Sandown is bright and seasidey. It's busy and we just sort of stop when the town starts to fill out, thinking that the pier can't be far. The place is bigger than we think, and we pass real shops and tourist ones. Cafes waft noise and bacon as we hurry down a sloping alley to the front – it's good.

A jogger goes past. I wait the appropriate distance before saying:

'I think I would jog, but you never see a jogger smiling, do you?'

'It ruins the knees,' says a deep Geordie accent. We look around to see a friendly witch, dressed in a shabby, black raincoat and mad skirt.

'I've heard that.' I smile at her, for fear of being turned into a toad.

She laughs like I've told a joke and because mine and Jon's pace has slowed to allow her to overtake us. We watch as she walks ahead, still chuckling. All three of us turn to each other with raised eyebrows and head towards the pier.

I've been worrying that we're not talking to enough people to get a true flavour of the places we're visiting. I'm reading Priestley and have been thinking that also, in a way, I'd like to do more reporting, like in Orwell's *Road to Wigan Pier*.

Sandown Pier has been through the usual cycle of deterioration and rejuvenation, including a disabling during World War Two. The most recent issue was a fire in 1989, which ripped through the pier and caused nearly £2m worth of damage.

In 1989 I was 11 and I liked to spend my weekends with my nan. This was partly because, as the first-born grandchild, I was worshipped like Mithras the golden-born and fed steak and chips for every meal, but mainly because my nan would take me to work with her. She worked in the Penny Arcade (known as that by everyone not least because of the 7-ft-diameter backlit penny coin on its front) at Lickey Hills in Rednal, also known as 'the Doss' by the local bikers who used it as a meeting place.

I remember the bikers well: a nice bunch of guys that smelt of patchouli oil and grease. They all cheered when I showed them my smile lacking the two front teeth, and when I got into a fight with my brother that resulted in a scrape on my arm. The smallest one let me sit on his bike and gave me a cloth patch with a panther on that I still have to this day.

I grew up in and near the arcade as my aunties and my mum also worked there. No visit would be complete without visiting 'Gran', the owner's mother who lived upstairs. To be honest I never enjoyed visiting Gran, because her flat smelt musty and of slightly off milk but she always gave me a 50p coin. Even better, to get to her flat you had to go through the back room, which was a mad professor's workshop of wires, games with their guts out and facades of clowns hanging in the dim light. Never getting to explore the cavernous workshop floor of the arcade properly must haunt me, because it's a background that my mind regularly drags up in dreams.

After being in the arcade all evening the owner would close up by tripping the main electric switch, turning the machines off all at once. The weird thing was that you could still hear them; all the whistles, jingles and electric barks would ring in your ears. Ghost noises.

Occasionally on this trip I hear one of those ghost noises from my youth, a certain sequence of beeps, three bars of a song that jog a memory. But it is only on Sandown Pier that I see a side-scrolling arcade game, a favourite of mine, the four-player Teenage Mutant Hero Turtles. Just seeing it in its original casing flips me back to my childhood, a time of ice-cold cans of Cherry Coke from the machine that stood by the pool tables, and of swiping money from the fruit machine one of my aunties would be playing to get enough money for a go on Street Fighter. Jon nudges me with a sharp 'come on', as if he hasn't been doing a weird little thing every time he encounters an image of Elvis, which, surprisingly, turns out to be incredibly often owing to the amount of Elvis poker games, fruit machines and grabbing cranes that appear in the arcades of Britain's coast.

SANDOWN, Isle of Wight

Opened: 1879

Length at start: 360 ft (110 m)

Length now: 875 ft (267 m)

Burn baby burn? A fire caused £2m of damage on August Bank Holiday, 1989.

At the bottom of the pier several bathing machines were installed in the 1890s, and it was in Sandown that Lewis Carroll wrote 'The Hunting of the Snark', which includes the lines:

> *The fourth is its fondness for bathing machines,*
> *Which it constantly carries about,*
> *And believes that they add to the beauty of scenes –*
> *A sentiment open to doubt.*

The theatre – now an arcade – was the largest on the Isle of Wight and hosted The Nolan Sisters, Jimmy Tarbuck, Gene Pitney, Jasper Carrott, Diana Dors, Roy Castle, Cannon and Ball, Jim Davidson and Matt Monro, amongst others.

As we tell people who ask – which is nearly everybody – we're not going to Wigan. There isn't a pier there. Sandown has one, though, and it's 'A whole day's fun in one!' according to the sign there. Nonsense, we'll prove that you can do nine in a day.

In the arcade, Danny indulges his Snake Plissken fantasies, pistol-shooting on a machine where you win tickets for a correct hit. You can imagine him in a post-apocalyptic New York fighting for his life. Until the roughly printed tokens collect round his black boots. A day's fun indeed. We get going.

As we approach the docks at Yarmouth, the petrol warning light comes on. We've been told that the prices are significantly higher on the island, so we decide to wait until we're on the mainland – but it still worries me and I try to manoeuvre my line of sight so I can tell just how much petrol is left. The queue is longer than we anticipate and I worry that the engine idling will burn away the last few drops of our juice. It's warm and the music in the car is loud.

————————

As we board the ferry what I presume to be one of the officials in a luminous yellow jacket holds up a sign that says 'All Must Appear In Judgement Before The Seat Of Christ', but we don't see any other signs on the ferry about it so we sit on the deck and write postcards instead.

CHAPTER FIVE

JEKYLL AND HYTHE

I don't recall seeing a garage near the port on the mainland – I don't recall seeing anything much – so I suggest we trust the satnav and program it to take us to the next pier via the nearest petrol station. It takes a few minutes to kick in and then directs us back the way we came into the town.

It takes a while and it's starting to become evident that we're running on fumes. Midge is cheerful for once. He casually said 'okey doke' to a guy telling him where to park on the ferry and was mortified with embarrassment. The teasing he got for it seemed to perk him up, possibly made him feel a bit more part of the gang. After a few missed turnings we make it to a Shell garage and fill right up. It's over 50 quid.

After a bit longer we're a little confused about the way we're meant to be heading. Logic suggests we should now double back on ourselves and head roughly east, but we're not. I check the 'dashboard Nazi', as Midge has taken to calling the satnav, and it's saying we've a four-hour drive ahead of us. I'd given up with postcodes after our experience the other night. The postcodes of piers aren't that useful anyway: you hit the sea, you've gone too far. I'd just typed in the name of the next town assuming we'd be able to find it.

It all looks okay, until I click through and read the map.

We're going to Hyde. Hyde somewhere by Manchester.

Not Hythe near Southampton, just up the coast. The one with a pier. We reprogram. Half an hour. That sounds more like it.

Almost every road we follow is a narrow one, boxed in by hedges. I ponder what the countryside would have looked like before the various enclosure acts, what would have bordered the way, how we would have found a path. The consequences of setting off in the wrong direction would have been a little more important. We make Hythe in good time and hurry through the tight pedestrianised streets to the seafront, spotting the thin and fragile pier framed as it is by the back of a car workshop. This side of the pier is the back garden of the Lord Nelson pub, and they are very insistent that you are not to go through the bar to get to the pier. As transitory types, the urge is to just ignore and plough on, but something about the gentle, slow nature of the town – it's busy, not bustling, low-rise and heavy – means I don't want to do anything to ruffle anyone. We retrace our steps and work round to the real entrance.

———————

Hythe has the oldest pier train in Britain and since we, the British, invented history, that means it's the oldest in the entire world. Which explains why the entrance looks like a tiny train station, a small hut for the ticket booth and all the signage branded like any rural station. The train itself leaves every 20 minutes but, as we have no time to wait, we walk the 700 yards to the end.

———————

It's not very warm, but the sun is bright enough. Something of the town reminds me of Bournville on the outskirts of Birmingham, a place that manages to appear twee on the surface despite being within a huge conurbation and existing purely because of the huge factory it was built to serve. Bournville was built by the

Cadbury family to house workers for their chocolate factory; it's very nice too – sports facilities, trees, social club and so on. The head Cadbury did it not because it was cheaper than finding a small orange tribe to kidnap, but because his Quakerism led him to believe it was possible and desirable to improve the lot of the workers. It's a little paternalist for my liking – especially its no pubs rule – but well enough intentioned and the place is quite nice. I doubt many chocolate workers can afford to live there now. It's a particular type of middle-class place harking back to the fifties.

Quakerism, I announce, is 'jazz religion'.

'It's free-form, Dan, man finding his own path to God... It's not really been that popular since the thirties.'

Danny isn't interested. And there's no one else to talk to on this walk to the pier end. The pedestrian doesn't get much width and the railway track is separated only by a thin rope propped up at intervals by splayed poles. In the huts at the end we can feel some movement underfoot, so we quicken our step, but not heavily, lest we fall through.

HYTHE

Opened: 1881 on New Year's Day (Architect: J. Wright)

Length at start: 2,100 ft (640 m)

Length now: 2,100 ft (640 m)

Burn baby burn? Nope, but a drunk boat captain did collide with it.

Has the world's oldest pier train (which is an official Guinness World Record).

From the end of the pier a ferry service once ran to Southampton. The only things there now are two large waiting rooms. One of these is empty and, by the looks of it, derelict. These long huts have rotting wood and extremely suspect floorboards. The waiting room that's open to the public has tables running around the edges and one down the middle, all holding all manner of nick-nacks and whojamawhats. The sort of treasure that looks delightful and eclectic at first glance but on closer inspection contains not one thing that you would want to own.

I make an effort to say 'hi' to the lady looking after the stall as I enter. I'm fighting my natural urge not to talk to people in order to satisfy my desire to get more from the places we're visiting. To start with, at least, I look intently at the junk in order to deflect conversation. It's not cheaply priced. I pick up a couple of books relating to the area and had they been 10p I'd have bought them, but they're approaching two quid. I flick through them and smile – replacing them carefully. Danny is outside, taking snaps of the decay on his phone and fiddling with packets of salt. I pick up a hardcover Enid Blyton book and decide it would make a good present. I like giving books. It's a pound, which isn't too bad considering it looks good and old. It's *The Island of Adventure*, which is sort of what we're... it feels relevant.

'Thank you,' says the stallholder. 'It's all for the upkeep of the pier. It needs repairing, as you can see.'

'It is a little dishevelled.' And I tell her in the broadest terms of our quest.

She's early fifties. Hennaed hair is showing growth at the roots. Her clothing speaks of a thrift that's studied – grey cardigan, blouse that doesn't quite go with the rest of the outfit.

'Many come here looking for something. But it's not here. It was, but it is no longer.'

'I'm not sure we are looking for a particular thing, for the past maybe.'

'That you'll not find here either. The community isn't what it was. We're commutable from London, there are too many people who don't care for the place really, don't interact. There's a magic where the land meets the sea, not everyone attracted by it can harness it. I control the ships; I make images of them, crude images in watercolour and ink. And I can decide if they float or if they sink. I can control you, if you become part of my art.'

'Then I can control you, because we're encircling the land. We have the power to rewrite real life in our image.'

'...'

Dan enters.

'They don't like paintings so much round here.' Calmer now. 'When I lived in Wolverhampton people liked paintings of the landscape, of the factories. Here they like photographs. Too real, no interpretation.'

In 2003 a group of Southampton football fans narrowly escaped when a drunk dredger captain steered his craft through the pier, completely severing the pier head from land. The incident cost £308,000 and the captain eight months of his life in prison. The cost of repairs has yet to be recouped, which is one reason for the jumble sale. The possibility of being smashed into any minute by a hammered sea salt on a joyride explains also the nervous scanning of the horizon by the troll guarding it.

Killing time until the train next leaves we mooch around. Occasionally she recommends some trinket and we politely refuse. Jon, made awkward by these interactions, engages her in conversation. It turns out she's both an artist and photographer lulled into a false sense of competency by boredom and the lack of any real competition from the Hythe craft community. Jon mentions our project and she seems engaged up to the point where he buys a set of postcards from her (in addition to an Enid Blyton book), pausing only to have a crack at Boscombe Pier. It seems they receive more funding than this one. The lull comes, the horrible gap where two people who have no intention of ever meeting again run out of polite things to say. Despite the bright sun and a reasonably upbeat mood up until then Jon senses my anstyness. I have a horrible habit of filling those particular lulls with the first thing that pops into my head. Jon knows this.

'What the fuck is up with your hair?' I feel my mouth form the words but, luckily, before they are articulated Jon cuts in, 'We better get going, if we're going to make Southampton.' He flashes me the stretched mouth and raised eyebrow expression that denotes 'don't say it, let's go'.

She has postcards of her ink work for sale, and it seems remiss not to buy some. Take control of her art and incorporate it into our own. They are of the *Titanic* and other liners.

In Jon's eagerness to get away, partly because the pier troll is both awkward and boring, and partly so I don't say something terrible to her, we leave before the next train arrives. Having missed the train both ways, we leave Hythe looking out for pissed boat captains all the way to Southampton.

A final decision. We've completely given up on the satnav and I've pulled a large-format road atlas from under the passenger seat.

'Where the fuck did that come from?'

'It's always been here, Midge. I just thought the satnav would be better.'

'Bastard.'

In fact we're not even using the map; we are following signs to Portsmouth and assuming we'll see Southampton on the way. The pier might be more tricky, as it no longer quite exists. The physical Southampton Pier has not been demolished as such – I don't think – but all that remains is a restaurant. Our notes say 'we must have a curry on the pier', but as we crawl through industrial estates and retail-park, landscaped roundabouts at around 11 a.m, Thai food is not on our minds. We've been following signs to the docks, but when we see the pier we also see that the sea itself is obscured by hoardings and that the pavements are guarded by yellow lines. We decide that there's not much here for us.

———————

Following a complicated one-way system we pull up outside Kuti's Royal Thai Pier, the sun high and lonely in a cloudless sky. The building, a revamp of the old entrance pavilion painted startling white, is grand and seems at odds with the scaffolding, temporary fences and vinyl banners that spill over from the Southampton International Boat Show. The mood is sour.

Angry and slightly drunk white guys in deck shoes are exchanging driving advice as they queue to pull their Land Rovers in through the gates. These are manned by security guards who are sober, but irritated by wearing the hot hi-vis jackets in the sun and being ordered about by middle-manager types who are as unaccustomed to being told 'no' as they are to the boats they pretend to sail.

Southampton Royal Pier was opened in 1833 by Princess Victoria before she was crowned queen and it enjoyed rapid expansion. The pier was expanded several times to accommodate the railway station and it became a hub of transport as well as leisure. But eventually disrepair and neglect by a private company caused it to be declared no longer 'viably maintainable' by the British Transport Docks Board. This, along with a couple of fires ten years later, effectively put an end to the pier's history.

Ideally we would have arrived late in the day and eaten, perhaps dropping our writers' credentials to score free food, but it is early in the day and we have no time to stop even if we did fancy curry for breakfast. The bad vibes from the ugly, rich white guys and the weight of hitting four more piers that day keep Midge and Jon in the car. I pull together my Hawaiian shirt, run my hand though wind-blown salty hair and walk in, my flip-flops flapping conspicuously on the polished floor.

I grab a menu and walk out again.

'Come on then, you old twat,' shouts one old white man to another equally old and privileged white man as we pull away.

SOUTHAMPTON Royal

Opened: 1833 by the then Princess Victoria (Architect: Edward L. Stephens)

Length at start: 900 ft (274 m)

Length now: Almost nothing.

Burn baby burn? One in 1987 pretty much finished it off.

Once docking up to ten steamers at a time and offering entertainment, food and even roller skating. There's now nothing but a Thai restaurant in the former gatehouse. The reviews for this place are generally good, but one review website does include this gem: 'The "manager" was unapologetic, rude and, might I add, needed to improve his oral hygiene.'

We're in a dull city, no friendly faces or distractions. There's traffic and confusing ring-road systems. As we pull out and try to get back on the road we're honked by a white-and-black security van. There's something dustily apocalyptic about the combination of stark brick, building work and demolition. The van is liveried with the name of Loomis – like Group Four, security is what you know them for, but you're not sure what shadowy things they really get up to – it's a word that makes me feel uneasy.

I spent far too much of my early teens mulling the prospect of sudden, uncontrollable death. Looking at grey-printed halftone heat maps of kill-zones, dreaming of frozen moments, clouds above the houses across from the playground. Some weeks there wasn't a day when I didn't wake half-unsure if the bomb had dropped. The constant Cold War news and films didn't help, but the thing that I think affected me most was a book we'd read in school. It featured a young girl in a patch of countryside which had somehow escaped nuclear fall-out. She was coping with the loneliness and learning to be self-sufficient when a man in a radiation suit turned up and destroyed the peace, and I remember something about rape. I can't remember how it ends, but the name of the guy always stuck with me: Loomis. The vans make me feel alone, fear being alone.

Danny is asleep in the back less than five minutes into our journey to Southsea.

———————

I wake up with a layer of sweat cooling on my skin and the menu for the Kuti's Royal Thai Pier glued to my face with spittle. My semi-conscious brain is already picking the perfect moment to open my eyes and interrupt Midge's and Jon's conversation about how best to rouse me. The truth is, a-rousing me would be an easier task. Three days without any private time and the gentle rocking vibration of the car by this point is leaving me with an erection I could knock doors down with. I shuffle awake before one of them turns me over and ends up with an eye out.

———————

It's not easy to see the first pier at Southsea, or even that it's a pier. After driving down the promising-sounding Pier Road, we park up and walk between low-rise, cheap fun to the main entrance. Across the funfair that's either closed or just deserted you can see the water; but the angular thrust of a pier just isn't there.

———————

Arcades and hotdog shops flank each side. They all show the signs of a busy season, and the free-standing cartoon hog dog covered in cracks, dirt and pro-vegan graffiti looks more like a prop from a Mad Max film than anything that would encourage me to eat food. I see my first black family of the trip, which is jarring when the realisation hits.

———————

The stalls and shops are open, but render is peeling from the walls where they're not covered in signs. This is the faded commerce we've been expecting but hadn't found as yet. The cheap fast food smells awful and inciting. I ate a few nuts, dry roasted, last night but haven't had much in the past few days. We're not eating, and we read nothing but postcards. We're here in Southsea, at the Clarence Pier. Southsea is either in or so close to Portsmouth that it makes no odds. But it doesn't really want to be.

Postcards of here there are none. There are postcards of dogs – I buy a set of golden retriever ones that fray at the edges and sing the Super Furry Animals song of the same name – postcards of 'historic Hampshire', postcards of 'Austen country', rootless perhaps. The pier entrance is well signposted, and we enter the same arcade we've seen a lot of. Machines burr and beep; metallic voices beckon.

Then, cutting through all of it, is a voice I recognise. A voice I love. Flashing from a busily carpeted alcove is the king. The King.

Elvis is a touchstone, a godhead. He transcends the ages and age. We see him bedecked with lights in arcade after arcade; the games are all gambling ones and the connections tenuous. I've taken to keeping myself grounded by touching his image, reminding me of a time we had control over what we consumed. If I have control of a stereo for a long-enough period of time I pretty much always pick a combination of Elvis, fifties, seventies, gospel, films – there's good stuff in much of it. But what Elvis really does at the moment is make me feel safe and connected to things, to memories. I quietly cross myself and touch his image. Danny puts 50p in the slot, is blinded by choice and loses some sort of game based on cards.

SOUTHSEA Clarence

Opened: 1861 (Architect: 1961 rebuilding by A. E. Cogswell & Sons and R. Lewis Reynish)

Length at start: A lot longer

Length now: 132 ft (40 m), but wider than it is long

Burn baby burn? Bombed during World Tar Two.

After destruction by the Germans in World War Two, it eventually reopened in 1961, 100 years to the day after the original pier opened.

Clarence Pier was a Victorian pier in the grand tradition and the first stop on any trip over to the Isle of Wight a gentleman would take. It was opened in 1861 and continued expanding right up to when it was destroyed by a German bomb on 10 January 1941. Rebuilding began in 1953 and, perhaps as a way of avoiding further bombs, the structure now hugged the coast and became a 'horizontal' pier. It's often billed as 'one of the largest amusement parks on the south coast'.

Confused by the lack of actual pier we head to the beach to try for a side view and are stunned by the launch of a giant hovercraft. An impressive and noisy beast, it's my first time seeing one for real and I'm immediately struck by how improbable, inefficient and silly the whole affair seems to be. Noble even in its silliness, it is English hubris dressed as advance.

We hunker down, making our notes as Midge scans the horizon. I look over at Jon in 'that' coat, Midge adjusting his day bag on his shoulders and at my own dirty frame. We're surrounded by an exchange school trip, all taking photos of the hovercraft, and even after five days we stick out like homeless 'Nam vets at a fashion show.

Without us really noticing we've become surrounded by a school trip of teenage girls, who start to giggle and gasp as a hovercraft emerges from the waters, its wet blousing clinging to the air, showing every fold. We feel a little uncomfortable.

We're looking at a rope course called Pier Pressure and we're deliberating the question we're all thinking but, as a result of our three-day-old proximity to one another, nobody has to ask: is one of us going to have a go? Jon shakes his head dismissively. 'Nah.' I think a bit longer and say out loud: 'I definitely would.'

Everybody looks up, the girls from the exchange school trip wrinkle their noses and pull their cardigans closer to themselves, and the guy in charge looks over pointedly. We leave shortly after.

———————

Pausing only to photograph Dan hugging a battered sausage, we climb back into the piermobile and head just a mile or so down the coast.

The south end of Southsea is approaching suburban, but looking run-down. We find a parking space beneath overhanging hedges. The roads are quiet but full of parked cars. We tessellate between a dropped kerb and a battered Vauxhall. I get out clutching my Priestley hardback and we stand on a pavement looking at semis as far as we can see. We've no view of the sea, and that's disconcerting for a moment. There's a vibe of a transient population, as many of the houses are divided into flats and other indications are there too: many, many bins, some overflowing; and numbers and messages for postmen scrawled without artistic thought on any available surfaces.

More than that, it's a feeling: there's little care of the area. If a household is poor, it's not usually immediately obvious from the outside. You can't tell how expensive the curtains are or if the paintwork has been done by hired help or a harassed resident. If a house is uncared for, it's different: sheets drape across windows at off angles, paint flecks. There are discarded things in drives and uncut gardens. And that's what we see here, along with takeaway remnants.

———————

Southsea South Parade Pier is technically younger than Clarence, but a lack of bombs makes it the more traditional of the two.

Although traditional isn't how some pier enthusiasts would describe it, due to it having a concrete deck. But as I said, I'm not a pier enthusiast, not by a long chalk. I didn't start a pier enthusiast, I'm unlikely to finish a pier enthusiast, and I can only describe three or four times during the entire trip so far where the piers even piqued my interest, apart from as a logistical challenge.

That is not to say I dislike piers; they seem to be important. But at this point in the trip the fact that South Parade Pier is mostly closed relieves me more than disappoints me. The pier head itself is wide and populated by fishermen. If fishing is merely a man's excuse to enjoy the sun then at this moment I understand why they go through the pantomime. The sun is hovering near the horizon, like an office worker on a Friday afternoon that has already logged off his computer and is in the process of shuffling papers on his desk waiting for the clock to turn five.

SOUTHSEA South Parade

Opened: 1879 (Architect: G. Rale; 1904 rebuilding by G. E. Smith)

Length at start: 1,950 ft (594 m)

Length now: 600 ft (183 m)

Burn baby burn? Fires in 1904, 1966 and again during the filming of the rock opera *Tommy* in 1974. The fire began (according to director Ken Russell) while filming Ann-Margret and Oliver Reed dancing together, a spotlight setting fire to some drapes. Smoke from the fire can be seen in the film. There's a shot of the pavilion fully ablaze during the destruction of Tommy's Holiday Camp in the finished movie, which must have saved money on special effects.

David Bowie, Peter Sellers and organist Reginald Dixon have all played the pier.

We pretty much ignore the arcade and skirt round onto the pier itself. It's flat and uninteresting, the faded tarmac coming loose and making it sandy and scuffy underfoot. There are lumps, bumps and kerbs all around – the surface has a crazy-golf course built into it. The pier is unloved; weeds force themselves through the deck. It is being reclaimed from commerce by nature, almost folded back into the world away from organised fun. It's busy, though. The seaward edges of the concrete are being fished heavily and, surprisingly for us, by people of non-white-British ethnicity. The absence of other cultures until now should perhaps have come as a shock, but we've been focussed inward on ourselves and outward on the water. This pier reflects the modern working class, rather than the McGill postcard or *Carry On* class of the early part of the last century, which isn't quite what we expected.

The sky is still warm when we arrive in Bognor, even though the mechanical shutters of the beachside huts on this most English-looking seafront are ratcheting closed as we hurry past them. Along the front, signs blink 'Mr Whippy' and 'Cassino' – maybe the King who gave the place his seal of approval was as dyslexic as I am.

Bognor earned the 'Regis' (literally 'of the king') suffix when King George V took the sea air during a convalescence from pleurisy and a nasty bout of septicaemia. World War One and a gradual eroding of the empire had taken its toll on a, by all accounts, terse and grumpy bloke at the best of times. It's often said his last words were 'Bugger Bognor', but it's more likely that he said those words when he was presented with the petition for it to have the suffix. His actual last words were more likely to have been 'God damn you', addressed to a nurse shortly before his physician took the brave but not unheard of option to euthanise him with a mixture of cocaine and morphine. Another version is of a tough, well-travelled man with a magnificent beard who, on his deathbed, summoned his secretary to ask 'How is the Empire?', only allowing himself to fade into unconsciousness when told that 'All is well with the Empire', but this was probably a generous fantasy concocted out of kindness and decorum by Stanley Baldwin, who was Prime Minister at the time – a story protecting an angry old man who had seen too much and had to be put to sleep with the same speedball cocktail that took John Belushi.

———————

Seaweed hangs tautly from the crossed metal under the pier. Rust and wear are obvious. Which is a bit of a shame as the pier looks – like much of Bognor at this quick glance – to be well cared for. If a little dull. I don't spend too much time on the pier or in the arcade. It's our sixth pier today and they're starting to blur. Instead, I clamber over the heavy blocks meant to stop people crossing the road directly outside the pier and cross the road. I say I'm off to post the approximately 30 postcards we've spent most of today's car miles scribbling on, but really I just want to stand in the ebbing sun.

BOGNOR REGIS

Opened: 1865 (Architects: Sir Charles Fox and J. W. Wilson)

Length at start: 1,000 ft (305 m)

Length now: 350 ft (107 m)

Burn baby burn? A little fire in 2011, but suffered massive storm damage in 1964 and 1965.

The pier was named HMS *Barbara* when 200 men were billeted there during World War Two. The Bognor Birdman event, where contestants attempt to fly by the use of home-made devices, has taken place at the end of the pier almost every year since 1978. A man called Ron Freeman has won the event the most times (and has set the world record for such an event at Worthing Pier just along the coast).

The pier itself is pretty standard. During World War Two it escaped demolition on account of its status as a Royal Navy base. The ballroom has been turned into a nightclub named Sheiks: it seems the appeal of dancing above the waves is universal. It's understandable. One of my secret thrills when walking on a pier is looking down between the cracks and wondering what would happen if I stepped on a rotten board. This small flirtation with mortality has always been humanity's drug of choice. Spending the night dancing above the black water, defying time's wing'd chariot, is as romantic as it is advantageous from a wooing gentleman's point of view. The link between sex and death has long been established. I mean, who doesn't get horny at a funeral? Even the body gets stiff.

I do that skippy jog that isn't quite a run, speeding up as a car rounds the corner from out of sight. Safely and less embarrassingly on the pavement, I post the cards. Whenever I put anything in a postbox I'm gripped by indecision and terror. As I lift my hand and am about to release, my mind goes into a terrible dead-end. 'What if I post my keys in there by mistake?' 'What if I post my phone?' These things are both safe in my pockets but I really believe that I'm about to fall prey to the urge and do it. It's a fear of doing something that you can't repair. Alone here, I get a bit of that, but not too much.

I've done lots of posting on the trip already, and will have to post nearly 400 cards by the time I'm finished, so maybe it has been a sort of aversion therapy. Maybe on the trip there is so much I can't control, or that can go wrong, that the worry of losing something isn't too overwhelming. I walk back towards the guys and pass a gypsy fortune-teller's hut.

I can see Danny and Midge ambling around the arcade, prodding at buttons and pointing out oddness, but I'm happier outside. I perch on the barrier and stare over the road again at the crazy-golf course. It's virulently green in its astroturfed landscaping. The obstacles – including the obligatory windmill – are stark in their whiteness, bright in the early-evening light. We've no time to play as we plan to hit Brighton this evening and still have Worthing to go before then. There is one family playing: mum, dad, teenage son and daughter, who's about 18. She's got cropped hair and a mod-ish dress, and I enjoy watching her play. She moves with the unconscious grace of the young. I feel very lonely. And old. And conscious.

Conscious of all my faults and doubts. Doubly conscious that lusting after a young woman who's bending over to play crazy golf is a seaside cliché.

As we're about to get back into the car my phone buzzes at my thigh. It's bad news.

I see his face ashen. Jon hates answering the phone at the best of times but recently I have got the impression that time spent away from the real world, faced with the enormity of nature, is more useful to him than just a holiday. He steps away and when he comes back he's running his hand through his hair:

'You know that bag?' he says.

'The one that definitely wasn't yours?' I ask.

'Yeah, that one – well, it is.'

'Well, we can't go back for it,' I say, stifling a smile. 'What's it got in it?'

'My T-shirts and my toilet stuff.'

To the left, underneath one of the sea barriers on the beach, a shrug of teenagers sits chatting and throwing stones at the sea, not laughing at Jon, but laughing.

Grand, ornate, domed, difficult to find the entrance to: Worthing Pier is a huge structure, its front dominated by a seated theatre that's closed but preparing for a more modern English oddity. Tonight the Pavilion Theatre is going to host a Sex Pistols tribute act. We won't be able to stick around to see the facsimile punks entertain a sit-down crowd.

WORTHING

Opened: 1862 (Architect: Sir Robert Rawlinson)

Length at start: 960 ft (293 m)

Length now: 984 ft (300 m)

Burn baby burn? Storm-damaged in 1913; the Southern Pavilion went up in flames in 1933; the pier was partly demolished during World War Two to stop enemy craft from landing on it.

The 'New Amusements' sign that featured on the cover of the album *To See the Lights* by Britpop band Gene was changed in 2006 to 'Pier Amusements'. In November 2009 Lewis Crathern and Jake Scrace became the first people to kitesurf over the pier.

It seems every pier has had a major fire at some time or another. Worthing Pier's happened in 1933 when possibly a discarded cigarette started a fire that would, at its peak, have shot 60-ft sheets of flame into the air, fanned by the stiff breeze. Onlookers destroyed part of the promenade to stop the fire spreading further and chains of women, still in their swimming costumes, passed buckets of water up and down to the firefighters. Worthing Pier didn't escape World War Two either, having a hole blown in it in 1940 for fear of the Germans winning too many tickets on the amusements and bankrupting us of novelty items and stuffed toys.

Now it's a massive art-deco monument with three buildings: the entrance, which houses a theatre and café; a middle-of-the-pier amusements arcade; and a nightclub called Angelik that was soon to open. All have the soft modern curves and domed roofs that hark back to a time before glass and concrete panels. Jon, still reeling from the loss of his hair products, absent-mindedly brings with him onto the pier his copy of a J. B. Priestley book that I haven't seen him read once.

It no longer surprises me, the range of bands that have touring, money-making tribute versions. The arguments against them are well told: that they are dull, that they stifle new artists, and so on. But they're easier for the venues to sell, guaranteeing an audience. Or at least they do in the back of a pub where an audience drawn in by the beer and atmosphere won't be drawn out again by anything not too challenging. But the Sex Pistols offer a different thing, because – despite years of commercial and cultural assimilation – they are still resolutely unpalatable. Sure, jukebox favourite 'Pretty Vacant' isn't going to upset the punters but lots of the rest of the 'hits' are discordant, stuffed with bile and lyrics that have to be spat with venom to work at all. In short, a Pistols tribute can't work unless it's harsh, and only 'real' punks will like that.

And shouldn't real punks care enough about authenticity to reject a tribute show as the antithesis of everything they are? Midge is a man rooted in the punk of the now, his bank holidays much more likely to be spent in a sweaty pub at an 'all-dayer' than at the seaside. I've picked up a flyer for a punk festival here, a mixture of old bands I've heard of (Buzzcocks, UK Subs...) and ones formed after 1980 that, if I've encountered them at all, it's been on hand-cut flyers on pub tables. Due to the fonts used, their names are hard to read to start with but get even more illegible as beer drips and condensation leave pools on the melamine.

'Booze and Glory, Johnny One Lung, 5 Shitty Fingers, The Bots ... are any of these any good, Midge?'

'I have absolutely no idea. Most modern 'old school' punk bands all sound the same. Dirt Box Disco are not too bad.'

I like punk, especially as an attitude, but the cider-drinking, whiffy, denim scene it's become is not one I want to spend too much time in. It demands commitment, like all subcultures that somehow survive in aspic. I've dipped my toe into mod and northern soul, but could never really dive in head first. To really do it right you have to exclude all sorts from your life.

We eventually slip round the side. The pier is nice enough but nothing we probably haven't seen before. A girl with long dyed-red hair is taking artful photos of the structure. I quickly think 'on holiday with parents' rather than resident. We've taken nothing but memory-joggers. I wish we had more time.

In many ways the rate at which we are consuming piers is becoming a little concerning. The details are being lost. But, honestly, how long does it take to enjoy a pier? The seaside is a short-term thing. The beach, even in summer, is weather roulette, the arcade a diversion for an hour. Even with a show at the theatre it's only one night. Bed & Breakfasts are inherently short-term, too. The English seaside, for working-class city folk, either by design or nature, is a temporary thing to be enjoyed on a long weekend away from work rather than over a leisurely two weeks.

––––––

On our way into Brighton I make us stop at a large Sainsbury's. I figure I can get toiletries, maybe a T-shirt or two and a towel. I know I could have waited till tomorrow, got stuff in the centre of town, but, disorganised as I am, when there's something outstanding I just want to get it done as quickly as possible. The place does homewares, shower stuff, shaving stuff – and booze. I need booze. But there are no clothes. I'm stuck with what I'm standing in till tomorrow at the earliest.

This is the second towel I've bought since we set off. It, being new, will leave fluff stuck to me when I wash in the morning. For us slightly bookish, slightly alternative kids of a slightly certain age, the towel means Douglas Adams. And it means much more than that. Because if a traveller has a towel, if they've managed to negotiate deep space and keep hold of their towel, then they're clearly someone to be respected. You've got to know where your towel is.

I'm Arthur Dent, but even more adrift. Except, I know where my towel is.

The Isle of Wight.

Along with my wash bag and T-shirts, and the shirt I'd packed in case we go to a nightclub: maybe a white-stilettoed Essex nightclub. I want an epic night now, too. We have come to Brighton with the avowed intent to disrupt the lives of its inhabitants.

We booze and press on. Arriving outside my friend Adam's flat – beautifully set on an Edwardian grassed square which is open on one side to the front – we park up remarkably easily but find ourselves under a sign announcing a parking restriction. 'Residents-only parking between 8 a.m. and 8 p.m. Monday to Friday.' It's half past seven, so as long as we watch it for a bit we'll be okay till the morning.

'Early start for you in the morning, Midge. You can move the car before we get a ticket.'

He says nothing and starts unpacking some stuff out of the car.

CHAPTER SIX

BRIGHTON ROCKS

We arrive at Adam's flat with an eagerness for excess. We have planned our first night of true bacchanalian worship in England's party town, London-on-Sea, Britain's unofficial gay capital, the magnificent newly minted city of Brighton.

We're stopping with Adam, who Danny calls 'Wes' and Midge hasn't met. No one calls Adam 'Wes' to his face. No one calls Adam 'Wes' at all apart from Danny, and me when I need to explain 'who this Adam is' to Danny. Dan has met Adam, but knows him much better from his regular guest appearances on my radio show where he played the anchorman of The Sweary News.

Rhubarb Radio was the appallingly named Internet radio station that both Danny and I had shows on until about a year ago. When we first found out about it we both excitedly got slots talking rubbish in between records. My show, the Saturday breakfast slot, featured a news slot where the presenter needed to be heavily bleeped – and the man I know that most needs bleeping is Adam. Late on a Friday night, often audibly inebriated, he would write and record a real news bulletin peppered with some of the very worst and most inventive swearwords, and then email it to me so that I could censor it pre-show, often hampered by sleeplessness or hangover.

Most weeks at least one would slip through. Adam, wisely if unusually modestly, hid behind the pseudonym 'Wes Mundell'. Adam buzzes us up to his flat and we bring in our bags. Well, the other two do. They get changed, ready for a night out. I pace the bay window chugging lager, paranoid about what my parking fine would be if I got one – £60 would break the bank. I can't change until eight o'clock strikes and wonder aloud if my retro Birmingham City shirt (yellow, seventies, away) will cause a problem at any nightspot we go to.

———————

The first time I came to Brighton it was on a city break when I fell in love with the second-hand bookshops and other independents. I've always bemoaned Birmingham's lack of independent shops, but I'm at least partially wrong to do so. The fact is, Birmingham has a good few non-chain retailers in the city centre. It's just that most of them are the expensive sort of boutique selling 'deconstructed' (read: poorly made) or 'distressed' (tatty) jackets for the sort of money I would normally reserve for holidays or moon landings. Either that or they spend so much effort to look like one of the generic high-street staples it would take a somebody who gave more shits than me to tell the difference.

The second time I came to Brighton was the way most people will experience it: on a stag do. The details probably shouldn't be recorded here, but we did meet Joe Mangel from *Neighbours*, we weren't really sober enough to be go-karting, and me and my other best friend, Mat, got ostracised at the end of the last night because we had no desire to pay money to have our crotches rubbed by bored-looking women going through the motions of arousal. I've never really understood the strip club. If I were to list the ideal circumstances in which I wanted to be aroused, 'with my mates, in a dark public room that smells of sweat, despair and money' doesn't even feature in the top 20. We chose to go to the beach and watch the sea writhe soothingly as we chatted about the big things – sex, death, the future – with the earnestness of two men who had drunk themselves sober. I had a lot of fun that weekend, but that bit, that moment with Mat and the sea, is a moment frozen in time. Locked in my head-cave for safe keeping.

But Brighton isn't just a favourite of hen dos and stag nights. The hosts of the party are the gay community. The first recorded gayness associated with the city was in 1822 when a George Wilson, a servant and prude from Newcastle, was outraged to be offered 'a sovereign and two shillings' to go down to the beach and commit 'an unnatural act'. Whether it was the act itself he objected to or the price he was offered (in today's money it would be worth around £25), we will probably never know.

Less than a year later Brighton's first pier would be built.

Adam is excited now, too. In preparation he's taken a day off work tomorrow and looks like he's about to break into a huge grin. 'Yes', I say as I hand him a tin and explain again the plan. His teeth shine through his thatchy beard.

'Yes, we're going to write about you.'

A chuckle.

He disappears, reappearing in a brown jacket and jiggling his keys. We're off to find where the action is. Where the faces are.

Men getting ready to go out give off the scent of caged animals. They pace, swig from cans and spritz themselves with the same deodorant for the thirteenth time in a row, finally spraying down their crotch 'just in case'. It is obvious to all involved that me and

Jon intend to paint the town rainbow tonight. Adam is along for the ride, but Midge is firmly miffed. Having been driving for a few days I think he imagined a night in with a cup of cocoa and maybe a slow wank by the fire.

'It's not going to be a big one tonight, is it?'

I open a can of cider one-handed while finishing the last one with the other.

'Eat me – it's booze o'clock, mate,' I say as I stifle a burp.

'I've been driving and I'm knackered, so not too late.' The losing battle is clearly getting to him.

'Sure, just till a quarter past booze o'clock and we'll get some kip,' I say as I apply eyeliner and a sprinkle of glitter.

'But it's always booze o'clock to you,' he says as he trails out of the room.

Luckily, with Midge I've learnt there is a certain amount of brooding time before he really gets cross, so the mission is simple: get Midge out of the flat and enjoying himself before he actively starts getting angry about getting out of the flat and enjoying himself.

'Did I tell you a friend of mine is meeting us? She's single...'

Brighton *is* the film *Quadrophenia*. Mods and escape from the city, from the grind. At the seaside, hiding from the nine-to-five and the truth. And I can't think of a much better pub to hide from them in than the Lion and Lobster. Like some vertical shanty town, it's hard to define a path to any part of it. Nook becomes bar becomes rooftop decking becomes overhead-heated, densely packed smoking terrace. I'm drinking two-to-one and my head is spinning down the same old tracks. I want to explain to people why I'm not quite 'right'. But Danny knows and it doesn't seem fair to break his spell. He's expansive and loud, glorying in his headgear, calling up an old friend and inviting her to join our rolling revue. Midge is quiet, so I want time to talk to my old mate.

I did my degree with Bobs. She lived in a shared house of girls that would feed, pet and take care of me when the house full of girls I lived in couldn't or wouldn't. She has long blonde hair, 14 types of smile, and despite the cut-glass RP accent is, in many other universes, the daughter of a governess turned ruthless pirate queen. We arrange to meet in a pub near Adam's house and, despite appearances, she is the type of girl more than willing to meet a friend and three strangers on any curious adventure.

The Lion and Lobster is a plush, red wonderland. It's the sort of pub I love: independent, eclectic and with booze in it (I'm willing to compromise on the first two). The walls are filled with every type of picture in the manner of how the National Gallery used to be. If you follow some stairs you come to a room without a roof; follow them further and you can look down and see the room below.

It's busy but we manage to find a large table. The four of us are crowded together at one corner of it:

'No room! No room!' we cry out when we see Bobs coming.

'There's PLENTY of room!' says Bobs indignantly, and she sits down on a large stool at one end of the table.

'Have some wine,' Jon says in an encouraging tone. Bobs looks all round the table, but there is nothing on it but beer or cider.

'I don't see any wine,' she remarks.

'There isn't any,' says Jon.

'Then it wasn't very civil of you to offer it,' says Bobs angrily.

'I'll get them in,' grins Adam as he disappears to the bar.

'I love this pub. How mad is it?' I say to keep the conversation going, mainly to stop Midge the grumpy little mouse from getting the chance to complain.

'All the pubs are mad here,' Bobs says primly. 'Here's mad, the pier's mad, everybody in the city is mad.'

'I'm not mad,' I say.

'Of course you are,' replies Bobs, 'otherwise you wouldn't be here.'

Then it goes a bit hazy. I remember falling down a rabbit-hole of a staircase on the way back from a toilet and a big white dog looking at me with resigned acceptance as the fifteenth drunk person that night to fall in love with it.

I'm clinging to what I know and want to talk, jabber really, get everything straight in my increasingly muddy brain. The drinking isn't really helping; it's not strong enough to cut through the fog. Let's go somewhere else.

The pavements are damp with expectation. The people move with staggering purpose, to join tribes, to drink, to eat. I strive to be part of whatever will have me. There are no longer two tribes to go to war, but diaspora of every fashion from the twentieth century all on top of one another, intermingling and cross-pollinating. I spot a guy that looks like he might be homeless, were it not for the well-tended and expensively coiffured Rod Stewart haircut. A sort of grunge-mod. Unsure whether I'll remember this, this vision in feathered hair, I get Adam to text me. 'Rod Stewart tramp to you.'

I'm trying hard to lose myself in the group, instigating conversations as wide as I can make them. Talking loudly and pointlessly about the nature of art and friendship. I'm buying drinks on a debit card I've long since stopped having a firm idea about, ordering more than I need. A double gin to wash down the premium lager. Extra trips to the toilet to punctuate the consumption. Desperately searching for a grand gesture. Making statements I can't back up and phone calls I don't want to make.

We hit bar after promised bar, each offering nothing but the dark. We buy cans on the way back.

One of the survival traits that I picked up early in my drinking career is falling asleep in the recovery position. If Hendrix had had a friend to roll him onto his side, he'd be married to Joplin right now, about to release an acid-inspired, guitar dubstep album that would permanently open our collective third eye and finally usher in the golden age of Aquarius. Somehow I make it to the airbed stuffed next to a coffee table but not into the covers far less my pyjamas.

And I know Jon has passed out where he sits, because he's fully dressed and leaning on his arm, frozen in mid proclamation of some thought.

I wake with a burningly dry mouth and a dull and fuzzy sensation where cogent thought once lived. Midge closes the flat door as he comes in, not carefully to protect the sleeping dead but loudly to wake them. He's moved the car:

'Down on to the front. I put three hours on the ticket – that should be enough, shouldn't it?'

I'm filling a scuffed pint glass with tap water, throat biting at the smell of stale lager from the cans and bottles that litter the worktop. Danny stirs, bare chest flecked with downy hair, from his sleeping bag. His head misses the TV stand by inches as he hoists himself up, puffy with excess.

'Sleep well in that... bed,' the word spat out, but with comedy venom, 'Midge?'

'Aye, yeah. Three hours. God, you two were pissed last night.'

'Drunk ourselves sober, I think.'

Danny crashes towards the bathroom, crashes himself clean. Crashes out and dresses.

I guzzle liquid and spray deodorant.

'I've got to go to Primark.'

Primark is where you go to get clothes in a hurry, clothes that you don't want to have to think too much about. Clothes that are cheap and you won't be bothered if you lose them – which seems likely, the way things are going.

Clothes shops, Danny informs me, put the women's stuff downstairs at the front, as women won't bother to go in to look unless something catches their eye as they browse past. Men, our behavioural expert says, know what they want and will hunt – looking to the horizon for the boxers or briefs, stalking their underpant prey. I'm not sure if all that cave-conditioning really impacts so much on our modern lives. I normally actively like clothes shopping, consider myself both a browser and a connoisseur of design, waiting for the right jacket or shirt to come along. Today, I'm on instinctual autopilot. I've got to get four or five T-shirts: I select the plainest and most fitted on offer, almost vests, except one. A stark yellow top, printed – ironically, one would assume – with a coloured-pencil sketch of a Labrador. The dog is stuck mid pant in the facial expression that we can anthropomorphise as smiling. It makes me feel safe and warm, so I buy it to feel better and don it as soon as we leave the shop. Exposing my torso the high street.

I also pick up a present for Midge, a cheap, rubber watchband to replace the one he destroyed showering a few days ago, and a pair of the most Audrey Hepburn sunglasses the shop has for under three quid. I've forgotten to bring any sunglasses and I need to hide my eyes.

I look up after putting my jacket back on. The day looks darker, there's a mean movement to the crowds on the high street. I call out to the guys and pick up the pace towards the seafront. Waves of people brush in all directions, like they're being manipulated.

A van streaks across a side road and effectively blocks the flow of people. Crushes look possible and confusion reigns. The forces are intent on stopping us. There is chanting and pushing, as Adam and I duck down an alley laughing and head into a coffee shop. The brew is urgent and refreshing. We sit outside and wait for the others to catch us up.

I sort of apologise for how messy I was the night before, for unburdening myself on to him.

'I'll be all right,' I lie to myself and him.

He changes the subject, and is happy when Danny and Midge reach us. We've a pilgrimage to make and Adam prods at his iPhone to find Mecca.

While recovering from the awful headaches Midge is smugly not having, we take tea at the Tic Toc Cafe, an overtly 'kooky' French-owned restaurant. It's replete with earnest young men working from MacBooks, Lego cutlery holders and a mosaic of newspaper clippings. The toilet is a stall that I trip over the mismatching furniture to get to.

Somebody hasn't flushed, leaving behind wadded toilet paper and presumably other things. In my hung-over state I decide not to flush before using it so just go ahead and unleash a stream of near neon-yellow piss over the existing mess. I finish and it won't flush. I rattle the handle a couple of times and it remains unflushed. Now I have two choices. I can tell them, say the toilet won't flush, and they can come and try and fix it while dangling their faces over the effluence. Or I can leave it and the next person that uses it can deal with the problem. Thirty seconds later I'm back at the table telling Midge, Adam, and Jon:

'Drink up, guys – lots to see today, lots of things to do.'

In this case it's not the pier I'm worried about. We could see the pier as we drove into town in the drizzle yesterday evening. It's big, pier-shaped and echoes the famous pavilion. We drove past the second, ruined and burnt, pier too. We'll go there, but I think we've sort of made the ticks to the list anyway. We're heading instead to an alleyway, what I've been ungallantly referring to as the Leslie Ash Memorial Alleyway. In *Quadrophenia*, our hero Jimmy eventually gets what he wants from the young Steph (Leslie Ash), not that it turns out to be the solution he needs. Instead, it was fitful and disappointing, as all success proves to be. And it was filmed on location right here.

So we pose for photos next to some large bins. I'm red-faced and slouched, and I'll delete them when I get the chance. We step back to admire the sheer number of pilgrims that have made the journey before us. The wall is doused in the signatures of groups and tribes: 'Walsall Mods', 'Jason + Marie 2011 Crewe'. I try to add our mark but all I have is my pencil. We're through without trace.

Brighton Pier is okay, a bit commercial, but still essentially a fancy shell over faded wooden boards. The arcade is massive and the funfair still closed at the early hour we get there. I know from previous trips that it is actually possible to go right to the back railing and look out to a surprisingly blue sea. Facing out from this point it's easy to forget the lights, litter, and litany of machines calling out for coins. You can actually hear, see and smell the sea.

BRIGHTON Palace

Opened: 1899 (Architect: R. St George Moore)

Length at start: 1,760 ft (536 m)

Length now: 1,719 ft (524 m)

Burn baby burn? Hit by a barge in 1973, which wrecked the theatre and the landing stage. A small fire in 2003, but they opened again the next day.

Properly called Brighton Marine Palace and Pier, it features in *Carry on at Your Convenience*, when the warring management and unions put on hold a strike to go on the annual works outing. It's also been in *The Persuaders*, *Doctor Who*, and The Who's film version of *Quadrophenia*.

Palace Pier is a novel by *Billy Liar* author Keith Waterhouse, set in Brighton and featuring a writer throwing a manuscript off the end of the pier. The pier also famously features in Graham Greene's novel *Brighton Rock*.

The Royal Suspension Chain Pier pre-dated the Palace Pier in Brighton by decades, but it doesn't exist anymore and therefore isn't on The List, but it does appear in a couple of famous paintings (a Turner and a Constable). It politely fell down in a storm in 1896 to save the people building the Palace Pier the bother of pulling it down. Palace Pier is prone to bits of luck like that, including the 2003 fire that stopped the rebuilding of the (also not on The List) West Pier shortly after the Palace Pier had raised objections to the Heritage Fund about the unfair competition it would present. The shore end of the old West Pier is now the i360, a Jetsons-style observation tower.

The pier itself is one of the best-kept we've seen. It's obviously working for the different personalities that Brighton simultaneously cultivates: gay, boho London-by-the-Sea, stag-and-hen town, party-conference venue, day-tripper's paradise. Here you can get married, gay-married, equal-married. You can play the slots and eat candyfloss. You can turn the irony dial any way you wish. It's all in your head. We get Midge to snap us with our heads through the obvious holes – I wonder just how many times we've done this now. I always go for the mermaid, or the bathing beauty. Danny is happy with a harpoon in his hands.

We planned only three things when we decided to undertake the trip: jump off a pier, get a tattoo and have a fight on Brighton beach. I'm a mod, Dan's a rocker – we should ruck. We should fight in Brighton.

But it didn't stay so simple. The idea of a fight is too easy. Not enough references, too straight. It probably says something about our minds that the only fight scene we felt we wanted to recreate was the Alan Bates, Ollie Reed one from *Women in Love*. Where they wrestle naked in front of the fire. The one we're told that they had to get halfway through a bottle of scotch to perform. We really couldn't think of a more resonant fight, because we don't hate each other, and we're no longer teenagers within the push and pull of gangs. And so, once on the beach, we leap over a wooden groyne and whip off our tops – our tops only, mind, thereby preserving some modesty – and stride unsteadily into the pebbles.

I've never had a proper fight: I've been hit and I've been angry, but never a sustained bout. I'm not sure how a fight ends.

We pantomime a bit of grappling, but it's clear that neither of us really wants to lose. We soon overbalance and sprawl onto the stones, arms round each other. Dan pushes me over and holds my hands back against the ground. I feel that he's not quite giving it his all and that, if I do, I can get on top. The embarrassment, and some of the clouds in my head, are moving further away. It's difficult to get a grip, though. We're both hefty guys and grabbing a handful of flesh seems uncouth. There's more of a slapping as our hands and bellies flop against each other. I make a grab for the belt of Dan's trousers and he attempts to hook his elbow under my leg. He gets me and I fall backwards heavily, catching sight of Midge and Adam laughing at our flailing. I'm surprised, though, to see that we've not attracted the attention of anyone else. Old ladies shuffle past our part of the beach, and people stroll up and down the boardwalk, but no one notices. Danny isn't concentrating. I see his eyes wander. I've had enough, heave him over and make like to hit him in the balls. I win.

Manly hugs all round as we leave Adam to return to his home to sleep. We've driving, piers and camping ahead of us before we can rest. We pull out of town with the sea on our right-hand side. The buildings drop away and we're left with grass and cliffs. I've prepared something for this moment. I plug my phone into the stereo and search for just the right music.

We start a slow climb, Midge as usual driving steadily. Rain starts to fall and a piano tinkles. The drums rumble gently, a cymbal splashes. If we weren't in a car the stereo panning would kick in.

The beach is kissed by the sea. I sweat beer sweats. Anxious sweats. I am starting to wonder what we're doing. Fake strings stab and I swipe the volume higher. It swells to fill the car, as we swoop down over the brow of the hill. The view is filling my mind, emptying it of worry. I can't sleep and I lie and I think. I need a drink.

The Who save me again. 'Won't Get Fooled Again' hits the speakers. As a pop aficionado I often remark that almost all songs are too long. Or their recorded versions are anyway: 2 minutes 45 seconds is the length that a tune should last. But 'Won't Get Fooled Again' is, at nearly nine minutes, way too short. I often reach the end and put it back on straight away. It is bombastic, symphonic and urgent all the way though. Every time you think it's about to die you get another battering from the drums of Keith Moon or a howl from the lusty lungs of Roger. It speaks directly to the bitter soul of all those who have felt treated unfairly by life. And that's all of us. It's me. It's me in the way that my dreams always seem to get thwarted, in the way that the things I really want I've no idea how to get. It won't happen again, not this time. But it will work out, as long as the trip does.

We get a break in the clouds. We really do.

CHAPTER SEVEN
BIG DEAL

We're heading to Eastbourne, one of the few places where the local media expressed any interest in us before the trip. We'd contacted the press more because we thought it was the sort of thing we should do than because it would do us any good. We filled in a questionnaire for a publication based in or near Eastbourne and I had to reveal my ignorance of the place.

I'm vaguely aware of it being the butt of sitcom jokes. The Major in *Fawlty Towers* defends the 'most badly run hotel in the world' by saying, 'No, no, I won't have that... there's a place in Eastbourne.' And that's about the extent of my knowledge. You could say under-researched; I'd say open-minded.

Eastbourne Pier is a grand and beautifully designed Victorian pier with round huts dotted along it. It looks like a traditional, if somewhat successful, old pier. But the amount of redevelopment and the number of commercial enterprises should tip you off. Yes, the buildings are old and the paint somewhat peeling, but you feel like something is weird. It works a little too well, the shops have none of the erratic opening habits of other piers and the stock is too consistent.

The pier is owned by Six Piers Ltd, who also own all three Blackpool piers and the one at Llandudno. Leisure tycoon

Trevor Hemmings put the pier up for sale in 2009 after a couple of terrible seasons and a loss of £7.3m. He managed to sell Southsea's South Parade Pier but withdrew the sale of Eastbourne after a £9m season. His current net worth is somewhere around £500m, which is not bad for someone who left school at 15.

And he knows the market. Eastbourne feels old and the pier reflects that. To highlight that fact, the crown green bowlers in front of the pier seem to foreshadow the facilities on it. The shops are definitely aimed at the older generation, including a glassblower, a clothes shop selling cream windbreakers and elasticised slacks (I had always wondered where those come from and, for the record, even new they have that old-person smell), and an ice-cream parlour that sells the generic Italian ice cream you find in every shopping centre in England.

EASTBOURNE

Opened: 1870 (Architect: Eugenius Birch)

Length at start: 1,000 ft (305 m)

Length now: 1,000 ft (305 m)

Burn baby burn? In 1942, a mine exploded: it had been tied to the pier by the police, who thought it was fitted with a safety device. A fire in 2014 damaged the central domed building.

A theatre added in 1888 soon blew away in a gale and landed 17 miles away in Lewes, where it was later used as a cowshed. Police visited a seller of saucy seaside postcards on the pier in 2012 after a complaint about their content from a minister of a local church. Both the *Agatha Christie's Poirot* episode 'Jewel Robbery' and the 2010 film remake of *Brighton Rock* used Eastbourne Pier as a stand-in for Brighton Pier.

The one thing we'd found out about the pier in advance was that it had a camera obscura in the building at the end – we reach it with hope and ice cream. To find it closed. The bar is playing Westlife and there's piss on the floor in the toilets. I feel a real need to touch the icon of The King. There's something about the way the place is both open but closed – the way shopping areas are on Sundays – that makes the tiles and the walls scream about the fading caused by modern commercialisation. Elvis is my current totem against that, as his commercialism was naked but homely. A touch is a connection, so I touch Elvis.

Danny has a Slush Puppie. That's as faded as it gets.

'Don't look now – but that grey van is following us,' says Midge, making it very clear he's not turning his head.

'What?' me and Jon say together. Jon's 'what' is incredulous, mine is more surprise because I have yet again begun to doze off. And, of course, we both turn around to look at an innocuous grey van behind us. Midge makes a noise of frustration.

'Why would a van be following us?'

'Could be the DSS,' Midge replies. Jon laughs and I join him when I see that Midge is serious.

'How can you be the one losing his mind? You had the bed last night,' I say to Midge. He just shakes his head.

I can see why things could be coming apart. Everything has started to get a bit odd. Like the landscape is unfolding just for us to have a giggle at. A bed shop passes by with a full-size *Jurassic Park* raptor outside. We laugh. We see a late-night chippy calling itself 'The Kebab Centre' and we get a good ten minutes out of wondering which workshops they offer and if they do a playscheme in the holidays.

We see a house with 'The Murder House' painted on the roof in broad red letters, but we don't really laugh at that.

There's not a battle in English history more remembered than the one that is named after Hastings, the site of which we pass on the way now. We don't follow the brown tourist sign any more than we followed the one for the Sussex Ox Country Pub on the way to Eastbourne. Thatcher's government deregulated the tourist sign and since then anyone who cares to pay for one can point travellers to their castle, ruin, patch of grass or garden centre (always garden centres). Which means that we've no idea if any of those we've seen advertised are interesting or not. I do like the signs, though, and I love the symbols and am becoming increasingly obsessed with getting the pier one tattooed on my arm.

Midge obviously thinks our jovial mood is a good enough time to bring up the reason for going to Hastings at all, or not.

'It's closed, we know it's closed — we could just say we'd been.'

'The List is king,' we both chime. I don't know when we'd taken to shouting that to nip any of these conversations in the bud. I also have no idea when the list gained capital letters and became 'The List'.

I'm undecided as to whether we are using the shorthand of fanatics as a way of explaining to Midge how 'it doesn't make sense, but we're compelled to do it now' or if The List is starting to become a religious text on a par with the Bible or the Torah in our heads. Perhaps both, maybe neither.

The thing is, when you separate yourself from your normal rhythms and routines for long enough, your brain retracts and waits for more information, waiting to find the routine again. Even on holiday you quickly fall into a different routine: your dad will get up way before you to go for a walk and 'get the papers' and then berate you for sleeping in and 'missing the best part of the day'. Little does he know that sleeping is for you, the teenager, the best part of the day for exactly the same reason his early-morning jaunt to the shop is for him; you don't have to interact with your family in any way. Deprive a brain for long enough from routine and it can have a tendency to seek solace elsewhere.

Hastings' signage is tastefully done in a mosaic style, with one such sign comprising a seagull and a landscape view that features the pier. The pier that we know burnt down a year before. Hastings Pier is somewhat of a music legend: it played home to the voodoo alien love god, Jimi Hendrix. It also hosted the last ever gig that the mental-pixie-acid pioneer Syd Barrett played with prog-rock grandfathers Pink Floyd.

'I don't trust your handbrake.'

'It'll be okay; leave it in gear if you're worried.'

I'm more bothered about checking the conditions on the parking sign. I'm oscillating between not caring at all about the money we're spending and being terrified that it's already all gone. I've not had a lot of work this year and my bank account is fragile, but my bank account is where the pier fund lives and I'm not going to be able to do the maths en route. A parking fine really would be costly and stupid, but my brain is as sandblasted as the rough wall I scrape against when weaving and staggering down to the sea.

As we approach the front we see the metal fence that stops you stepping onto what is basically a wooden platform, all that is left of the pier. It's sad, and it feels like all the memories and cultural ghosts are hovering above the water on that platform, kept behind that fence as if in a spiritual zoo.

We decide to discover the town some more and head towards the shops we can see open in the distance. Mainly because we're all busting for a slash. Obviously our bodies still have some more toxins to get rid of from Brighton. The base for the 'Save Hastings Pier' campaign is a shop set up in an old millinery. It's all dark-wooden panels and shelves, and they have done an amazing job of filling the glass cabinets with merchandise, from cool T-shirts that exploit Hastings' rock-and-roll history to books and poetry that actually tell the local history of the area and the building of the pier. There's a great exhibition space at the back of the shop, occupied by a sculptor who modifies books and other objects to look like Victorian oddities, which only adds to the vibe. Even though this is a community-driven venture, it's all very slick and smart. Proof that this sort of thing doesn't have to be a bit naff and run by people who wear cardigans.

HASTINGS

Opened: 1872 (Architect: Eugenius Birch)

Length at start: 910 ft (277 m)

Length now: 910-ish ft (277-ish m) (see below)

Burn baby burn? The pavilion burnt down in 1917 and the seaward end was damaged by storms in 1938. Since then various cycles of disrepair and damage have included a lightning strike in 2007 and a devastating fire in 2010.

The pier was opened on the first ever Bank Holiday – 5 August 1872 – after the law creating them was passed in 1871. A number of famous names have played on the pier, including The Rolling

Stones, The Who, Jimi Hendrix, Pink Floyd, The Hollies, The Clash and the Sex Pistols. In 2013 a community shares scheme was launched to sell shares in the pier at £100 each to provide funds towards its refurbishment. The pier is now run by a charitable trust, who are overseeing the rebuilding and eventual reopening.

I'm hung-over and hurting, so I lose myself in the merchandise; I want to buy things to cure me. Top hat, T-shirt, those metal wall hangings that are reprints of bygone adverts. Danny's perhaps a little better, Midge is buzzing. He flicks through the free postcards and fiddles with stickers he's made with our website address on, using Impact and a photo of a donkey.

'We're visiting every pier in England and Wales,' says Midge.

And perhaps for the first time someone is actually interested. David, the guy running the shop, listens.

'Hastings is our twenty-sixth. It's really good, getting to see loads of things.'

'That's great.'

'Yeah. Yeah... it's er... they're writing about it, I'm just the driver.' He re-adjusts his backpack strap on his shoulder. Excitedly hopping between feet.

There are lottery bids and fundraising efforts on the go here, a real community effort, and a CD that I can buy without looking profligate, as it's a good cause.

We cross the road, looking for a better angle, trying to see the pavilion that's worth saving, as the front doesn't seem to be. I dip down an incline towards the sea and find myself in a sort of promenade mezzanine. Columns frame the sea and nooks and benches form a colonnade of expectation.

At the first bench is a couple of what officialdom terms street drinkers – not homeless, but exhibiting few signs of a comfortable home environment – and one has an old purple tin and a festival jester's hat. The second guy has an odd-shaped acoustic guitar, battered and looking a little fire-damaged.

'Hey, man.'

I don't want to make eye contact. You never know with the trampish.

'Hi.' Hopefully friendly but non-committal.

The first guy, long hair and a wild look in his eyes, but too sad to be dangerous, says, 'No, man. We might be able to help.'

'We've seen some things. Maybe the things you're looking for.'

'The white dog, he owns us all. Cold, cold.'

They stare out to see across the charred lines. I mutter something that's meant to sound like 'okay' but could be something else if challenged.

As calmly as possible I walk down to join two slightly saner people.

We're playing the CD in the car as we move on. I put the case into the glovebox with some difficulty and there's a faint sound of plastic under stress when I close it – the car is full to the brim and tightly packed. Almost as soon as I've reconfigured my bag and other stuff around myself, spreading the map back over my lap, I want to read who this song is by and have to dismantle it all again. It's all local bands, well or at least competently produced, a mixture of rock and acoustic. King Bathmat is a great name for a band but the track itself doesn't quite live up to it.

Midge beams and to my mind's delight, but my stomach's chagrin, presses a little harder on the gas. It's a fair distance to Deal.

———

On the way to Deal the clouds make it darker earlier than it should be. Autumn is coming, the sky is telling us. Don't be fooled.

———

There's something ordinary and suburban about Deal. London suburban at that. We park in a side street outside a gloss-painted, shuttered snooker club. It's a regular town. The closed doors on the vaguely municipal building in front of the pier sit in a neat row, and the bus-shelter things along the pier are evenly spaced and uniform in their emptiness.

DEAL

Opened: 1957 (Architect: Sir W. Halcrow)

Length at start: 1,026 ft (313 m)

Length now: 1,026 ft (313 m)

Burn baby burn? It is the third pier to occupy the site. The first one (1838, J. Rennie) was lost due to storm damage and sandworm, whilst the second (1864, Eugenius Birch) had a boat drift into it. The current pier suffered some storm damage in 2013.

A notice on the pier says that it is the same length as the *Titanic*, which was actually over 100 ft shorter.

The grey sky complements the concrete of Deal Pier. And highlights the loneliness of the single fisherman. Fishing is silly; all the benefits that anglers boast about – you get to sit and relax, it's an excuse to drink, it's nice to be out of the house – could easily be achieved without having to potentially stove an animal's head in. In fact I have been able to do all three of those things most days without having to get up at 4.30 in the morning. I'm secretly suspicious of people who fish, because it's like they enjoy hurting the fish but have managed to wrap it up as a harmless pastime. The guy fishing looks innocent enough, but if you really look at his equipment – the hooks, knives, clubs and net – you realise that if he came into your bedroom in the middle of the night with it you'd shit yourself.

The lasting image I have is the stained-red concrete of the benches that run the entire length of Deal Pier; fish blood and bait. The only sign that other anglers were ever there.

The cafe at the end of the pier looks clean and modern, and a waitress sits outside smoking, looking out to sea. I don't think that the fag break is an excuse to do that, though. She looks like she really, really needed that cigarette. It occurs to me that piers are quite peaceful places. Being this close to the sea quietens people, stills them as they try and take in the sheer magnitude of it. Weird that the first thing we do, then, is build busy, loud palaces of neon and noise on them. Although no one ever got rich off people wrestling with the infinite.

———

The seafront is not relaxing, despite the pie and mash shop and the *EastEnders* vibe, but the main street of the town is more welcoming. I squint at some independent boutiques as we drive out into the sun.

Talking in the car is getting harder. I'm out of things to say. I don't even bother to tell the guys about the tramps in Hastings. My mind is empty and I'm worrying that even if the quest succeeds the book will fail. I'm not sure my observations will be enough; I'm just not feeling literary. I think it's the drink. We're drinking to kill time. I'm drinking to sleep and to maintain the illusion of being sociable.

I could murder a pint.

Our camp for the night in Whitstable doesn't seem to be really anywhere. It's not near the sea or the town, just a turn up the dual carriageway from a supermarket. The air has turned colder and the wind is getting up. There's grass and gravel and a low cabin that shows some sign of life.

———

We arrive at Primrose Campsite late, but, for once, someone is in the office. He's a large man with receding hair cropped short. That, coupled with his very cockney accent and amicable nature, puts me in mind of a Disney version of a London cabbie.

'Where shall we put the tent?'

'Anywhere you want, mate. The wind might get up so put it over there might be better.' He gestures to a place that seems to be no more or less sheltered from the wind than anywhere else.

'Do you want to sort the money out now?'

'When do you want to do it? I'll wait till tomorrow if you like,' he says.

'Shall we get our tent up then? We'll come over when we're finished,' I venture.

'Sure, whatever you want, chaps,' he replies so amicably I'm surprised he doesn't offer to come over and put it up for us.

The tent goes up with remarkable efficiency, each of us now comfortable in our roles: Jon standing looking confused, hoping that he hasn't lost even more of his kit; Midge disappearing; and me, well, putting up the entire tent.

We go over to pay.

'Go whatever time you want, chaps, no rush in the morning,' he says as he takes the payment.

We ask him for recommendations for a local pub.

'Well, if you want to go to the big supermarket and getcha wobbly water there then it's just over the road.' You can tell he likes saying 'wobbly water'. We like it too. 'Or the nearest pubs are in town, down the hill down there and right on the high street.'

———

I drift off to the toilet block to keep out of the way. I check my eyes and my shakes in the mirror. I look tired, but good. My hair especially has a great texture. I usually use a sea-salt spray to keep it from being too fluffy but actual sea salt seems to be much better. I could save around 20 quid a year by moving to live by the sea. I'd have no job, no girl, no money, nowhere to live, but my hair would look good. Maybe.

With nothing to keep us here, we turn down the lushly verged gradient. The place doesn't feel like the seaside or a resort. We stride uncomfortably downhill past semis and green-sheathed wire fence.

———————

He may come across as the most amicable used-car salesman in south London, but his sense of scale when giving directions is definitely rural. That is to say, after about 20 minutes of walking down a country lane that seems to separate the countryside from a suburban housing estate we decide that doing this journey uphill slightly pissed is an untenable situation. And that the Pier Review fund will be springing for a taxi back.

Up until now I have avoided thinking about the money, because both me and Jon know that the money we've raised isn't quite enough to cover the trip. And, knowing Jon, the money is sitting in his account with his money and, as I haven't seen him take a receipt or write even the petrol costs down once, I can safely assume that there will be no delineation between when our money runs out and his begins to be spent.

———————

Green forces its way through the cracks in every surface: we're not at the end of a hot summer, we're not in a place where the council or the residents have been pruning, and we're not at the touristy bit by some stretch. We turn a corner and just aren't feeling positive as we exit a side alley opposite a Co-op. If a town has a Co-op, it's a certain level of suburban. Not disadvantaged enough to be served by a Select and Save, or a blue-carrier-bagged kwik-e-mart, but not posh enough either to sustain independent boutiques. It's not small enough to have a village shop, or no shop at all, but it's not big enough to sustain a Metro or Local version of any of the major chains. It's a drive-to-the-retail-park kind of place, which is to say it exhibits modern tendencies, rather than being preserved in a candyfloss-based aspic.

Huge piles of oyster shells lie like guardians to the beach. It takes me a while to realise what they are in the dark. They could just be stones, or some trash – I first think bin bags, glinting in the damp.

We find a pub with barely room to stand. There's a sense of anticipation and liveliness that doesn't so much include us as overwhelm us. And that's okay, as I've nothing to say.

We're at a pub practically on the beach called Old Neptune. It's a nice little place with slightly too many people in it, which is the perfect amount for a cosy pub on a Friday night. Okay, at this point I have no idea whether it is Friday or not, but it feels like one. We sit outside where the picnic tables look out on a dramatic sky and a calm, black sea. In the distance I can see some loading cranes. This is a guess, because I can't really tell you if that is actually what those things are. Big crane-like things anyway, lit up so they look like a queue of electric giraffes striding towards the horizon. I feed crisps to a dog of no determinate owner, but soon it gets too cold and we shuffle our way back inside.

One of the reasons for the pub being full is nearly a quarter of it being occupied by a bunch of older gents in ten-gallon hats and long, white hair setting up steel guitars, a keyboard and a reduced drum kit in one corner. The music stands read 'Happy Trails', set out in the shape of the shield used for American road signs. One of these hatted men has a coat with a fringe.

'What sort of music do you reckon they play?' says Jon with a straight face.

'New-wave punk probably,' I say.

'I thought they were going to be drum and bass myself,' Jon says, finally cracking as we both pull our coats on.

'Are we going then?' says Midge, seeing us get up.

'Yeah Midge, do keep up, mate,' I tell him, realising now that neither me nor Jon had mentioned it. We'd just got up.

On the high street we see kids playing, treating a metal fence and a set of steps as their private playground. I can't see any parents. These elves playing in the night under the yellow-mist-coloured moon make the town feel more foreign than it actually is. More connected to history, and more an image of an English fishing town suited to a fairy story than a story about three prats in a car.

And I'm not talking about the sanitised fairy stories either. I mean the mean ones, the ones where fairies aren't annoying magical balls of light, but vicious little bastards with an angry streak and a sociopath's sense of humour. The ones where weary travellers are lured over cliffs as pranks, or sent home with hooves for hands so that they accidentally beat their loved ones to death in their panic.

Further up the road we find a more traditional pub, the Royal Naval Reserve. A warm, well-worn place with dark-stained wood and horse brasses on the wall. The sort of pub that interior designers have in mind when they cough up another Wetherspoon's onto the street. It's empty apart from the bar staff and the old woman at the bar, who I presume is the manager by the way she's smoking with the nonchalance of someone who carries a stun gun and a real-life 'get out of jail free' card. She's dressed like a traditional cockney barmaid.

For someone who looks so severe, though, she turns out to be quite amicable. She proudly states that we are in the oldest pub in Whitstable, and she tells us of the alleys at the back of the pub where smugglers could escape the burly police officers because of their very narrowness. And, sure enough, at the back is the entrance to Squeeze Gut Alley, which is very narrow indeed. It is a little depressing imagining a clearly malnourished smuggler chuckling as he slid down the alley, waving two fingers at the red-faced police officer pushing breath out from underneath his moustache. She also tells us of the Oyster Festival, which happens every year. By the way she describes it, with parade and bonfire, it sounds a bit *Wicker Man* to me.

———————

Drinking from thin glasses while sitting on a wall on the pebbled beach, we can see activity nearer the water; flickering lights and a small dog jumping around excitedly. Figures are illuminated by torches, and then suddenly hidden by crashing bows. There are boats landing and nets clacking as they hit the shore. This is a joyous catch, not a workaday one. Light suddenly fills the scene from behind us, the doors from the pub having been thrown open. Music thrusts out, foreshadowing the flow of people towards the sea.

Summer is coming in at last, and the celebrations at landing the crop of the sea are raucous and obviously about to go on all night. Wooden barrels of beer are slid down the jetty, smashing into the foam and flavouring it as they either split or are hacked open. The town is getting a round in for the English Channel, as a thank you for their livelihood. And drink with the sea they do, pint after pint and song after song. For the first time on the trip, there's something genuinely welcoming and communal about a place we've stayed.

I have one desire. That is to be part of this earth, to have that deep eerie connection to the history and the land, to exist with the green and blue that has always been there and feasts upon the blood and bones of everything that has gone before. It will consume us and continue to grow. Our only survival is by passing on ideas, the way our ancestors have done. Some we will remember.

I want to make an engraving like that, either scratched into oak or in flesh itself. In flesh with history, and with words. With songs that follow the rhythm of growth itself.

The local vicar blesses the oysters to cheers, and toasts. He slurs a little, but his voice booms above the carousing.

'You are the salt of the earth. But what good is salt if it has lost its flavour? Can you make it salty again?'

I've never felt so connected as I do now. I feel at one with my compadres and with the world. In an almost post-coital daze we sit, after-hours drinking, talking of folk songs. At one point I ask Danny to marry me.

'No.'

'It'd make a great book.'

'It would, but I'm not doing it.'

'Two heterosexual guys, going through the whole process of planning a wedding. An unusual perspective, it'd be sure to get loads of interest.'

The soft strains of Clannad drift through the empty pub. Jon leans over and tells me 'Theme from Harry's Game' when he sees me go to note it down, knowing full well I wouldn't be able to name the song. If there is a better definition of friendship than 'someone who knows the exact boundaries of your pop-culture trivia' then at this moment I'd be hard pushed to name it. The soft Celtic noodling seems to be the signal for closing time as the landlady sets about closing the curtains and shutting the door. Our long-hibernated, last-orders instincts kick in and we're debating exactly how many drinks to get up and order before the final bell when people start coming into the pub. About 20 or so in groups of three or four come through the closed door, filling up what, up to ten minutes ago, seemed liked the roomy bar area.

'Is this a lock-in?' I smile at the landlady. I clock her eyes flick towards the notebook on my table.

'No,' she says, I look at the clearly closed door and the closed curtains. She says hello to a couple of people.

'So these are regulars, right?' I ask, trying to make sense of the sudden rush.

'Not at all, luv,' she growls in a voice gravelled by years of smoking. 'Never seen them before.'

I don't pursue the subject or mention the legal extension of the closing hours that happened six or so years ago, but something is clearly happening. Maybe later they will hold hands and sing traditional folk songs while swaying, something I'm not in a hurry to see – especially through the wrong side of the torso of a giant wooden figure.

The heavily made-up landlady collects our glasses and we bid the town farewell and stagger away.

After the worst kebab I've ever tasted and a taxi journey I don't really remember, we retire to the tent. Tents are uniquely bonding experiences. With the sheer proximity it'd be hard not to have a relationship with the people you are practically spooning, but it's more than that. Maybe it's the vulnerability in seeing someone asleep, or the glimpse into their private night-time rituals – Midge methodically removing his rings into a specific pocket of the bag he uses as pillow, or Jon's ritual of straightening his sleeping bag. But seeing them both asleep, the filtered light of the tent allowing me to see the shape of their skulls as they lie there vulnerable and unknowing, all the annoyances of the day slide away like raindrops sliding off the canvas.

CHAPTER EIGHT

LAST CLACTON HERO

I wake earliest again and have a cold shower. Shaving for something to do I decide to clip my sideburns down. I've had these sideburns since I was about 18. No one really taught me how to shave or what to do, so I sort of decided that the jawline was the best leveller for sidies. I also hate looking in the mirror, so shaving by touch is easier that way.

This particular a.m, though, I stare hard into the glass at hairs and pores. I notice remnants of food round the corners of my mouth. We went to a takeaway on the way back last night. There were scant veggie options, so my food – just chips – was gone before our minicab arrived, leaving only ketchup traces.

We're soon back on a damp and featureless A road. Heading to Gravesend.

We see a 'pier' sign and find a side street to park in. I get the feeling we're now within the orbit of London. We see evidence of immigrant populations, and there is litter: KFC remnants strewn on the parking-restricted back roads.

As we pull up to Gravesend, Brett Anderson's 'Brittle Heart' pleads at us from the radio. Due to the amount of airplay it is getting it's rapidly becoming our unofficial theme tune, and not one any of us would have picked. With the skies grey and foreboding, the indulgent woe of a 40-year-old writing songs on the poetic side of teenage angst seems appropriate.

The rain lazily drops on our heads and arms in fat, wet drops that seem to laconically trip out of the sky as an afterthought. I look up.

'Antiseptic skies,' I say under my breath and immediately hate myself for it.

We head downhill, which seems to be where the water is normally kept. Sure enough, after passing a giant bronze statue of Neptune (also a good sign you're near the sea), we come to a grand wooden structure. It's essentially a giant shed that juts out over the bay. This is Gravesend Port Authority Pier. A quick peek through the window reveals it to be a giant, empty bike shed. We piss about at the entrance for a short while, marvelling at the old English phone box painted in army-camouflage colours, and childishly giggling at the solemn notice commemorating the 'fallen tug men'.

The pier we come to is closed for repair, and has a door plaque that says 'Pier Master'. Danny, in jeans and a black mac wrapped around his usual T-shirt (and I mean usual T-shirt; I think it's the same one he started in), poses beneath it. He turns his head into profile to have his photo taken. He looks a little puffy and not quite as masterful as he thinks he is. I'm about to tell him and duck, but then it dawns on us. The pier we're looking for must be somewhere else.

The actual Gravesend Pier is about 200 yards away and is disappointingly nothing more than a fancy restaurant with an art gallery along its entrance. The art is terrible.

GRAVESEND Town

Opened: 1834 (Architect: William Tiernwey Clark)

Length at start: 260 ft (79 m)

Length now: 260 ft (79 m)

Burn baby burn? No.

Gravesend Town Pier is the oldest surviving cast-iron pier in the world and is Grade II listed.

We're back on that A road, in what I think is the other direction.

The sun has beaten off the last of the antiseptic skies by the time we reach Herne Bay. Jon and Midge are openly arguing about where to park and my back is beginning to show signs of sleeping on floors all night and sitting in cars all day. We walk to the front, me creaking audibly as my spine cracks and pops into an upright position.

Herne Bay Pier is closed. Very closed. Metal railings bar the way and 'Danger, Demolition' tape covers those railings to underline the point. The first thing that strikes you is the wonderful municipal building. Big and angular, it has the striking ugliness of all council places built in the seventies – the locals' nickname for it is 'the cowshed'. It has a yellowing sign that says 'Roller Skating, Sports Hall, Fitness and Dance Studios and Squash Courts'. It was built when the grand pavilion ironically burnt down at the end of a £158,000 refurbishment, the victim of what they suspect was a stray welder's spark during the finishing of the entrance.

Herne Bay was the second-longest pier in Britain until a storm destroyed sections and isolated the pier head. You can still see it from the shore: an architectural fly preserved in amber. Because of the distance and the sun's hazy-heat blur, it almost seems a mirage. A Polaroid from history, developing in reverse, framed by the very real but pleasantly ridiculous wind farm behind it.

HERNE BAY

Opened: 1832, rebuilt in 1873 and extended in 1899 (Architect: Thomas Telford, then Wilkinson and Smith, then E. Mattheson)

Length at start: 3,633 ft (1,107 m)

Length now: 320 ft (98 m)

Burn baby burn? The first pier that occupied the site was sold for scrap in 1871. The theatre burnt down in 1928. In 1953 floods damaged the pier. After £158,000 was spent on rebuilding the Grand Pavilion in 1970, it burnt down before ever being opened. In 1978 storms destroyed the main neck, isolating the pier head out at sea.

Ken Russell used the pier as the backdrop to his first film, *French Dressing* (1964).

We spot a 'Pier Trust' shop opposite. I can almost feel the excitement building in Midge – he loved the one in Hastings.

This one is different, white and pastel, with very little shop and very little trust, as the guardians eye us with a form of disdain reserved for the unwashed. I've washed often, but not well. They are completely uninterested in our mission, and it seems like they are willing the demolition of the pavilion rather than hoping to preserve the heritage. When it's gone the space will apparently make a 'lovely spot for a farmers' market'.

———————

The lady behind the desk largely ignores us for a good ten minutes, even though a good portion of those ten minutes is spent with us at her desk trying to talk to her. Her desk is covered with the mild sort of women's magazines, the ones with puzzles, true-life 'it happened to me' stories, and tips for recycling jam jars. We do chat for a bit, but you can see she is neither impressed nor happy that three scruffy, working-class men are poking around her shop. Jon starts paying attention and stands a little closer, something he does when I'm about to do something stupid, or dangerous, or say something he'll regret. It must be something in the dismissive tone of her answers or the increasing contempt in my voice that has put Jon on high alert. She eventually tells us the plans for the pier.

'Still, it's a shame to get rid of such a glorious example of seventies architecture,' I say, and it is, because the current trend to pull down any buildings built between 1970 and 1985 is going to leave a massive gap in our architectural history.

'Well, some people don't like it,' she sneers down a nose that is spider-webbed with red lines. I look at her, from her Marks & Spencer elasticised trousers to the milky coffee in her Winnie the Pooh mug, and see her and the Herne Bay Pier Trust for what they are, retired NIMBY do-gooders with no real agenda apart from the destruction of the building they probably wrote letters to the local paper about 40 years ago.

'Well, we better go,' says Jon looking at the watch on his wrist that doesn't exist.

I fume inside and start my swearing as I'm guided out of the door. 'Did you hear her? The snooty, pinch-faced, old hag woman.'

'She wasn't that bad,' says Jon.

'Wasn't that bad? Drinking her fucking Mellow Birds from a Tesco mug, judging anyone that disagrees with her. Bitch.'

'Is your back sore? You might be overreacting a bit.'

'I spotted every inch of her and saw into her soul,' I say, ignoring Jon.

Midge walks ahead saying nothing.

Dan bristles at one of the women in particular; the self-appointed curators of heritage are winding him up something rotten.

'It's a decision to destroy a building on a fashion whim.'

That's something we know about from Birmingham: the really quite stunning Central Library is being knocked down essentially because the Council don't like it. Lots of fun in new, fashionable buildings; lots of meetings and admin in keeping the past working in the present.

On the front here is a classic piece of Englishness, a coin-operated stall that promises a glimpse of something. Danny puts 'any coin' in and starts the ball rolling – literally. The ball drops into a wheel, like roulette but more slowly and with a dull, rubber thud rather than a ping of excitement. It falls into a slot and a striped can rotates in primary colours. It shows us the Tweenies – children's TV characters already starting to fade from view. We could have seen the Fraggles, which no child now can remember, or Miss Piggy. Characters frozen in time, picked up cheap and as necessary. That's how a culture builds.

There is news on the radio that an old cinema, now a bingo hall, round the corner from my house is on fire and is probably burning down. We're losing the past.

Sitting in the car watching suburbia melt into the countryside like a boring zoetrope, I reflect that I am hopelessly fucking lost. All the long-term plans I can imagine sound as pointless as the ones I've tried and found wanting. The ideals of my ancestors are as empty as a Coca-Cola billboard and the only joy I've achieved has arrived in three- or four-minute bursts, no longer than a punk song.

It wouldn't be an English journey without a traffic jam, and the M25 is the classic English place to have one. We sit stationary, then moving, almost organically jockeying for position with cars in other lanes. Danny, fed up with losing count of how many piers we've seen and now aware that it's the second question anyone asks us, has started a tally chart. The army-camouflage pier in Gravesend has its own 'bonus piers' section, and the five-bar gates are building up.

The chart is on the writing side of a Linda Lusardi postcard – an eighties Page Three version of seaside raunch, which says as much about the mainstream eighties as any number of archive shots of men in shiny suits talking into large mobile phones. The eighties, or what we saw of the culture of London in the eighties, were a place without warmth, humour and compassion – and full of tits.

Linda faces out and Dan much enjoys the reactions of those that spot it from the next lane.

Driving in to Southend, we go down a road called Orwell Street and I think about my literary hero. The place seems unconnected to anything about him. It's truly suburban; the sort of suburb where cars are being 'worked on' on the grass in front gardens.

I mention Orwell to Danny. Some time ago we had an idea for a computer game, based around my obsession with the Spanish Civil War. We imagined a first-person shooter – you know the sort, where you just see the end of your gun at the bottom of the screen – in which you would take the role of Orwell fighting the fascists. And to make it a two-player game, a friend could pick up a rifle as Ernest Hemingway. They were both in Spain as the war raged around them, but came away with very different views of the same thing.

Who on our trip is Orwell, who is Hemingway?

'I'm Orwell,' says Dan.

'But I'm the big Orwell fan. I do the politics.'

'I'd rather be Orwell.'

'I don't think I'm butch enough to... '

'I'm Orwell, I'll fight you for it.'

And that's the point at which Danny became Hemingway.

I have a good sulk in the car, and slowly my mood shifts. I may have been a little unreasonable and a bit tired and in a lot of pain earlier. Jon starts trying to find a local radio station and ends up on a local dance station. I think it's called 'Funky', because they use the term once every three words in every jingle they play. Which is approximately every two minutes or so. It's a good job too, because the DJ is as unprofessional as they come – even for local radio.

'Thanks for all your requests, I just got round to looking at the post from a couple of weeks ago, so thank you if sent anything in,' comes the voice between indistinguishable dance tracks and funky-laden jingles.

At one point he openly berates the last DJ (for drinking the lager out of the fridge without putting anything in the kitty) for the length of an entire link. And after one song, he sounds distracted. 'I've just been on the phone about a job, so that's good news, eh?'

Me and Jon dub him DJ Slapdash, Essex's fourteenth-best dance DJ, and take it in turns talking over him, providing lazy, half-arsed links in our best radio DJ voices.

'That was a song by those guys with the funny hair, it's got a dog on the cover if you want to seek it out.'

Funky nights in funky clubs that the funky listeners must get funky down to.

'I might nip to the shop during the next track. You want anything, Steve?' And eventually just the jingle we invented:

'SLAPDASH
DJ
DJ
SLAPDASH
funkyFUNKYfunky'

'Shut up! Just shut up, will you,' Midge erupts from the front.

At first I'm shocked, but it can't be easy driving and navigating on as little sleep as we've all had. I feel bad at first, like being told off by a dinner lady.

We drive along a packed seafront looking for parking spaces. The nearest is 300 yards away from the pier and costs a small fortune from a ticket machine that is 100 yards further on from where we park.

Southend is full of beachfront stalls, and shops, and funfairs, and commerce – it's as tacky as anything we've seen so far. Mostly it's full of people, people with what our ears detect to be London accents.

———————

There is no real beach to speak of, just a concrete slope into a brown sea with suspicious brown foam. In the distance over the water you can make out the mills and heavy machinery of industry. You can never be sure if something's a silhouette or it's actually just black in colour. As we walk, someone is emerging from the water and a crowd has gathered. I imagine them bemused as to why he went in there to begin with. We pass the occasional hut selling cheap fried food or plastic swords for the kids.

Before we get to the pier we see a funfair that, while not being totally pirate-themed itself, is having a pirate weekend in order to squeeze the last out of the summer trade, and it's working. Southend is pretty full.

The reason the pier exists is to grab the visitors that were previously skipping Southend in favour of Margate. Most people in the early 1800s travelled down the river on boats, which often had trouble docking. Southend, for example, has an incredibly low tide, and when the tide is out it leaves a mile or so of mud between the shore and the sea. So in 1830 they built their first pier, and when they discovered it wasn't long enough a few years later they added to it, and then they added to it again until it became the longest pier in Europe.

We find the entrance and speak to the people in the office, who aren't quite expecting the reaction they get when we find out that the pier was closed after a boat had drifted into it earlier in the year, which rotates between disbelief, swearing and at one point falling to our knees and crying with laughter. Probably it's just as well. Brummies don't do well on Southend Pier. In 1931 a drayman from Ansells Brewery, Ernest Turner, while here on a works do, fell from one of the trains on the pier and landed under the wheels of one coming in the opposite direction. Let's face it, he was probably absolutely pissed at the time. In my childhood I remember my nan, as not only the matriarch of the family but also as a local figure in the community, organising coach trips to the seaside: entire streets of people piling onto a couple of coaches and drinking from five in the morning till gone 12 at night when you got dropped off. I only realise in retrospect that everyone was drinking, because at the time I was too young to know.

SOUTHEND-ON-SEA

Opened: 1890 (Architect: James Brunlees)

Length at start: 600 ft

Length now: 7,080 ft (2,158 m)

Burn baby burn? Southend Pier has had no fewer than four major fires and numerous accidents with boats drifting into it. The worst of these was in 1980 when the MV *Kingsabbey* crashed through it, entirely severing the pier head from the mainland and leaving a 70-ft gap.

There was a wooden pier on the site long before the iron one that opened in 1890. It had opened in 1830 and became the longest pier in Europe after an 1846 extension. Some of the boards from that earlier pier were used to make the Southend mayoral chair. The iron pier that replaced it in 1890 became the longest pier in the world after an 1898 extension.

In the end credits of TV show *Minder*, Arthur Daley and his bodyguard Ray are shown walking down the pier. When they reach land, Arthur realises that he has left his lighter at the sea end and they proceed to walk all the way back.

The pier is also mentioned in *The Hitchhiker's Guide to the Galaxy*. When the hitchhikers are thrown off a spaceship, Arthur remarks that it looks as though they're standing 'on the seafront at

Southend'. However, the set used for the pier in the TV adaptation (the show started life as a radio comedy) looks nothing like Southend.

In May 2011, plans to redevelop the pier were delayed by months because of nesting birds: ruddy turnstones.

We can do nothing but press our noses against the glass at the ticket desk. This place is the most modern pier we've (nearly) been on: airline-uniformed girls behind melamine desks inform us that it's not likely to open any time soon. There's no point in staying any longer, except that we've put two hours on the parking meter.

Midge has an idea of what to do with the time. He broke his sunglasses at some point and has been driving with them on in the style of Eric Morecambe doing van Gogh for at least a day. He's got very exacting standards and this leads us from Primark to Poundland to Poundstretcher, in fact any shop noted for its cheapness.

The shopping centre is odd. Actually, that's not true. The shopping centre is completely normal. It could be any shopping centre anywhere in Britain. It has the same shops and the same music, and even the temperature is air-conditioned just this side of comfortably cool. It's us that are odd. We don't know how to behave around these people. We stride around with the confident purpose of those that have a very specific goal. A purpose is rarely seen in a place made specifically for browsing. The roof seems too low and the smells too strong. We soon leave and head to the front, hoping a gift shop might have a pair of sunglasses that will fit Midge's unusually small head.

This is a little more interesting, and I focus on a set of Frank Sinatra plates. Another bit of culture that will be forever stuck in time.

On the way back to the car I buy a plastic sword for the car. Midge rolls his eyes but if we are attacked by plastic pirates I will be ready.

As we drive away from Southend, the sun starts pushing solid rays of light through the cloud that has gathered over the dramatic Essex skyline.

On the way to Clacton we listen to more of Rich Gold Funky FM – the banter is not so much inane as deliberately artless, simply repeating banalities about everyday life – it's media as one of us. Afraid to challenge, recognition is how we connect these days.

It's the sort of station the teenagers we pass quietly under an ornate bridge by the front of Clacton Pier would listen to. Making what I realise are classist distinctions based on their clothing and deportment, we hurry past with our heads down. We fear a shouted confrontation given our 'outsider look'. It will come after we've passed and there is no response that won't just provoke laughter. No wit that will hit home, we will just have to keep going. I don't confirm this with Midge or Dan; I just know that it's how 'alternative' people think.

From underneath the footbridge the white edifice of the pier unfolds in front of you: the sign promising free admission is clearly visible and certainly more legible than that of 'Clacton Pier'. Through the doors are a selection of rides, including the 20p single-person rockers normally seen outside supermarkets, cups and saucers and dodgems, all painted the usual gaudy funfair colours.

These rides and bunko magic booths spill out onto the open large deck that extends before us. The sky is the same grey colour as the sea and they merge together like an image placeholder until someone can be bothered to fill them in.

CLACTON-ON-SEA

Opened: 1871 (Architect: Peter Bruff; Kinipple and Jaffrey for the pavilion)

Length at start: 480 ft (146 m)

Length now: 1,180 ft (360 m)

Burn baby burn? A 1973 fire caused significant structural damage.

Clacton Pier was officially the first building erected in the new resort of Clacton-on-Sea. In 2009 the pier was taken over by the Clacton Pier Company, who installed a 50-ft helter-skelter. Originally built in 1949 and used in a travelling show, this slide has also featured in a Marks & Spencer advert. Clacton's famous Cockney Pride pub is now the Boardwalk Bar & Grill, and you can attempt the Stella's Revenge roller coaster to cure any hangover the next morning.

Clacton Pier itself looks well. It's expansive and cared for, without being glossed. I spend some time taking photos inside the beautifully tiled toilets, admiring the way that the old Edwardian workings have been allowed to stand, to gather just the right amount of chips and scratches. There's something about older architecture that allows this growing old gracefully. Decay as design, working with the ageing process. I manage to take a few shots without getting mistaken for a sexual pervert rather than a pier one. A 'piervert'.

The boardwalk is wide and welcoming, and rides and concessions are placed around in a not exactly ordered way. The place feels organic and homely, like it's evolved to how it now is, but I know from friends that stuff has changed. I've been talking about a 'scary clown' we are supposedly looking for but I know now it's long gone. Things change, people change.

Then, standing with all the grandeur of an A-road cafe, near to the coin-op dodgems, is a yellow hut, and I almost see a reason for us to be here. The windows are guarded by bars on the outside and covered with faded graphics on the inside. The front is festooned with pictures of dogs and poor cartoons. It's a T-shirt-printing stall and I know we have to get one each.

Getting to the door, we see it's shut. The sign says 'back in ten minutes' but it looks as if it's been there for about ten years, and the transfers displayed on the windows are so faded with age we're not sure the place is still open.

'We have to wait,' I say to Jon. The shack is untouched since the eighties, and I remember begging my mum for a T-shirt with rude versions of the Mr Men ironed on it when I was a teenager.

'Well, even if we just missed 'em, they'll only be ten minutes,' says Jon.

Clearly Midge is annoyed at this, but he knows us well enough by now to know this is one of the things that we have to do that he won't understand.

———————

I sometimes mistake the act of buying as something that will comfort me. In the tatty souvenir stalls we've looked at, my guts cry out that I should make purchases. If I get the right thing, I'll be happy for a moment. So far the present on Hythe Pier and postcards are the only things I've bought. I really wanted something stupid, just to have it and remind myself that I exist in a world with other people.

On a school trip back in juniors – I must have been ten at the most – to Barry Island near Cardiff I made maybe the most disastrous buying decision of my life. (Except maybe that Crash Test Dummies album.) I had saved the money my mum had given me all day and splurged it in the joke shop as we were about to get back on the coach. I saw a box that was labelled 'Fart Detector'. It cost a couple of quid, everything I had, but I knew I needed it. I had visions of some amazing machine that would smell them and know who had dealt them. What fun there would be on the bus on the way home, childish fun of course, but I was a child.

And it turned out to be a false nose. Capitalism disappoints.

We do the slow waltz of shy people around the T-shirt shop, pretending to make decisions and admire the stock rather than striding right up to the counter and getting what we want. Only the supremely confident, the posh and the foreign can do that. We have to do this dance, and as there's two of us – Midge having snorted derision and being off looking for chips – we also have to do the nudging for the other one to do the actual interaction. I win this. With most people I do. I'm the best at being shy.

———————

Inside there are wall-to-wall transfers of metal bands from the eighties, generic football teams, dolphins in the moonlight. For

20p a letter we can get whatever we want ironed onto a T-shirt in lovely red velour letters in a font we both spot is the traditional Cooper Black.

Dan orders the shirts: he wants XL and white; I want L and black. I think a large will probably be a little too tight on me, but I am enjoying pretending to be slimmer than Danny. While the guy behind the counter places the furry letters on the cloth we make a kind of aggressive small talk with him. We're both unfailingly polite, as we always are with strangers, even one that seems to be trying to trip us up with questions about the quest, about The List. Danny does most of the talking and is doing well – apart from being unable to remember the chap is called Peter and not John.

'So, how long have you worked here, John?'

'Peter,' I say quietly.

It's been a long time.

'Is business getting worse or is it about the same, John?'

'Peter.'

It's okay, but not as good as it used to be. We hopefully make the overcast afternoon a little bit more profitable.

John speaks as he moves, quietly and in compact sentences that reveal no strong emotions. He has a scruffy Zen about him as he carefully aligns the letters of 'piervert' in an arc across the chests of our T-shirts. He's been on Clacton Pier for 29 years. Before that he was a tailor. As one of the first people in the country to import Lacrosse he was partly responsible for the soccer-casual look of the eighties. You really get the impression he loves what he does, but business isn't great after three bad seasons weather-wise and the recession.

'It'll get worse before it gets better,' he warns darkly as he sets about aligning the second set of letters on Jon's shirt.

'Weird thing to have on a T-shirt, we know, but we're doing this thing, you see,' I stumble to explain.

'You're visiting every pier in England and Wales in two weeks. I wondered when you'd get here,' he says without looking up.

Stunned, me and Jon look at each other and he lets it sit in the air for a few moments.

'You were in yesterday's paper.' He reaches under his desk and produces the paper. Sure enough, in one of the corners there's a couple of paragraphs about our trip.

'How many have you done so far?' There's a smile to his eyes.

'No idea – we started at Weston.'

'What's the shortest pier?' It isn't a request for information, it's a quiz.

'Burnham,' I say automatically.

'It used to be the Harwich, called the "halfpenny pier", did you know that?'

'Yes,' I lie.

'The longest pier?'

'Southend,' I say. 'Easy,' I think.

'Largest by square footage?' he counters. I think for a moment. I don't know this, but I do want to make it look like I used to and have merely forgotten.

'I don't know,' I concede.

He raises his eyebrows and tilts his head slightly.

'This one?' I ask, and he smiles for the first time, happy to have caught me out.

'There's a really good book I've been reading about the Victorian seaside and piers.' He reaches under the table and brings out a beautifully illustrated book. We chat some more. He seems clearly a little bitter that the trade relies too much on just the dwindling tourists. Midge arrives and that's our cue. We thank John for his time and leave the wise man in his cave.

_____

Peter, who shall be known as John, represents the slow decline of this type of pier and seaside life. It seems that the attractions are built for the transient tourist and don't have anything to offer the locals. The pier isn't part of the community. He's no time for the locals: they'll come on to the boards when it's a handy viewing platform for the air show but 'they want something for nothing' and he'll not see them for the rest of the year.

_____

Someone had painted 'LIFE IS BEAUTIFUL' on a wall near Frinton. I think about John and wonder whether he'd agree. I think he would, with just a small nod of his head.

_____

Walton-on-the-Naze is another in a series of place names that I had preconceptions about without any real knowledge. I had no idea it was anywhere near the coast. I had pictured a sleepy Cotswolds village, thatched houses with climbing roses bookending a babbling stream.

_____

By now the grey that had become the sky and the sea in Clacton has enveloped the land, bleaching out the colours, making everything seem like a depressing documentary. We park on a hill with the coast a steep walk down. We pass the Thames MRCC (Maritime Rescue Coordination Centre) and outside are black-marble panels with names and dates. Reverently I take a look and realise that, far from being a list of people who died at sea, this is a list of all the people they have saved over the years. This cheers me until we crest the hill and see the pier.

Iron, colour powder coated, and lettered in the same seventies font that adorns our chests. While it is warming and fuzzy over our hearts, it is bland and unwelcoming over the gaping entrance to the pier. It looks more like a parcel depot than a palace of fun. It's dark and dingy, chintzy name or not. The day is ending, but the sun's waning doesn't make the large youths hanging around the entrance threatening – that's just their stance and their presence. The 'open all year pier' looks like a warehouse.

WALTON-ON-THE-NAZE

Opened: 1898 (Architect: J. Cochrane)

Length at start: 2,600 ft (162 m)

Length now: 2,600 ft (792 m)

Burn baby burn? 1942, and serious storms in 1978.

Up until it closed during the war, passengers were transported along the pier on an unusual battery-powered car.

The pier is big yellow bastard the size of a small aeroplane hangar squatting on the coast, with the promenade emanating from behind it. Ugly in its desperation to appear fun, the bright yellow seems perverse in the grey climate. Three men stand in the doorway next to the closed shutters.

'Look, it's closed,' says Midge, clearly hesitant.

'And it's fucking spooky. Looks like somewhere Scooby-Doo would visit,' I say.

'Do we have to go?' asks Midge

'Yes,' me and Jon say in unison.

The three gentlemen outside look very much like Eastern European movie gangsters, their cheap tracksuits and roll-up cigarettes matched with all-too-obvious jewellery and unnatural nonchalance. We say nothing as we walk past. Neither do they. Both groups pointedly saying nothing.

The structure is massive inside and dotted about are the funfair rides and arcade games of 20 years ago. Most of them are turned off, which highlights the empty space. We are alone and it feels like no one has been here for years. Near the exit to the pier itself is a run-down bowling alley. Four or five people are at the bar; no one is bowling. The barmaid looks suicidally bored. We quickly walk up the length of the bleak, wet and unnecessarily long pier. By now a fine rain is making the wooden planks slippery and the wind has picked up to the point where I can't hear what Jon is saying. A well-timed gust of wind and we could lose Midge to the sea forever.

———

In the semi-dark the traditional hillbilly shooting range almost looks like a place to sleep. I'm struck with the question of what makes it okay to shoot the hillbillies in these games. They're human lives we're meant to find disposable. I've worked this up as a speech over the last week or so, and am about to foist it on the guys.

This is halted by Danny about to climb into something a little bigger than a shower. It's a 'Hurricane Simulator'.

I'm not about to let him have first go, or spend any money I don't have to spend, so I pull the door open and climb in too. It actually turns out to be very much like a shower, except with wind. I think two of us being in here weakens the strength of the experience, or maybe I'm just not standing under the jet. We pantomime enjoyment for Midge and our antics do not go unnoticed by the surly inhabitants of the pier.

———————

The vibe is bad and we try and shake it off on our way back to the car.

———————

I know Harwich is a ferry town. That means confusing road signs and odd turnings of different types, plus elevated roundabouts with no immediate purpose or obvious correct exit. Midge nearly drives us onto a freight carrier of some sort, before we start our now traditional skirt round the back streets of a town looking for free parking. The town is damp, and dark, and empty except for the bar of a hotel we pass. It has no curtains or glass frosting so the view inside looks like an illuminated screen. A super HD broadcast of a normal, snug life we can't be part of at the moment.

The pier is dark wood, and slippery. A droop of benches and railings, sheathed with nets and boats. Somehow the dull light makes the flowers left on the memorial bench, flecked as they are with rain, seem sadder even than they would otherwise be.

———————

We walk the length of the pier in silence. On the bench near the end lie some yellow roses. Yellow roses, traditionally, are the flower of jealousy or a dying love.

HARWICH Ha'penny

Opened: 1853

Length at start: Twice as long as it is now.

Length now: Half as long as it was.

Burn baby burn? Originally the pier was twice as long as the present one, but one half burnt down in 1927.

The pier bends around to hug the coast and creates a sea area known as the Pound, which also makes its length difficult to measure. The pier – named after the original toll to enter – houses an exhibition on the *Mayflower* ship and her captain, Christopher Jones.

As we leave town we're assaulted by signs saying 'DRIVE ON LEFT'. If Midge can see them, and I'm not too sure of his eyesight in the dark, I wonder if he too is fighting the anti-authoritarian streak to drive on the other side just to piss them off.

CHAPTER NINE
THE BEAUTIFUL SOUTHWOLD

Jon fiddles about with his phone and a punk song comes out of the piermobile's stereo. There are no speakers at the back so I don't hear it very clearly, but because of where we're going, and because Jon would never normally play punk, I know that it must be a song about the siege at Castle Inn called 'Never Had Nothin'' by the Angelic Upstarts. It's a pleasantly melodic song for the genre, with a surprising handclap refrain and breakdown in the bridge. It reached number 52 in the British charts in 1979. We listen to it a couple of times as Midge swears at the ever-patient and slightly patronising woman who lives inside the satnav.

I can't remember who found out about the Castle Inn: punk credentials would suggest Midge, but I don't remember him suggesting it. Once we had read the story of the place, though, we had to stop here. The pub was the scene of a shotgun shoot-out between the police and a man called Paul Howe after a botched burglary. Gun sieges are still unusual enough in our country to make one from 30 years or more back notable.

We arrive around half seven. When we stick our head in the pub we find that it's painted coffee-house bland, obviously wearing a recent makeover. We ask the small, unwelcoming woman behind the bar where the campsite is. She tells us that we've parked next to it. She is managing to look harassed and busy despite the only customer being a very old gentleman wearing a suit who's impossibly balanced on a bar stool. We go out and discover the campsite is the small beer garden at the back. Hastily we put up our tent, eager to get some pub food.

Back inside, we are joined by another customer, obviously a regular by the way he didn't have to order a drink. We ask to order some food.

'Food's finished, kitchen's closed,' she says and goes into the kitchen switching off the lights. I'm looking at the menu that says the kitchen doesn't close for another hour, but she seems definite. We're obviously crestfallen.

'Why don't you guys order a takeaway?' shouts the regular from his seat. 'You could eat it here, she'll give you some plates.' The manageress gives him a filthy look.

'Would that be all right?' I ask.

'I'm not having curries stinking up the place,' she says. I again can't help glancing at the menu, this time at the 'curries' section.

'How about we have it ordered to here, and we take it into the tent?' She looks cross. The regular looks delighted at her discomfort.

'Do what you want,' she says.

'Great, could we borrow some plates and cutlery?' I'm chancing my luck but I want to punish her.

'How will I get them back? We don't open till 12,' she counters.

'We'll leave them on the table just inside the door.'

'Course she'll let you have the plates,' shouts the regular, enjoying himself.

'All right then,' she spits as she storms off to fetch us our plates.

The pub shows no sign of what went on 32 years ago. I ask at the bar, but she aggressively pretends not to know what I'm talking about. I figure that I'm standing there like a tit anyway, so I elaborate further. Eventually she points me to a small display, comprising no more than a press cutting and the Angelic Upstarts vinyl single framed on a far wall.

'I took over the place six years ago when the refit happened so don't really know anything,' she dismisses.

The old man in a suit points to part of the wall above our heads. 'You can still see some bullet holes up there.'

We look. You can't.

As we get up to leave when the food arrives, the regular makes eye contact and gestures at the woman and the old man.

'They've been miserable bastards since they took over this place.' He winks as we go.

I go back to the car to get something. It's still only closing time or thereabouts and I don't have a torch. I'm relying on the glow though the bar windows as I open the boot and start rummaging. I'm now not sure what I was after, but I can remember the feeling of being watched and turning around.

'Dan, have you brought the torch? I can't find shit.'

But it isn't Danny. Or Midge. The silhouettes don't match. Instead of a tubby, ponytailed guy and a matchstick punk there are other people, bulkier people. Silent and threatening people.

The light from the pub throws them into shadow but reflects off the tallest guy's white baseball cap.

And then it drops that these are the blokes from Walton Pier. They were watching us. They have followed us.

'I hear you're not popular, yeah?' says baseball cap. 'The Cool White Dog has a message. Stop. Now.'

'Stop doing what? Me and DANNY and MIDGE.' They must hear; the tent is only 20 yards away in the unkempt beer garden.

'Just stop. There's nothing for you in it.'

'Hey guys, what's going on?' Danny, fronting it as usual. Suddenly beside me, like he was there all along.

We're outnumbered, at least four to two and a half. And crap at fighting.

'Fuck off, I've got a hammer.' I have, a claw hammer from the car toolkit we've used to knock in tent pegs. But despite raising it in anger I can't bring myself to strike a blow. We struggle and flail, taking blows to head and body.

I swing a kick at some bollocks and connect. It hurts him but it doesn't stop the pounding. I can taste blood and grit and feel warm from kick after hit. One of them feels strangely like a kiss. There's a loud blast from the pub and the next thing I know it's 6 a.m.

The dawn chorus lulls me awake. Feeling hung-over and groggy, I remember that we went back to the tent last night and I was asleep before my head hit the takeaway. The dawn chorus is soon joined by some robust DIY from across the fence and I drag myself out of the tent. It's too early to wake the guys, though. I've a pain in my stomach like I've been hit in the gut. I'm hungry.

We've no food, so I decide to walk through the village, hoping to come across a shop. The village is pretty, but nothing stirs. Eventually I turn back towards the pub car park where we've camped and pull a couple of apples off a tree on the way. They look edible, but I know nothing about what should or shouldn't be pulled off and popped in between one's lips. Biting in, it doesn't taste bad, so I grab a couple more and fill my pockets.

––––––––––

The shower has cobwebs everywhere that the jet of lukewarm water doesn't directly hit. It runs on tokens that were begrudgingly sold to us last night. The shower unit is a seventies cream and brown affair, with white streaks where drops of water run down through the thick dust. I look out through the gap in the door at a pale blue sky, a couple of long, thin, knobbly clouds running diagonally through it, looking how my back feels after another night of sleeping on the floor. My clothes and wash kit are on a garden chair that is the perfect distance away for them to be not at all in reach but still thoroughly wet from the shower.

As we leave, I try and post the plates through the letter box, but they won't fit.

———————

Felixstowe is dominated by ships, big ships turning. I get a fair amount of time to stare out to sea. The pier is almost gone. Demolished, or awaiting demolition maybe. But what remains, electronic bingo and a cafe that uses those squat, thick, white cups, is closed. We're here too early.

I'm scanning the horizon, looking at the ships and looking for windmills. I feel alone and helpless, hungry and powerless. I'd look to Danny and Midge for help, but I'm not sure they have the capacity to provide it. Dan is distracted and distant, and while I see Midge as a stoic and a strong presence, I can't get over how old and frail he looked this morning.

As I watched him cross the patio area of the pub towards the shower in the grotty shed, I noticed that his hair was starting to grow. The pattern revealed just how little of his baldness is there by choice.

If I really need help, they'll be there for me, but how much will they be able to do?

The only chain of shops that seems to have made it to Felixstowe is Job Centre Plus, the sight of which unnerves Midge into a succession of wrong turns on our way out of town. A week left for us to get him back and 'available for work'.

Waiting to get on to the main road, a bike gang burr past. The Iron Crows. As always, these gangs are not as scary as they first look, as they consist of guys in their forties or older. Whether it's just a weekend tribal thing for them or not, the idea that leather and a mode of transport are inherently scary or dangerous just doesn't wash. When we're scared of youth tribes, it's the youth bit that frightens us, because that's the bit that we know we can't compete with or hope to understand. You can research the past, we're trying to do that on this trip, but you can't hold on to the future. I know that this whole thing is an attempt by all three of us to stay young.

Looking at the aches, the hobbling, the quiet we yearn for, it's not working.

We arrive at Felixstowe Pier. It originally had its own train station and used to be one of the longest in the country, but, as with a lot of piers, the seaward section was destroyed by the Royal Engineers as a precaution against invading troops. It's always chilling to imagine when you see these piers how close we were to being invaded, exactly how close they thought that the enemy troops would get. And how much we were willing to sacrifice in terms of history, culture and architecture for the sake of a few hundred yards. At Felixstowe, disrepair has done the rest. Plans were released in 1996 for a £2.5m repair job but nothing came of it. And in 1999 a charity trust was set up, but quietly closed again soon after. In 2004 a demolition request was made by the owners.

The amusements at the front of the pier are still open, however. The wheels of local government do turn slowly, but they don't turn that slowly, so maybe the amusements do bring in enough money to make ends meet. And maybe the owners could be persuaded to invest the money to do up the pier. With the recent rise in home tourism, it could happen. It's a sliver of hope, but it's there, and sometimes that's all you need.

We walk under the pier and the light reflects off the pebbles, still wet after the tide went out.

FELIXSTOWE

Opened: 1905 (Architects: Rogers Brothers)

Length at start: 2,640 ft (805 m)

Length now: 450 ft (137 m)

Burn baby burn? No fires. The pier was sectioned for defence reasons during World War Two and the seaward end was demolished after the war ended. In 2011 a hole opened in the floor of the building after one of the pillars shifted.

A shorter, but wider, pier is due to open in 2017, which will mean the pier we visited will be replaced. The new pier is slated to have a huge entertainment complex with 'bowling and leisure attractions', which can only be an improvement.

It's a cold day in mid September, and my phone buzzes thirteen. Southwold Pier is buzzing too, with pastel. Checking the day, I realise it's an end-of-season weekend. Despite the cold, the sun is striking the sand and the painted wood in a pleasantly bright way. The light blues of Southwold Pier give each of its hand-lettered signs, gouged and painted into swinging driftwood, a charming air. Even if their sheer number and their wordiness do give off a passive-aggressive vibe.

Getting on to the main thrust of the pier means negotiating a busy bottleneck of steps around the side. Once on, you're immediately in the way of tea-taking older people. Wicker chairs and condiments, Saturday-job teens in black slacks and starched shirts, the deck is trying to do too much too soon.

The smell of lavender is giving me a headache and my vision is fuzzy around the edges already, softening what is basically a chocolate-box, Marks & Spencer, middle-class smugfest. The pier is aggressively pleasant; pleasant people, pleasant weather. The gift shop is also pleasant, and I'm beginning to think that's my problem. Everything is so bloody nice. I look at the organic nick-nacks. Turning over a hand-made pot I spot the price and bark out a laugh. Everyone is far too polite to stare, but the sideways glances make me glad I'm wearing the only clean T-shirt in my possession. Unfortunately it says 'piervert' on it and I have to wrestle down a snake of shame. That's why I'm so uncomfortable around the middle classes; they're so reasonable, so polite. They control us through our natural subservient inclination, whipping us sharply with shame. You alter your own behaviour and they expect you to be grateful for their tolerance.

Holding my breath I make it to an exit and suck in the sea air. Okay, I'm not that annoyed. Strong smells tend to do that to me, overwhelm the other senses. The weather is perfect, and the whole vista is like a day at the seaside as described by a child, or an idealised memory recalled by an adult. The beach is the perfect, platonic ideal of a sandy beach and a row of brightly coloured beach huts, which delineate the beach from the Tellytubbyland green hills behind.

I make eye contact with Jon. Jon is as bolshie as they come, and we recognise each other's discomfort. Various families run about being 'delighted' at things and for the first time on the trip I feel like an intruder rather than a visitor.

Everywhere is cramped, and busy. This is a popular place. It's got telescopes, a cafe and a shop that manages to replicate the end bit of a garden centre, but it's got a quirk to it too. We gather with the rest of the crowd at a quarter past the hour to hear the clock strike. No one is sure what will happen or which angle it's best viewed from.

'Is that it?' I ask Midge.

'Dunno, maybe it's better on the half hour. I like the guy who built this, he does good stuff. Hunkin, his name is.'

Midge is a hacker and machine builder too. We bullied him into making a steady-hand-buzz-wire machine for a summer fete once. He's a talented man, who can turn his hand to all sorts of practical and technical things; I've often wondered what makes him unemployable. Polite, clever, handy, but jobless. I resolve again to actually ask him at some point, knowing that I won't.

The arcade here is the most individual we're likely to see. I change a note and wait for families to leave space. The machine I want to try is called Rent-A-Dog. I've never had a dog and the more gambolling, panting companions I see on the road, the more and more I want one. Danny's panting is not comforting, and his gambolling is limited by an old back injury.

I step on to the treadmill and grasp the lead, the metal hound cocks his head at me and we are off. The lead tugs, the path moves and the screen shows a suburban street from a dog's point of view. I pull away from cars and am pulled towards other dogs. I am held back and dragged forwards. All in all, the machine isn't exactly fun, but like the others here it's an idea executed. The fun is to share the idea.

Paying a quid to simulate a quotidian experience like this is somehow deeply English. The whole pier has a deliberately eccentric bent, a middle-class one, a *Reggie Perrin* or *The Good*

Life suburban eccentricity. The clock, the signage, everything has just enough quirk not to spook the posh. Our working-class-hero inner dialogues are spooked a little, though.

SOUTHWOLD

Opened: 1900 (Architect: W. Jeffrey)

Length at start: 810 ft (247 m)

Length now: 623 ft (190 m)

Burn baby burn? A T-shape at the pier head was washed away in 1934 by storms (but rebuilt in 1999). A drifting sea mine struck the pier in 1941, and more storms in 1979 reduced the pier to 60 ft.

The *Rough Guide to Britain* named the Under the Pier Show – the arcade machines and simulator rides of inventor Tim Hunkin – as number nine in its 'Top 10 Things to Do in Britain'. Jon went back a year or so after our trip. He's still not clear what the clock does.

Southwold Pier has none of the grubbiness of other piers, no tacky branding intruding and none of the sticky charm of the piss-cheap, candy-apple wrappers that seem to blow around the feet of most piers. It's nice, like waking up in someone else's dream.

Just off the end of the pier some posts stick out of the sea, freestanding and level with the rail. Onto the flat ends people have thrown coins. I root around in my pockets for any of the loose change I didn't spend in the arcade, wondering if people made wishes as they threw them. I get five pence balanced on my second try but don't wish for anything. I never do.

And so with a back that is getting more uncomfortable and our pockets getting ever emptier, we head to England's most easterly point.

———————

On our way out of Southwold, passing through real rural England with its rusting cars in gardens and Sunday-morning football, we spotted a sign to a 'maize maze'. But we drive up to where we think it is and can't see any evidence of it. We must have missed a turn.

'We must have gone too far.'

'I didn't see a turning.' Is Midge taking this as a slight?

I'm trying to Google, but can't find anything. Midge sighs and does a three-point turn up a dirt track. We drive and we miss again. We turn again.

'Let's get back to where the sign was, it must be near there.'

It isn't.

'I'm aware of the irony,' I say, 'of getting lost trying to find a maze.'

By this point I've developed a verbal tick – 'all grist to the mill' – to wipe away bad things. I say it now.

———————

From now on we will be in the east. A place casual with history where, according to the peasant traditions of the moors dwellers whose language goes back further than records, travelling widdershins around any fairy ring puts you at the mercy of the fey folk. These are not the Disney fairies of the films, but the fairies of England, a wild feral personification of nature's cruel sense of humour. Will we come under the influence of the Seelie, those kind, good-natured wood spirits? Or the Unseelie, dangerous agents of disruption and change? Are we here to create or destroy?

I've never believed that journalism is neutral. Any quantum-science pervert will tell you that the act of observing something changes it. Are we here to chase images of our childhood, and if we are, what can we do with them? Pin them down like butterflies under glass? And if we do, would other people even see them as butterflies? Or just half-transformed caterpillars? Or as cocooned, liquefied words still squirming with nostalgia and defiance.

Lowestoft appears after the countryside recedes into suburb and then town again. One thing about coastal towns is that everything seems very flat; buildings don't need to grow up if they can grow out. And, being a city boy, it's always weird the amount of room you're afforded when not in one. The directions to the front are clear, and a good indicator of how much the town values tourism. Lowestoft is part of what is poetically called the 'sunrise coast' and, being our most easterly point, it is the very first place the sun hits as it make its golden cameos in the movie of our lives. I read that Lowestoft is where Captain Birdseye employs over 700 people and I'm a little disappointed that a giant, wooden frigate isn't moored by the first pier we come to, staffed by salty and surprisingly non-abused children, eyes narrowed at the distance, searching for the signs only shoals of wild fish fingers leave in their wake.

The first of Lowestoft's piers is perfectly pierish, nothing we haven't seen before. The only thing noteworthy is just how bored a teenage girl fishing off the end is. Pink top and tracksuit bottoms and the deepest glower against the world I've ever seen.

LOWESTOFT South

Opened: 1846 (Architect: unknown, but an earlier wooden pier was built in 1831 by William Cubitt)

Length at start: 1,320 ft (402 m)

Length now: 1,320 ft (402 m)

Burn baby burn? A reading room was added in 1853 and a bandstand in 1884; both were destroyed by fire in 1885. In 1987, the seaward end closed due to structural problems, not to be opened to its full length again until 1993.

People often gather on the pier to mourn loved ones. The Lowestoft lifeboat crew will scatter ashes at sea near the pier while carrying out their weekly training exercise.

South Pier is as disappointing as the concrete jetty that is Felixstowe Pier. Only a slightly tacky 'entertainment complex' squats near it. We dutifully walk its length and then we're off down the seafront towards Claremont Pier. There's a massive seagull sitting on the concrete wall. I've never believed the usual stereotype of seagulls as angry, mean bastards. To me they always look slightly surprised that they're birds, like they half-remember being human and are confused about why we are so reluctant to share our food. The one on the wall staring at us is a big bastard, though. I half-joke to Midge that that one could probably overpower him and take him back to its nest, but he pretends not to hear me.

'Hey, look – don't they make shower fittings?' Midge has already moved on. He is pointing to a large statue of who I presume to be 'Neptune' but it is in fact labelled 'Triton', who, according to the sign, was Poseidon's son. I hate not knowing that sort of stuff, so I pretend that I do.

'Course,' I say casually, 'who did you think they named the company after?'

'You know all sorts of weird stuff,' says Midge, not sounding impressed at all.

I am surprised that this is the first time the Greek god Poseidon had been referenced, though. Around the seaside the statues and place names so far have favoured Neptune, the Roman god of water, which is interesting because Neptune to the Romans was a fresh-water god, not connected to the sea nearly as strongly as his earlier Greek form. I go to mention this, but Midge and Jon have already moved on. Okay, so I do know all sorts of weird stuff.

I step, blinking, out of the light, letting the random flashing and disjointed bloops of the amusements welcome me back into the dark. We make our way as far back as we possibly can. Part of our ritual to try and reach each pier's furthest point. What we don't know is a storm back in 1962 washed a large part of it away, so we are soon at the entrance of the roller disco that occupies the last half of Claremont's 720 feet. We look at each other.

'We've got to do it,' says Jon, with a mixture of playfulness and resignation.

'What?'

'We're going to have to go roller-skating, aren't we?'

A pang of guilt hits me. 'I'm not sure my budget can stretch, to be honest, mate.'

'That's okay, it's part of the trip budget.'

I stifle a wince. To be honest, I lost count a while ago, and I am pretty sure he has too. Anything over is coming out of his bank balance.

'Are you sure?'

'Yeah, it'll be fine.' But with how excited my face was, in retrospect, I'm not sure he could have given any other answer.

LOWESTOFT Claremont

Opened: 1903 (Architect: D. Fox)

Length at start: 600 ft (183 m)

Length now: 720 ft (219 m)

Burn baby burn? No, but in 1962 the pier head was destroyed by storms, along with some of the main structure.

When a pavilion was built in 1913 the pier reached 760 feet, which was reduced to 720 feet in the 1962 storms. More recently, artist David Ward was commissioned by the local council to create a visual link between Claremont Pier and South Pier. St Elmo's Fire was unveiled in 2001 and consists of a group of lights on tall poles, which are reflected in the water.

I can't roller-skate; neither can I dance in a way that brings pleasure to anyone. And I don't believe that any white man over 20 can do both together. So, of course, I'm handing over my Adidas trainers, sandy inside and scuffed on the outside, along with a tenner for roller boots for me and Dan at the end of Claremont Pier. This, I'm pretty sure, has broken the bank of Pier Review. Organised people would be keeping these receipts and noting down just how much the trip is costing. It's not that I'm profligate or careless. In fact, there have been times when I've done nothing at night but turn over financial scenarios in my restless mind. I'm just at the extreme end of the scale of British reserve that doesn't like to talk about money, even to myself.

As we lace up, it strikes me that I can't remember if I asked Midge if he wanted a go.

'You sure you don't fancy it?' I say, pretending that I have but also covering my arse.

'Nah. Give us your coat and stuff. I'll just watch you pair of idiots,' says the tiny punk Passepartout.

Roller disco is a sport that both seven-year-old girls and 70-year-old women are somehow built for. It's something to do with the intensity of interest and practice needed to do anything more than roll warily in a circle. These seem to be the ages of female obsession, of getting so engrossed in one activity that you can devote to it all the time it needs – and that can be any amount of time that strikes them as necessary. For men the age of obsession is 12 (football or *Dungeons & Dragons*), then 18 (music and girls). Ah, who am I kidding – the male psyche is much more prone to obsession anyway. That's why most youth tribes are based on male fashion, and it's why model-train shops gather just enough custom and not too much dust around the corner from the main shopping street in towns around the country. It's why two blokes are willing to leave home and work, and drag another from home and dole, for two weeks for no purpose.

———————

Skating over to Jon I tell him to bend his knees a little and loosen up. He listens because he knows that I spent a whole bunch of time in my late teenage years rollerblading, or, as me and another friend put it, 'roller bleeding', because for a couple of summers we did nothing but hang out watching hidden-camera police shows until it got dark and then go to our skate spot, drinking miniature bottles of absinthe along the way. The skills are similar, but not the same, and after a while I adjust and am able to glide at some speed. And for brief moments I feel it – the rush, the level you get to in your brain when you're just flying. It seems no effort at all as the world hurtles past you and nothing can touch you – not worry, not fear of crashing, just the sensation of the wheels that you feel on the soles of your feet, as connected to you as your toes, spinning smoothly around.

If I'd practised this, or even tried it before, I wouldn't be clinging on to the side while dead-eyed anthem 'I Will Survive' drives the glitterball around clockwise. Clockwise against the stream of embarrassment that is ages seven to 70. A portly, long-haired Brummie whips past me over and over again. I should have known. Danny, it turns out, is good at this.

On one trip round he gives me some advice: let the wheels run, don't pull them up, glide. I try it and it does seem to work. But my nervousness takes over, makes me think that this can't possibly be right and I walk my feet. This immediately unbalances me and I windmill into the barriers for safety.

Eventually I manage to get a bit of a hang of it, and it's fun. I lose myself in the activity. And then Danny falls flat on his arse. Legs splayed in a 'v' and a surprised look upon his face.

I hit the floor hard and look around to see who's seen. There's the young mum teaching the toddler at one end and, of course, the two young girls running circles around Jon making his baby-giraffe-like steps. So far, so good, but I turn to our seats and Midge is laughing openly as he sits next to our pocket detritus and the extra layers of clothes me and Jon peeled off for him to look after.

I scrabble back to my feet, and the two young girls glide past, placing each foot over the other in a way that looks so easy it must be really bloody difficult.

Danny let himself go, fell over and bruised his coccyx. He enjoyed himself, though, I think. I went gingerly and didn't fall. But nor did I have a great time. Midge sat watching and seemed to piss himself laughing. Is all of this a metaphor for life?

Walking back towards the car we are hit by what I'm hoping is a local radio roadshow. An outside broadcast with Beach FM one-oh-three-point-four, including some contest that will involve judging by how loud the crowd shouts. That would be perfect.

Turns out, though, to be the end (or the start perhaps, we never work it out) of a sponsored walk in memory of a local guy. I'm not quite sure now what fate befell him, but in a way it doesn't matter: for the people who loved him it won't be the cause of the loss but the loss itself that hurts. And for those that didn't, the feeling of doing something and being a part of something won't be heightened or lessened by a particular illness or other tragedy. That we have an excuse to come together with T-shirts and balloons, to talk of our loss to strangers behind the prop of a sponsorship form, is enough.

Lowestoft and Yarmouth are very close to each other, and to almost nothing else. This I know, as I've been here before. Yarmouth is a day trip from Pakefield, where I spent many a holiday in my late teens. The Pontins camp there was discovered by my Uncle Nicky and something about it determined that our already large family should be further extended with many extras in order to spend a week there in late August that year.

The east coast almost couldn't have been further from Birmingham, or more difficult to get to. In the early nineties there wasn't a motorway in that direction, so our convoy of ageing three-door hatchbacks and boxy family saloons took nearly four hours to bend and stall across the country. It's because of these journeys that I can do nothing but press out a thin smile and feel the beginnings of a furry headache when I'm reminded of towns like Thetford or Diss. We went a number of times, but on the first I was navigating – pre-GPS, of course – for my dad in our green Mini Metro, so the twisting red line of the A11 is etched into my subconscious.

Two things had attracted Nicky. One was that the place was still running a full-board dining system, at a time when most holiday camps had turned to slews of self-catering. In the last episode of fifties-set sitcom *Hi-De-Hi!* staff are told that the future is coming, and they're not required on the voyage towards it. 'Next year it'll be nineteen hundred and sixty. We've got that self-catering starting,' Maplins hatchet-man executive Alec Foster tells the assembled entertainments staff by way of letting them go. And while the redcoats and bluecoats, unlike the fictional yellowcoats, didn't all disappear in the time it took to say 'You have been watching...', the era of mass participation at these camps was fading. That it existed in such a pure form as it did on the east coast at that time seemed to bear testimony to how isolated and living in the past the area was. That longing for the past, a past with no responsibilities – not even cooking or deciding where to eat – other than to enjoy oneself might have been Nicky's thinking.

But maybe it was just the ability to load his tray with double and triple helpings, while calling 'I'll get yours, Fred' to no one in particular.

At Maplins, melancholically upbeat camp host Ted Bovis wouldn't have minded. It's very much the sort of fiddle he'd be pulling himself. And the staff at Pakefield couldn't have cared less either. They'd been there long enough to see all the fiddles, the sports bags under every table at night containing cans of lager and bottles of scotch. The nightly 'adult' comedians would let you know they were in on the joke – and that it happened at every camp they travelled to around the country. I remember one starting his act in the Hawaiian Ballroom by imitating the noise and action of ring pulls.

'When the lights go down... pssht, pssht, pssht.'

It was, and probably still is, a trope to liken Pontins or Butlins to POW camps, where you might stand outside the bar idly shaking your trousers to let earth from the tunnel fall out. Any terseness from the staff would result in references to them being guards, and there'd be mention of Red Cross parcels. The thing is, though, this camp we kept returning to – from when I was about age 14 until after I reached 20, the others probably still go – had in fact been a prisoner-of-war camp during and just after World War Two. An entrepreneurial post-war chap had seen the row upon row of basic accommodation huts and thought – that's just what people recovering from the horrors of conflict will need to come to in order to find relaxation.

Especially those who had escaped from Colditz, of course.

They'd done it up a bit in the intervening years since the war. I guess that not even the barbed wire that stopped you getting too close to the cliff was an original feature. I also doubt our German cousins had bars or a nine-hole pitch and putt course.

One attraction of those camps in those days was much more relaxed licensing laws: bars open all day and into the early hours, rather than being restricted to lunchtimes and evenings till 11 p.m. My family took full advantage of those laws to drink calmly, good-naturedly and amusingly, but essentially all day every day. And with their own drink where possible.

———

The first thing we notice about Great Yarmouth's Britannia Pier is all the Mini Coopers. It seems that we've arrived on the day of a rally. Most prominent in the crowd of cars is one that has a seat built on top of it. In that seat sits a giant golly doll. Jon nudges me with glee on spotting it.

'What kind of rally is this?' he says out of the corner of his mouth.

'I don't know, mate, but if they start pouring petrol on a cross we should leave.'

Pouring petrol anywhere near Britannia Pier would be in poor taste. Plagued by fires throughout the last hundred years, it survived World War Two intact only to catch fire again in 1954. It was reopened in 1958. The most notable of these fires was in 1914, reputedly started by one of the suffragettes who had been refused a meeting venue in the pavilions.

Looking at the predominantly male list of performers not famed for their liberal views advertised on the large hoardings at the entrance, I wouldn't blame the sisters for coming back now with a jerrycan for another go. Hopefully they can lock Jim Davidson in his dressing room before they do it.

Most of the amusements and the pier itself have opted for the pirate theme that seems to be clinging to the coast like a capitalist rash.

GREAT YARMOUTH Britannia

Opened: 1901 (Architects: Joseph and Arthur Mayoh)

Length at start: 810 ft (247 m)

Length now: 810 ft (247 m)

Burn baby burn? An earlier pier lasted from 1858 to 1899, when storms took it. The first pavilion on the replacement pier burnt down in 1909 and a second lasted only until 1914. A ballroom lasted from 1928 until 1933, and a third pavilion from 1933 to 1944. And then they gave up on pavilions until 1958; this latest one remains unburnt.

We've not had a beer on a pier so far. I've wanted to do so at every opportunity but there really haven't been that many. We've been on piers in the morning, hung-over, and in the evening, about to rush to the next campsite. A casual beer hasn't been on the agenda, but now five stops in and just another easy one to go today it seems like the atmosphere says we can. And we do, but it's immediately a mistake – sharp and stewed Carlsberg Export is served in thin glasses.

We opt for a pint in Long John Silver's, a nightclub bar halfway down the pier. The place is massive and set up for the night crowds. The huge space for the dance floor and the plastic cups swept into a corner are indications of the cheap cattle market it would become during the hot summer nights.

Something about the framed olde worlde posters makes me uncomfortable: it's one thing to glamorise the violent theft of the pirate, after all the very monarchy of the time did exactly that, but treating the slave trade as something quaint is not right. How many of the assembled – when they actually assemble (the place is empty) – parents would take time to explain about slavery to enquiring kids? Or how many partake of alarming casual racism like the cartoonish golly out front and think nothing of it?

Yarmouth is another one of those places where the sea recedes out past the pier.

With Jon lost in thought and Midge fiddling with something or other, I look over to the guy on the table opposite and recognise him. He's got a shaved head and is wearing a Nike vest top over a paunch he's showing no sign of shame about. His gold-sovereign rings reflect the sun as he picks up the dummy that the baby in a cheap pram has spat out. Pausing only slightly he wipes the dummy on his three-quarter-length trousers and dips it into his cider before giving it back to the child. I can't place where I know him from. But then it hits me that he's an amalgamation of every male adult I grew up with. I don't just know him, I nearly was him, or could have been if some quirk of genes hadn't sent me down a different path. He is my uncles and their friends, and the people I served in pubs and worked with in every temporary job I've ever had.

To the right, the machinery of industry dominates the skyline and I try and remember why and when I became the person I am. How did I get off that conveyor belt straight from my school to the Rover factory down the road? I suddenly resent his happiness, his contentment, how at ease he appears with everything. I have debt, a degree, and a brain full of memories that decay by the second. He has a life, a kid and, it seems, no doubts nagging him at all.

———————

The Mini rally is in some way raising money for Help for Heroes, which is sort of the tabloid version of the British Legion Poppy Appeal: all *X Factor* and passive-aggressive pressure.

———————

I can see the front stretching off to the right, the 'Golden Mile' which consists of 12 amusement arcades and the Joyland outdoor amusements. The Golden Mile in fact covers two square miles up to the second pier, Wellington. Everything about the seaside is here, rock shops, ice-cream stalls and cheap, plastic buckets and spades. You can buy fake plastic dog poo and a hat that declares your position as a member of the FBI, or 'Female Body Inspector'. There are practical, handwritten cardboard signs and makeshift bins by the side of the food stalls. In places it's old and battered by the weather, like the benches by the sea wall, but in others it's also glitzy and showbiz. The shimmering metal signs flicker like the scales of a fish. To be English is to embrace our contradictory nature, and own our hypocrisy, so it fits that our seaside should as well.

Yarmouth's second pier isn't much of a pier, and it doesn't reach the sea by some distance. It's as if Marine Parade is crouching over the sands to relieve itself. The crystal palace stands guard over an arcade with ideas above its station. In between the buzzing slots and the falling coins is an expensively monogrammed carpet.

Across the water an oil refinery doesn't exactly belch smoke across the North Sea, but it shadows the front and peels back the curtain on the rest of life.

GREAT YARMOUTH Wellington

Opened: 1853 (Architect: P. Ashcroft)

Length at start: 700 ft (213 m)

Length now: 700 ft (213 m)

Burn baby burn? No, none at all. However, it survived a demolition bid by the council in the eighties.

Named after the Duke of Wellington, who died the year before it was opened and had similar views on foreigners to eventual pier owner Jim Davidson.

The original Wellington Pier was opened in 1853. Five years later Britannia Pier opened just along the promenade and killed its trade. It struggled till 1899 when the local council had to step in with a bailout. They opened a new pavilion and shipped the Winter Gardens by barge from Torquay. The Winter Gardens look like something out of an old science fiction novel – a giant ornate greenhouse with chipped white paint and ivy growing around the trellises, and which hints of unspeakable horrors inside. The pier has almost gone and the pavilion is all that's left after comedian Jim Davidson sank his own money into renovating the inside but not the outside. The rest of the pier was demolished in 2005, and the Winter Gardens are often closed in high winds for fear of collapse or attack from the Elder Gods.

The inside of Wellington Pavilion is a densely packed arcade/ bowling alley/children's play area, a soulless mash of what a money-obsessed misanthrope might imagine ordinary families to want. We wander through in a daze, Midge disappearing to do whatever Midge does when he disappears – which could be talk to his 17 kids or report back to the planet he's originally from, for all I know. Jon beats me at foosball, something that gives him more satisfaction than he lets on and annoys me more than I let him know.

Outside, the building extends over the beach. We consider jumping off onto it, thereby fulfilling our promise to everyone before the trip that we would 'jump off a pier'. But we both know it would be a get-out, a non-satisfactory loophole. So we gather up Midge and head to the car.

———

We weren't sure we'd make Cromer this evening. In the plan there is a stop tonight just inland from here, but our spirits at this point are good and 30 miles more doesn't seem too much to take on. The piers really do start to stretch out along the coast now, and after Cromer there's a long drive round the bulge on the map.

Our plans are sketchy. The only one that really matters, the only one that needs confirmation and organisational skill is Pontins. I'm way too shy to let the organised side of my brain show, as it would mean taking on the responsibility of getting what we needed out of other people. I can't operate in that way, so I feign disorganisation enough for Dan to have to be the organised one. I hadn't quite calculated just how casual that would mean I had to pretend to be, but I'm having to act as if I really don't care, that I haven't poured over the logistics, that I'm not often fleetingly terrified of us miscalculating. I am in fact scared of missing Pontins; that's important.

Danny has got us this far, to Cromer, and the town scores highly on the Kurt Vonnegut Car Park Rating Scheme (8/10), leaving us with a view down a steep incline to a prom and a pier, which looks white, wide and well used. The road in front is alive with activity. I count the dogs and brood about my lack of animal companionship.

––––––––––

On top of the cliff overlooking Cromer Pier I look out at the sea reflecting the grey sky and look down at the structure, solid and white. At the moment it looks like the only real thing I have seen that day.

The vocal parts of Pink Floyd's 'The Great Gig in the Sky' stab into my ears, just the higher register, far away like in another wing of a mansion.

'Do you hear that?' I ask Jon.

'What?'

'Music?' I reply.

He answers with a look. And we set off down the cliffside stairway

'Look at this,' says Jon as we get closer. 'The Drifters, The Searchers, and a Bon Jovi Tribute.' He smiles. 'It's a shame we don't have time to catch a show,' he says with excited regret.

But I'm not listening. I'm staring at one of the biggest posters, advertising the Pink Floyd Experience. Got to be a coincidence, I tell myself, as 'The Great Gig in the Sky' once again swells up in my head. We head onto the pier past the crabbing families. The first person ever to eat a crab must have been really fucking hungry, and odd, very, very odd. I head to the end of the pier as quick as I can.

CROMER

Opened: 1901 (Architects: Douglass and Arnott)

Length at start: 500 ft (152 m)

Length now: 500 ft (152 m)

Burn baby burn? No, but damaged by storms in 1949, 1953, 1976, 1978 and 2005.

Reputably 'the most haunted pier in England'. Incidents of ghostly apparitions, poltergeist activity and the wails of lost sailors have all been reported on the pier. All of which failed to be caught by the cameras of TV's *Most Haunted* in April 2009, but the cameraman did get a headache so the jury's still out.

Sightings of Russ Abbot (who filmed for the TV drama *September Song* here), Stephen Fry (who opened the refurbished pavilion in 2004) and Steve Coogan (as Alan Partridge) are confirmed and a little scarier if we're honest.

The theatre on the pier, large but closed now as people fish and stroll around it, is about to feature The Barron Knights. Now, if you're not aware who The Barron Knights are, then you're probably younger than me, or less taken with the place where comedy and music meet. They've been parodying pop songs with skill and a certain type of wit since the sixties. A very English experience: a nod, a wink and a double entendre. At some point in my childhood they must have been getting regular TV work as otherwise I'd never have heard them. And I was really hooked. One tape of theirs I had was a real favourite. What strikes me now is that I didn't really know what the original songs were. The first track on the cassette was a version of the hit 'Angelo' by Brotherhood of Man – already a parody of a sort. 'Angelo' was a song constructed to be as close in feel to the Abba hit 'Fernando' as possible. The Knights' version transposed the Spanish Civil War setting for south London and kitchen-sink romance. Closer to home, but still something I wouldn't have known anything about at the age of ten. Culture spins around on itself, with *Ever Decreasing Circles* on in the background.

It's been a long day, so I don't disturb Jon as he meditates staring straight out to sea. I hear it again, the vocal solo of 'The Great Gig in the Sky', but not in my head this time. I move closer to the pavilion and it gets louder.

'Jon!' I hiss. Jon comes over. 'Can you hear that?'

'Hear what?' he says on reflex as he cocks his head to one side.

'Pink Floyd. You can hear that too?'

'Oh, yeah,' he says. 'Must be rehearsals, they're playing tonight. I was saying earlier that it's a shame we can't go, but you looked pretty spaced out. How many painkillers have you taken today?'

'Enough,' I say as I walk off.

In the kebab shop where Midge decides he must eat is a fruit machine themed around kebab shops. We're stuck in a loop. While I wait for Midge to be fed I scan the selection of tourist leaflets drooping in the window. At least four out of ten of the attractions in some way feature steam engines.

The campsite we find doesn't inspire confidence in me as we park up; it looks too ordered and prone to rules to be comfortable. There's row after row of static caravans with tended gardens around their concrete slab steps. I read something on the gate about a last check-in time, a time we've missed. I'm trying to keep disorganised and calm. Danny needs to sort this out. It's confrontation. It's a confrontation in which he has to essentially prostrate himself and beg to give them money to lie on an empty patch of grass. I waste the time during which he does this by making Midge pose on a giant chessboard on one of the lawns. There are no pieces, we just need another 30 Midges, I tell him, and he's not amused.

I charm the largely indifferent on-site manager to letting us having a pitch. I rush the tent up and grab my clothes, excited about the prospect of using the washing-machine facilities. Of course they're closed, so dejectedly I lug them back, trying to decide which are the least dirty to put on tomorrow. There's a rash on my inner legs and it's getting worse, becoming sorer by the minute.

I'm left alone as they both wander across the squared grass of the numbered pitches to the facilities.

It's the first time I've been alone in private since we set off, and I'm halfway through that when the front of the tent sways. I adjust my sleeping bag and suggest we all head off down the hill for a pint.

We decide to have a little walk to the pub, which Jon assures us is a 'little bit' down the road, but luckily we don't have to walk all the way down to the entrance of the campsite to double back on ourselves, because in the corner of the field is a gate. A sign tells us it is 'locked at 11 p.m. sharp'. It probably isn't, though.

———————

The first of the pubs we come to looks a little rough from the outside. If it was in a suburb of Birmingham I think I'd be walking past. When you're so much the stranger, though, you are able to assume that you'll be a novelty and not a threat, and so not be in danger of being threatened.

———————

The pub is a bit of a walk away, and the pain from the rash on my legs has set my senses sharp and bitey. So I see every inch of The Fishing Boat pub; the scuffed brass, the crayon on the table where a kid has been colouring, the fruit machine that is at least three years behind most others. But it's a good place, the crowd friendly and the jukebox a mixture of soul classics and new-wave punk. There are a number of teenagers in the pub, none of them drinking but all of them getting served soft drinks at the bar and being talked to by bartenders, regulars and strangers alike. It's hard to imagine these teenagers going out causing trouble: it takes a village to raise a child; perhaps it takes a pub to raise a teenager?

———————

Once inside the roughness reveals itself to be nothing but unpretentiousness and homeliness. Random tat adorns the walls and at least six dogs slumber near their owners. The jukebox is frozen out of time and comforts us all with things we wouldn't have put on but are glad to hear. I think I hear a guy at the bar, unkempt but welcome, say 'I live in Norfolk, why would I go anywhere else?'

Indeed, it's warm, and the beer is cheap. Like many before us we sit around a pub table, each doing our backs not much good by leaning over on short stools, and talk of our origin stories. Danny's silhouetted against the glow from a lamp through the window, as he lifts his leg up above the table edge. He hoists a trouser leg.

'Got that falling off my 'blades.'

'Nice,' Midge stutters and removes his cap to scratch the front of his head. He too reveals a mark. 'Came off me bike.'

'Well, you see this.' I rub the bridge of my nose. 'And this,' pointing to the left of my top lip. 'And this... ' I stand and turn, slowly pulling my jacket and T-shirt up my back. 'All the result of getting out of the wrong side of a taxi.' These are the scars I talk about.

A guy called Patrick is holding court at the bar, talking to everyone who will listen about how he loves camping and how it affords him an escape from people. For someone who needs to get away from people he's awfully keen to engage people in conversation. The pub is traditional, warm and welcoming, like how every chain pub aspires to be. It's hard not to like.

When we get back to the campsite, the gate, true to its word, is locked. But the main entrance is quite far away.

'I can climb that,' I say, having no idea if I can climb it or not, especially after no food and a few pints sloshing through me. I half climb over the gate, swinging my leg round the fence laced with the barbed wire that surrounds it. I feel myself start to fall so style it out as a jump, landing with a thump on the other side. Midge comes next, frankly making it look easy.

'Hang on,' says Jon from the other side. 'Hold this.' I look around and something lands on my head. It's his black Paul Weller/Liam Gallagher jacket.

CHAPTER TEN
SKEGNESS IS MORE

Again I'm awake with the remnants of the summer. It's not too long past five but there's no hope of further rest. It was cold as we clambered through the bushes half-cut last night, so I've slept in a hoody and tracksuit bottoms. Slipping on my pumps, I'm punch-drunk but feeling sporty and the cool damp awakens me.

I start with a jog around the football pitch across the hedge. The sun is red in the sky. I then turn back towards the cliff edge through the camp. Wild rabbits scatter as I plod past along the edge, white tails disappearing under bushes and under caravans. Everything else is still. There's no wind, and looking across the fields there's a game of chess being played on maize and earth.

I'm mentally moving Midge to king's bishop four to put white under pressure, when a glint of sun blinds me. Then I hit the deck hard, feeling the warm thud of a moving object, the wet grass on my back.

'You nearly went over the edge.'

Looking to my right, I am very close to the drop. To my left is a tall guy. He's lifting himself up and I can't see his face, only his tunic – tunic?

He stands over me and grips my hand in his. I feel the calluses in his palm scrape as he pulls me upright. The movement is swift, powerful, but not angry. I've met this guy before.

'We meet again, stranger.' I can see him more clearly now. It's the guy from near Weymouth. I think. I'm still groggy from the impact.

'You gave me water that I might drink and guidance that I might meet my quest. For that I thank you.'

I'm staring at his belt, off which hangs a sword. A bloody big sword.

'But I must ask more. Our quests are similar, I feel, and I need your assistance.'

'It's not exactly a quest...' I don't want to offend a man who's just stopped me pacing over a cliff, or who has a blade that big.

'You're circling the land, looking for the source. There's a magic afoot and the county must be saved.'

'Okay.'

'Albion.'

I say nothing. I'm not sure I get it. I'm not coming round.

My back is sore. The climb over the fence last night must have twisted something I didn't notice due to the cushion of booze. This morning it feels like an animal is biting the nerves on the base of my spine and dripping electric piss down the muscles of my right thigh. I've had a bad back for a few years. I dry-swallow a couple of Tramadol and grit my teeth as I pack the car. It's quite a drive to Skegness, which is either a good thing or a very bad thing.

In a trip that's meant to evoke our childhood, stopping off at a Little Chef, as I've spent every moment since we woke this morning persuading a reluctant Midge and a woozily truculent Dan to do, means nothing to me. Exciting as roadside dining seemed to me as a kid – and still does – it was not something that my family would ever have considered. If a trip really was to go on for hours over a mealtime, cobs would be prepared and wrapped in plastic. They would contain ham, or cheese. They would be distributed piecemeal without stopping to eat and accompanied by a bag of crisps. A Little Chef with melamine tables and menus seemed impossibly exotic.

Food has become a bit of an issue on this trip. None of us are ever suggesting we stop to eat, maybe because we're not that interested but also because it costs money and we don't really have any. I'm starving, and I bought some custard creams – the cheapest brand at the cheapest petrol station biscuit – when I blew another 50 quid on fuel just now.

I figure that even if it isn't within our own memory, the chain roadside cafe is part of our collective consciousness. It's just the right sort of faded for us; aesthetically we should be all over it, the red of the logo and the padded leather of the seats. But it's only as we turn the radio on that Danny and Midge are won over.

Joe Pasquale is not a comedian we'd profess a liking for. Too recent to be ironic and with a mainstream taint that tells our brains he must be doing something distasteful even if he isn't. This morning he's on some odd roll and as we hear the end of Brett Anderson's new single he's assuring the host that he can do an impression of David Essex in a chip shop. The impression isn't recognisable, but a Little Chef is a chip shop of sorts and David Essex is our thing right now. We pull into a car park and practise ordering sausages and chips in strangulated cockney tones.

Little Chef roadside cafes have recently and famously been given a celebrity chef makeover; they are at a fulcrum in the way culture's changing. Even if often it's no more than a modern cladding on the oldest of things, most places won't let you see beneath the reality-show gloss. Here, though, if there's cladding it's peeling off, revealing the inner workings – a reality-show extra on a digital channel, at best. Things haven't got a gloss here yet; there are tears in the padded bench seats and the open view into the kitchen is accompanied by the reassuring smell of grease.

We sit at a table for four and read the laminated menus: for a vegetarian the options are back in the seventies, so I order tomatoes on toast, which isn't on the menu but seems not to faze the waiter. Danny has toast, I think, but what I note is that Midge only orders a drink. I worry he has decided he can't afford to eat. That's uncomfortable because I understand but would gladly pay if only it was possible to offer.

I look across at the furniture and a table that is listing at 20 degrees. The alarmingly camp maître d' bounds over eventually and takes our money, and then returns to boyishly bickering with the short-order cook, who has bright eyes beneath a head of tight black curls.

A couple of hours later I take another pill, trying to take the edge off. I get the warm fuzzies, but the electric piss dribbling down the nerves of my leg has turned into a river of knives, so I figure I should take another as I've built a tolerance. We arrive at Skegness to bright sunshine. As Midge and Jon do the usual 'where shall we park' dance I take another couple of pills, as it's been four hours since I took the first couple, right? We pull up to the kerb and I'm out of the car before the engine's off. I fall out of the door onto the pavement, my back not quite taking the weight to stand. I need to stretch out a bit, so I lie flat on my back with my knees bent on the pavement. I let my legs fall one side and then the other, easing the nerves like my physiotherapist has taught me. It's sunny but my vision has soft edges, like an old movie or that moment just before you pass out.

'You all right?' Jon's looking down at me concerned. Midge is standing away, clearly embarrassed.

'Yeah, back's a bit bad this morning.'

'You look a bit pale, actually.'

'Shhhhh,' I whisper in pantomime. 'I took some painkillers.'

'How many?' says Jon with a hint of concern.

I hold up four fingers. 'Two or three.' I don't want to worry him. It doesn't work. He frowns a little, so I jump up as quick as I'm able and force the words 'I'm fine. Let's go.'

Skegness is so bracing, as the old railway poster had it. Today Skegness is also bright and sunny. We park and head straight for the arcade. It encompasses and overwhelms the rest of the pier, clad in beaten plastic. It's obsessed with tenpin bowling: a sport that occupies a space for early-teenage boys as one of the few places you can legitimately take a date to.

The pier seems something of an afterthought, as the tram sheds are the thing here. And they multiply, like outbuildings: the Pleasure Beach, stalls of novelty and sugar. An Anderson-shelter McDonald's mirrors the industrial-estate vibe. The pier juts out of the back, a lamp-posted boulevard to nowhere. Open sea and the distant thrust and parry of another wind farm are all that's out there.

I see from photographs – which feature a pier unadorned by bowling sheds – that the boardwalk once led to a smart white pavilion, but now it just stops. The lamp posts right now are festooned with tea-cosy-like knitting. It's an odd look, but it doesn't surprise me. I've known they were going to be here, as they've also been installed by some artists local to where I live in Birmingham. They call it guerrilla knitting, and call the group... wait for it... Stitches and Hos. It's a name that perfectly reflects the kind of ironic hipster crafters they are, and so that didn't surprise me either. The artwork being in Skegness is odd. Middle-class Southwold I can see, but one wonders heavily – and

I do, aloud to a blank-faced Midge – what the residents and holidaymakers here think.

'They'd be right not to like it. It does just look scruffy.'

Midge says nothing more. He's found the handle of a broken spade and is poinging it off the railings in an act of punk rebellion. Or boredom.

———

Skegness Pier started in 1881 at 1,817 feet long with a T-shaped head. Time and the usual disasters – storms, drifting boats and World War Two – have whittled it down to a mere 387 feet now. It's fairly busy when we get there and I bump through the arcade like a pinball until I reach the promenade at the back. The sea air hits me hard and my vision swims slightly. Jon looks up.

'You all right?' he asks.

'Yeah. Just thinking, we haven't interviewed a lot of people, have we? Let's change that now,' I say as I march over with a head full of drugs to an old couple sitting on deckchairs staring out to sea.

Brian and Sheila are a lovely couple. Brian is wearing a pair of sand-coloured slacks that you only ever see old people wear and a jumper that the office pest would have worn in the eighties to prove his wackiness. It looks neutral on him. Sheila is wrapped in a large anorak against the wind that I am aware of but can't actually feel.

'Excuse me,' I smile. 'My name is Danny Smith, can I ask you a few questions?'

Brian looks at Sheila and says, 'Yes, I suppose you can.' Sheila turns her head round and smiles. Either she's not all there or a little deaf. I ask if they come to Skegness often.

'Every year,' answers Brian. 'We've been to Yarmouth and Weymouth and north Wales, but we always end up coming back here.'

'Did you go to the piers in Yarmouth and Weymouth?'

'Oh yes,' says Brian. 'We like the shows.'

'Who did you see?' I ask. This cracks Brian a little. He visibly relaxes.

'Everyone, we've seen Morecambe and Wise, Des O'Connor, Bernie Winters, Matt Monro.'

'Tony Christie,' Sheila shouts up.

'Tony Christie,' confirms Brian. 'Oh, and the other two fellas.'

'Little and Large?' A stab in the dark from me, but it seems about right and we're obviously not talking about anything else until he finishes the list.

'No, they were policemen in that film.'

'Cannon and Ball,' I answer, thanking my years of consuming obscure English pop culture. The film he's talking about is *The Boys in Blue*, made in 1982 and Cannon and Ball's only film. I remember it being set on the coast and featuring smuggling, a crime that is serious enough to merit being investigated but not distasteful enough to turn a family audience's stomach (see also: all the *Famous Five* books and *Scooby-Doo*).

'How has Skegness changed?' I ask. This is it, our elders are a connection to the past and, if the past is another country like L. P. Hartley asserts, then the older generation are our explorers, bringing back exotic tales and objects. I focus, but the grey round the edges of my vision is starting to get deeper and sometimes the voices are switching from stereo to a flat mono but I pull it all together for his answer. Brian thinks for a second.

'It's more bloody expensive,' shouts Sheila.

'Yes, it is that,' agrees Brian, who then goes on to explain the increments in which the B&B where they always stay has gone up in price. They start to talk about the price of different holiday objects and I give in.

'Thank you, you've been very helpful,' I lie.

SKEGNESS

Opened: 1881 (Architects: Clarke and Pickwell)

Length at start: 1,817 ft (554 m)

Length now: 387 ft (118 m)

Burn baby burn? Hit by a boat in 1919 and sectioned during World War Two. Floods damaged the pier in 1953, and it was battered by a severe storm in 1978. In 1985 a fire gutted the theatre they were dismantling anyway.

An online review (in January 2015) says that the 'walk through under Skegness Pier stinks'. That might have been our fault, sorry, as it was okay when we got there.

Despite the ironic statue, the fairground, the bowling, oh the bowling, the copious amounts of sugar for sale and even volleyball nets on the sand, no one seems to be having fun. I eavesdrop on the conversation between three generations of Black Country cliché, gran, young mum and baby.' 'E wants 'is dinna.'

For sustenance we pay two quid for a plastic cup each and mix our own – non-branded – slush drinks. I go for one based on the lyrics of the Bob Dylan song 'Country Pie': raspberry, strawberry, lemon and lime.

I'm staring at the doughnut machine, which looks like something you'd see on Southwold Pier, a Rube Goldberg contraption where white Os of dough are shat into a pit of boiling oil, snagged onto a conveyer belt, flipped over and sprinkled with sugar. It's fascinating, all the parts working together. Jon nudges me.

'Come on.'

He begins to walk off. The row of stalls extends right the way down the front. I spot four different fish and chip stalls next to each other and give the logistics of that some serious thought. The crowd at the picnic tables in front of these stalls are in tank tops, gold chains and football shirts. Everyone is smoking. I get a push.

'Come on,' pleads Jon again. I take another long pull from my slushie, all crushed ice and syrup. I bought a 'large' and mixed cola with bubble gum to produce a delicious brown sludge. I can't complain though, as the sugar and E numbers are providing a decent-enough high to counter the painkillers. 'I'm speedballing on tramadol and sugar,' I think to myself and giggle in my head. Or was it out loud?

'DAN!' calls Jon. He's set off without me and I run to catch up.

Cleethorpes is the seaside of Grimsby. While coastal, it is more fishing port than resort. It's also the home of Grimsby Town FC, who made me the coldest I'd ever been when I was watching them play an FA Cup tie at some point in the nineties.

Cleethorpes' front is empty. The road runs right next to the beach and ends at the pier. The journey has been made uncomfortable by the sugar crashing out of my system, and my back hasn't taken kindly to getting in the car again, so I take another couple of painkillers. My guts have started to cramp up. My insides are not happy and need to vent.

It's a little warmer now, as we pull up in the shadow of the fences surrounding the pier, but the shadow is weak. The sun's low and drizzle is starting to form in the air. I offer my remaining slush to Midge, but he's not in the mood. Not in the mood for anything at all. He grumpily stays in the car as we unfold ourselves from the bags, clothes and bits of paper we're accumulating. I pop my slush into the first bin we come to.

The pier is shut.

So is most of the seafront.

Shops offering rock, candy and fun are shuttered against the gusts coming across from the North Sea. Some are closed for the season; others are concrete and boarded, desolate against the sand like the small towns outside Las Vegas. I walk up until the metropolis peters out and then back towards the car. It's a long drive to Whitby, where we've decided to spend the night.

CLEETHORPES

Opened: 1873 (Architect: Head Wrightson)

Length at start: 1,200 ft (366 m)

Length now: 335 ft (102 m)

Burn baby burn? A concert hall burnt down in 1903 and the pier was sectioned during World War Two.

When the seaward end was demolished after the war, some of the salvaged material was used to build Leicester City a new stand.

The sun is bright but the blurred bits around the edges of my vision are getting bigger. I stumble into the arcade, ricocheting off one of the fruit machines as I try to focus. I see a sign at the back and remember thinking, 'I hope that's a toilet sign, not a fire exit, because I'm shitting there whatever.' Feeling sick, stomach cramping and not really knowing where I'm going, I come to the toilets. It's a turnstile, 20p to get in. I pull my hand out of my pocket in an explosion of change. I've only got a pound coin and some coppers, not worth checking the floor now. I can't bend over. I run to the change cashier and slam the change onto the counter.

'20p pieces, please.'

She's gargoyle-impassive but I look into her eyes. She's scared. I smile and remember that we humans are the only creatures who show our teeth to prove we're friendly rather than the opposite. She pushes a button on a machine set to the left and 20p coins appear down a slide. I grab them and throw a 'thank you' over my shoulder.

The toilets are a familiar blue, lit by UV lights to stop junkies finding their veins so they can push drugs through spikes straight into them. Poor bastards, why don't they just get a Slush Puppie speedball instead? Oh, yeah. I don't bother checking if the door has a lock before I sit down. My stomach cramps for a last couple of times and I'm done. The relief swims my head, the blur in my eyes becomes a black and starts to thicken. My thoughts become not connected to much...

No. I refuse to pass out in a junkie, shooting-gallery arcade in Cleethorpes with my trousers round my ankles. Think. DEEP BREATHS. Okay, maybe not too deep. Concentrate. The song that plays in my head whenever I fuck up plays. I grab it and sing along.

'You do it to yourself, you do, and that's what really hurts, you do...'

Wipe, pull up your kecks, stand, a little unsteady but not too bad.

'... you do it to yourseeeeeeeeeeEEEEElllf.'

Right, vision fuzzy but better. Fluids, drink from the tap, warm but: whatever. Reflection, hair not bad, a bit eighties metal, eyes a bit sunken. I'm a bit grey, when was the last time I ate? Must do that soon, I suppose.

'WwwhhhhooooooOOOOOLLLN noooowlln whhhhhwl.' I'm singing the guitar solo now. I'm okay.

The arcade is bigger than I remember running into, and darker. I head towards the front that appears like a bright letter box in front of me. I notice a couple of attendants near the toilets as I come out. The change lady must have said something. I head out into the sunshine and the front at Cleethorpes is empty; a few food stalls are closed and a big fence is barricading the pier. Nothing is moving. It's like we travelled too far into the future, or maybe the past? Anyway, it's barren and spooky-quiet.

What we don't know is that earlier that month the pier, which essentially is just a large nightclub, lost its licence and had to be closed. This followed a long list of noise complaints, a couple of broken jaws (one fractured in two places), a slew of people being beaten unconscious or hospitalised, a GBH charge, and, the icing on the violent cake, two men being chased down the pier and having to jump off the end. One of them broke both his legs on landing.

'Fancy a game?' I say to Dan, nodding my head towards a fairly big windmill across from where we've parked.

'My back's fucked.'

'I don't think it's a physically demanding game, crazy golf. It's a seaside staple.'

Danny pulls the driver's door open. Midge looks up from his phone.

'Fancy a round of golf?'

Midge grumbles something like 'nah, you're all right, so we leave him to it.

Two balls and two putters is over a fiver, but we've the course to ourselves and nine holes ahead of us.

And we have a laugh, with that particular crazy-golf thing of trying hard for one or two hits each hole and then just deciding to whack it as there's no way you can calculate the path the ball is intended to take. We bash through boats, over humps, between flood-defence-type barriers. But before the windmill – here an impressive ten feet high, clay-coloured and with six white blades – this routine starts to become a chore.

Crazy golf just isn't much fun. It's frustrating for me, and although Dan is some way ahead in the scoring (or at least better at lying about how many shots each hole has taken), he is also just wishing it over. I take frustrated swing after angry swing, thudding the heavy little ball against the windmill. Eventually it goes through the hole and clunks off the back wall into the grass. This is the first windmill that's made me angry. Across the country people are protesting about the useful ones that provide electricity but not about these buggers that stop you getting balls into holes. There's no logic.

———————

Halfway round I can see Jon lose interest. This, of course, coincides with the moment that I pull into a nearly insurmountable lead. We persevere. The course is well kept, and the sun, the quiet calm and the idle concentration suit my fuzzed-up head. Of course I win, using a combination of applied maths, proper golf stance and grip, and a fluky hole-in-one at the last hole. Jon smiles. It's a real smile, which brightens me up from deep inside my fog.

'We'll put that down to performance-enhancing drugs, shall we,' he says.

'Put it down to whatever you want, you still lost.' I smile back. 'Where's Midge?'

'I don't know, where do you think he goes when we're doing stuff?' asks Jon.

I shrug.

I lose, we hand the kit back over the counter of the kiosk and return to the car.

We look over to the beach and Midge is a short way down, walking along with his head down looking at the shells. I'm struck by a flashback of my mum. My mum, the matriarch who rules absolutely and is and has been a lot of things – wife, mother, sister, auntie and childminder – and I guess that's only how I ever saw her. Except for one time. We were on a rare holiday to France and by the beach mum wandered off. I looked up and she was in the distance looking for shells, or pretty rocks, which she would then keep and take home. She's still got thousands of them in the garden. But I saw her in the distance with no one around her, no one to take care of, shout at, or natter to, just her. And I realised that she, my mum, was human. And with that realisation came the immediate knowledge that one day she wouldn't be here. I quickly took a picture. I still have it: my mum, a silhouette against a setting sun, alone, happy, mortal.

They say childhood is over when you realise that one day you're going to die. I don't know what finished that day, but I've always hugged a little tighter since.

Midge looks at me staring at him and, when he's close enough, says, 'What? What have I done now?'

'Nothing, mate, you ready to go?' I ask.

'Yeah,' he takes a final look around. 'It's shit round here, innit?'

We're crossing the Humber Bridge on the way to Whitby. The weather is bright and the drop at each side is sharpening. The List says that there isn't a pier in Whitby, but there is goth heritage. Goth is the most untouched of the youth tribes: its Victorian romanticism might be in a Venn intersection with steampunk, and emo kids might have the black hair and surliness, but goths are goths and, while the band names might change, the look and feel doesn't.

They congregate one weekend in Whitby every year to celebrate the fact that they are usually alone and that Bram Stoker sailed Count Dracula to the shores of the town.

We're driven here by necessity and the idea that it was a place where we should stay in a traditional seaside bed and breakfast.

But what is really driving us here is a grumbling old punk – and he's muttering about the roads as we trundle up and down the hills that hug the coast. I'm simultaneously Googling for places to stay and looking out at the old houses now converted into low-rent hotels and B&Bs. Dan is silent, and spaced, wheezing a little whenever he moves.

I sleep on the way to Whitby and by the time we arrive the sky is grey, the same colour as my skin. Woozy from the detox and the nap, I watch Midge navigating purely on instinct coupled with Jon's power of suggestion. We haven't booked a B&B, thinking that this late in the season there will obviously be plenty. I get out of the car. Jon clearly doesn't want to speak to the owners on his own.

'I don't know mate, words difficult me for a bit,' I stumble.

'It's okay, just hang back, I'll do the talking,' he says, unsure.

We walk to the nearest house with a sign and ring the bell. A man answers wearing a thick fishing jumper that he probably only wears for the tourists.

'Hi, we'd like a room for the night,' says Jon, noticeably cheerier than when he was talking to me.

'Just you two, is it?' he says suspiciously.

'Nope, our friend in the car as well,' says Jon, gesturing to Midge.

'Separate rooms?'

'No we'd like to share,' says Jon, probably thinking about the dwindling pot of money.

'I'm afraid we've got no rooms for you.'

The 'you' is pointed. At the time I was incensed at the sly homophobia, but looking back it may not just have been the possibility that we were gay. It could also have been how gay we were: an unshaven, mod bear taking his grey, detoxing chicken in a Hawaiian shirt to a room with a pierced, leather midget to do who knows what. It never occurred to us that we'd have any trouble finding a room so walking down the street looking at the 'no vacancy' signs starts to panic us a little.

My shyness and paranoia are kicking in a lot, as have various ticks. Annoying recurring thoughts about my inadequacies are all I can muster. I'm lonely and try to think about good things: cats, dogs, babies. That's the only thing I can do to control it, and if the thoughts get really bad then I have to sort of shout it to myself like a mantra 'cats and dogs and babies, cats and dogs and babies'; they're good things, good things happen when you're with them, they're warm, things are simple.

Midge decides there's better parking round the corner and I will a silent Danny to stand near me as I ring the doorbell of a potential place to stay. There's no answer, but we can hear the rumbling of a cider tramp sitting on a stoop across the way. There's cackling and there's talk of werewolves. And there's no answer.

One of us must look pregnant with our saviour as a procession of innkeepers turn us away. Their reasons are increasingly bizarre and their speech has the pattern of someone making up excuses on the spot.

'Try Mountbatten House across the way,' referring to a place we've already tried and been moved on from. I check the web for nearby campsites, but there are none: which is reasonable when you think how cold it must be this far north at this time of year. We round the corner and I look for Midge and my red Renault, but it's not where I think it should be. Has he decided to bugger off, taking our car and money? We don't really know him that well and he's had a week of not fun. Has he snapped? My heart and mind are turning over. Dan is non-communicative. The painkillers are killing most of his vital signs. I was thinking we might have to sleep in the car, but now even that's not here.

The next place that answers the door are apparently having issues with their boiler, but I guess that was a lie. We try the next street, and the next, until, rapidly running out of options, we come to Kimberley House. Even in our tired and worried state both me and Jon take time to do our best Victoria Wood impression. 'My friend Kim-ber-ley' – we pronounce the exaggerated northern vowels – 'my friend Kim-ber-ley, yer know, with the big dang-ley earrings.' Cheered by this we ring the bell. No one answers for a while and we're about to leave when a woman in a red top and apron answers the door.

'Hello,' she says in a broad northern accent. Me and Jon grin at the coincidence. Jon asks about a room and she lets us in. She tells us that she only has a double with a kid's bed but we take it, explaining that we don't mind 'Morecambe and Wiseing it' and, delightfully, she seems to know what we mean.

She has a welcoming smile and an accent that places her somewhere in Lancashire. I feel safe. I feel sitcom safe. I'm happy to pay, now after all the problems, a price nearing a hundred quid for a 'family room' (one double and a single), which is the cheapest way we can sleep three. It goes on my credit card. I go out to the car – which is exactly where we'd left it – to fetch Midge and bags. Danny negotiates the stairs and heavy fire doors with something that isn't quite ease.

After any time camping the novelty of being indoors is hard to shake. I lie on the bed and feel my spine unclick.

'Why do I get the kid's bed?' says Midge redundantly.

'Who would you like to share with? Either me or Jon?' I ask. 'Jon snores, and I get handsy.'

'Wouldn't surprise me,' says Midge, unpacking his sleeping bag.

'What are you doing?' I ask.

'Making my bed,' says Midge as he unfolds the bag on top of the bed.

'You can use the sheets,' I tell him. 'It's all part of the price.' He looks confused.

'Just didn't like to, we're only here one night.'

A toilet flushes and Jon comes out of the bathroom.

'Midge, do you want the next shower? I'm too comfortable to move at the moment,' and, I add in my head, I know what Jon was probably doing in there for the last ten minutes.

'Cheers, Dan,' he says, grabbing his towel and wash kit.

There's a knock on the door, and me and Jon freeze. We aren't doing anything we shouldn't, but I think we're just kids at heart really, waiting for the grown-ups to tell us to stop it. It's the woman who runs the B&B, a lady whose name we learn is Rachel.

We all check her out as she bends over. Terrible, but true. I'm really looking forward to the bed, even if I have to share with Dan. It's more sitcom material, although nothing really noteworthy happens, as I'll tell you later.

We try to engage Rachel in conversation, trying to find out how she came to be running a guest house on the other side of the country from where she's from. Danny does best, as he pretty much always does in conversation. I stare through the net curtains, across the dullness and the gathering night.

'I've just got to make up the little bed.' She looks at the sleeping bag on it. 'Is he going to use that?' she asks, confused.

'No, not at all.' I get up and pull Midge's stuff onto the floor.

Up until about six months ago Rachel had an office job, but with the threat of redundancy she and her husband took a holiday staying in this very B&B on a cold night in January. She chatted to the manager who was looking to retire, and by the end of their weekend away they had bought the place.

Midge bustles out of the bathroom in nothing but a small towel, sees Rachel making his bed, freezes, and goes back into the bathroom. I think for a moment. A new business in a new city is brave move for anyone, especially considering the pram I saw in the private front room. We explain our trip and that we might be writing a book about it. She spies my notebook.

'Will I be in it, then?'

'Well, it's partly about doing a potentially stupid thing on a whim and just seeing how that pans out. You might make it in, yes. How do you spell your name?'

She gives me the half flirty, half motherly smile that only some women pull off. 'R-a-c-h-e-l'.

Later we're walking through Whitby, which is a strange mixture of 'alternative' shops and high street. Looking at the windows it seems a lot of the tourist places are closed for the winter already. Whitby slopes sharply down to the River Esk. We, being weary, follow the slope down, slowly though, as the roads are cobbled and uneven with tight turns and shortcuts that lead nowhere. The first pub we come to is a place called The Ship, anonymous in a forgettable kind of way, but seemingly very proud of winning the Harrison Cup: Whitby's pool competition. Seeing it makes me sad. I can never imagine a time when I'll be that settled, a regular in a pub, nestled in a routine caring about a pool competition that no one has heard of. I don't know what this drive I have for constant novelty is. I don't know what I'm looking for. Which, of course, is going to make it very much harder to find. The thought is fleeting and everyone is cheery. A decent shower and the thought of sleeping in (or on, for Midge) a real bed have got everyone in a good mood. Even Midge, who has to drive across the country tomorrow, is drinking and joining in.

Jon has been communicating with a few people via our Twitter account. One of these is a lady who has offered to come for a drink with us if we make it up to Whitby.

She suggests a pub near the docks called, suitably enough, The Pier. The Pier is open and bright, big and used to tourism, but tonight we are the only customers. Susie turns out to be a lovely, slightly awkward, middle-aged woman, now a sculptor but who had previously worked in a school.

'So you want to go see the lighthouse then?' It stuns me for a second, but then I remember that one of the reasons she had got in touch with us was to offer us a look from the top of a lighthouse. Susie is a volunteer lighthouse keeper for Whitby's two harbour lighthouses.

There are 81 steps up to the thin balcony at the top of the lighthouse. On one side you can see a complete vista of the town of Whitby. From up here, lit by a smattering of windows and streetlights, it looks like a fairy-tale fishing village, a model built for a disaster movie, doomed to be flooded over and over by bored special-effects technicians. The unreality is breathtaking. While Midge and Jon ask Susie questions I'm on the other side looking out to sea. It's dark black, a complete absence of light, a darkness that sucks you in. I just gaze, trying to pull meaning from nothing.

After days of staring into sea, enjoying the emptiness, I'm staring back at the land. I blink, enjoying the red burn to the retina that the lamp provides. I'm not quite sure how we got to the top of a lighthouse at closing time, but here we are and it's the shadows and points of light from Whitby and its harbour that are drawing me in.

I see a ship on the horizon, and am confused between land and sea.

Susie has brought us up here, dragging us away from singing along to Fleetwood Mac in a pub, away from looking at pictures of the presumed fallen on the walls. Giving me a hug during which I could smell her pink hair, and buying us a drink. I don't know Susie. We met her on the Internet, but I sort of know her based on other people I do know. We are all – except ourselves, of course – nothing but a jigsaw of different experiences, a sort of cultural and environmental DNA code. She led us up the stairs, around a rough-concrete interior. Midge bangs his head somewhere near the top and I've still no idea how that happened.

We get Midge to take photos of us in bed reading back at the B&B, using my phone. Dan lifts a copy of the local paper from a heavily emulsioned pub bar earlier and I drag a bent but unread copy of the *New Statesman* from one of my bags. In the photos we look red, sweaty and wind-beaten. I'm feeling that hot way you do after being outside for long periods, a kind of scrubbed dirtiness.

The photos are despatched to the Internet to no particular interest. And we sleep, untouching.

CHAPTER ELEVEN

MEN IN BLACKPOOL

We wake naturally early, smiling at each other in recognition of a night spent comfortable and warm. Sharing a bed with Jon wasn't at all awkward or weird. It felt natural, comforting even. All three of us at some point or another had woken up with our faces dangerously close to each other due to sloping campsites. So that night was as far as I'd been from Jon during bedtime for a week or so. I turn the TV on while we take turns in the shower and find the news telling us that the *Cutty Sark* has burned down overnight. Given how prone piers are to catching alight, I consider this a good omen, but that could just be the solid seven hours sleep I've had. After the news comes the weather. As the weather guy is sweeping his hand over the country I can't help ticking off the places we've visited, like a boy swapping stickers. Swap, swap, need, need, need, got, got, got.

For the first time ever in a hotel I'm at the breakfast table as the window of full English opportunity opens rather than closes. We've already washed, packed and loaded the car by 8 a.m. – this is a lie-in. The breakfast is hearty and fills my cramping stomach to its edges.

The drive up to Saltburn is spectacular, deep green hills and glimpses of ocean. I twitch and grumble and try to banish dark thoughts brought on by history and sickening chimneys. Three men slide past in a bathtub and the handbrake is pulled taut on a cliff top.

'Was nice to sleep in a bed last night,' says Jon, half turning in the front seat so I can hear him in the back. I lean forward so I can join in. We'd had a nice breakfast and for once felt ready to tackle the day.

'Yeah, and that view last night was amazing,' I say.

'It was nice,' agrees Midge.

'That Susie...' I begin.

'DON'T YOU TALK SHIT ABOUT HER, SHE WAS LOVELY,' snaps Midge before I can finish. Stunned, we sit there for a while. Jon's eyebrows are raised.

'Mate,' I say, 'I was just going to say how nice she was to let us up there, that's all.'

Midge thinks about it. 'Sorry, I thought you were going to take the piss, you know what you're like.'

'No, mate, I was going to be nice.' I think about mustering some offence at his presumption but to be fair he's not far from the truth. The car is quiet for a bit, the window for somebody to say something funny to diffuse the situation is closing rapidly.

'Midge, mate?'

'Yeah,' answers Midge, furiously concentrating on the empty straight road ahead.

'If you're having feelings for the first time that are confusing you or you don't understand, you can...' I don't finish the statement. Me and Jon are laughing too much. Even Midge smiles.

Dogs run on the beach, pausing only to piss into the sand.

The car park for Saltburn Pier is high atop a cliff. So high and steep that after the pier was built in 1869 it was concluded that the cliff walk was putting people off visiting the town after their trip to the beach. More importantly for the pier owners, it was also discouraging people from the town from visiting the pier. The solution was the cliff lift. The lift we see today is the replacement opened in 1884, which is now one of the oldest, water-powered funicular rail systems in the world. Of course, it's not open today.

We look down at the pristine, muddy-golden sands of the beach in the distance. Two people are riding horses along the shoreline, and next to the pier a group of schoolboys are wielding the equipment of a field trip. The white cliffs jut into the sea and the dramatic grey sky is a swirl of cloud. It's beautiful and very English.

The pier is mostly red timber with cream panels and looks like a historical reconstruction, an element reinforced by the arcade being closed and forcing us to do nothing but enjoy the view. I also have time to admire the giant cock and balls the boys have drawn in the sand with the measuring sticks they're now using to hit each other with.

SALTBURN

Opened: 1869 (Architect: John Anderson)

Length at start: 1,500 ft (457 m)

Length now: 681 ft (208 m)

Burn baby burn? Storm damage in 1875, 1953, 1959 and 1961. Damage to the piles finally caused the pier head to collapse and wash away in 1974.

In early 2012 a 160-ft, Olympic-themed, knitted woolly scarf appeared unexplained on the handrails of the pier. In 2014, the Bollywood movie *Shaandaar*, starring Shahid Kapoor (PETA Asia-Pacific's Sexiest Vegetarian Man 2011) and Alia Bhatt, filmed a scene on the pier. Bemused pier-goers were roped in as extras.

Standing on the pier you can look into the future and the past. In one direction unspoilt cliffs loom over the waves. Turn and you can see shadows stretching into the sky from a comic-book factory. A fishing boat is pulled up onto the shore by a tractor just as jets roar our gaze upwards. It feels like war is warming up, armaments being made and landings hastily organised. Wet khaki, heavy with dirt and salt, struggles home.

Whether this is what I really feel, or whether being told that the Dunkirk beach scenes from the film *Atonement* were filmed here has filled in the paint-by-numbers tourism brochure in my mind, I don't know. We are interviewed by a guy making an anniversary documentary to celebrate the 150th year of pier. I manage to stonewall him and feign interest in piers. I hate them right now. I also attempt to sound chirpy to the local paper reporter from Blackpool who calls me as we set off.

———

Back at the car I try calling Pontins again. It has been a couple of days since I tried moving the booking back a day, and I haven't quite been able to confirm the booking in the first place. For ten minutes I'm passed from person to person, all of them changing their name shortly after speaking to me. I once worked for an accounts payable helpdesk in a large catering company and we were encouraged to give false names in order to delay payment.

This practice was stopped when the names we started using became increasingly surreal: I remember giving my name as 'Stroke' in a broad Texan accent once. Not one person knows anything about the booking, but I am told that the PR person who wasn't in the office yet does have a Post-it note on her desk about it. This is worrying.

'How did it go?' asks Midge when I walk back to the car from the top of a picnic table to get reception.

'Fine,' I say. 'All sorted. Bloody call centres, eh?' I make an eye-roll shrug.

Midge agrees and climbs into the car. He is driving from one coast of the country to the other in about five minutes – he doesn't need the stress. Jon, who has been using the public toilets to wash a couple of pairs of socks comes back and catches my eye.

'All sorted?' he asks as he winds the back windows up to trap the socks. I make a wide-eyed gesture of fear.

'Not at all, going to have to phone back later,' I say, out of earshot of Midge.

'Bad?'

'Not great, I'll sort something.' I have no idea what. It isn't just somewhere to stay. Southport Pontins is important. Both me and Jon have spent many family holidays there, it appears in both our memories as the typical family holiday, and our experiences are near exact copies of each other and probably tens of thousands of other working-class people of our generation. Plus, it would be the last night of the trip where we wouldn't be in a tent. Beds, hot showers and using the laundrette seem far more important than hitting any interesting nodes at this point.

———

We now have to cross from the east to west coast, the longest drive of the trip at nearly three hours.

Signs whizz past, places we've only heard of on news bulletins and sporting classified checks now exist in metal. I'm consuming the country. We pass the curious village of Works Access Only and turn at Scotch Corner. We've seen signs for towns rooted in Englishness, like Sheringham and West Beckham, and we've passed places we'd not been sure really existed, like Little Snoring.

Now we're on the M6, heading south towards Blackpool, and it would be so easy to ignore the M55 to the coast and just keep going on it. This road would take us home. We don't, and I wonder if that's because we don't want to go home, ever.

I put George Formby on the car stereo and attempt to enforce some holiday spirit, get us thinking cheekily dirty thoughts and cut through the fug. Near Fleetwood a huge graffito reads 'All MPs Are Thieves'.

Lulled by the hum of the car and the gentle thwipping sound of Jon's socks drying in the breeze, I sleep for the journey across the country. It is the gentle squabbling about directions that wakes me. We are driving in a mainly suburban area, but the grey, oppressive sky is getting bigger and you can see Blackpool Tower poking up in the distance. We approach Blackpool from its back and get to see behind the artifice from the start.

We're listening to a song about George's sticky penis as we enter a vile concrete runway. It traps us and spurts us onto a dented belly of a car park.

The car park is grim, the ground is littered with little squares of glass from a hundred busted windows and the ticket machines are badly defaced. Immediately the vibe is soured and we genuinely fear for the things we keep in the car, scrabbling round to hide anything valuable under the seats or in the boot.

Next to the car park a shop is advertised on a large yellow sign, 'JOKES – Masks, Wigs, Fancy Dress – Central Air Rifles – Naughty Adult Only Section Now Open'. The font is impossibly jaunty and the sign is grimy with age. Inside, the large shop is covered in every tacky plastic joke, gimmick and trick. Novelty sunglasses next to glitter wigs and flick combs. Fake vomit and dog poo, and chewing gum that turns your tongue blue. Some of the packaging has been here for years, the print gone yellow. Some things are relatively new, like the layers of tat hanging from the walls. The glass cabinets of the counters house air pistols and BB guns, but the staff discourage any real inspection. Grim-faced and angry at nothing, their eyes never leave us the entire time we are in here.

We stumble into the 'Adult' section, but it is harmless 'postcard-raunchy' stuff, the same things that have been titillating schoolboys since my dad was one: naked playing-card decks, pens where the bikini disappears, furry handcuffs and penis-shaped straws: the sort of tat that gets stapled to the bride-to-be's veil on her hen night. In other circumstances it would be adorable to see such things billed as 'adults only', a throwback to a more innocent time of postcard double entendre and *Carry On* raunchiness. But here, under the aggressive stare of the counter staff and the fading stock, it all feels like a lie.

It's the third circle of a dusty hell. Luminous cards and marker pens draw attention. Faded printing behind a beaded curtain offers incites to auto-stimulation and flaccid sadism. The floor is an ashy concrete, the smell is of cobwebs.

I couldn't muster an erection in here no matter whose help I had. It is a new and exciting experience, though, as our balls have been weighing heavier and heavier, as if the centripetal force of our circumnavigation has been pulling them outwards. We take in the stock with a circle of vision, stuck to the centre of the room by sour, hate-filled gazes, then exit.

'I'm not looking forward to this,' says Jon.

'What?' I ask.

'Blackpool. It's horrible, it's going to rain and it's terrible. Did you see in there?'

'Yeah, but it can't all be that bad, can it?' I reason, but realising that by the end of the sentence I don't seem so sure myself.

'Look at that, that's the type of place we're at.' Jon points to another large vinyl sign. It's advertising 'Braddy's Sunday Lunch' at a place called The Flagship, with the face of a man, I presume Braddy himself, smiling on the right-hand side. But Braddy's face is contorting into a horrible grin, like he's about to laugh and be sick at the same time, his red face squinting at the mirth of what I can only guess to be torture off camera.

'The thing that baffles me,' says Jon, 'is that they must have taken a number of photographs that day, and that, with his red sweaty face, must have been the best one.'

'He must be some sort of monster,' I agree.

We run for the front, Midge making sure we watch out for trams. This is the first place we've felt any danger. There's traffic up and down the wide road that separates the gaping shops from the gaping sea. The pier offers a familiar safety, and the high roof frowns over a low arcade door as I touch an Elvis. Then we hear, unmistakably, the theme tune to *Coronation Street*.

Outside on the pier a mini carousel spins howls from trapped babies. I feel like we're being followed, watched and circled by the malformed and misshapen. A stall hosts a lynching of waistcoated meerkats. Taller, heavier than Midge, they hang by the neck, swinging the creak of the dead. By one of the attractions, a man in a stained boiler suit sloshes blood from a bucket into a drain. The planks are slippery and stained.

BLACKPOOL Central

Opened: 1868 (Architect: J. I. Mawson)

Length at start: 1,518 ft (463 m)

Length now: 1,118 ft (341 m)

Burn baby burn? Fires in 1964 and 1973 gutted the theatre buildings. The jetty was demolished in the seventies.

The Central Pier has always been considered the 'fun' one and boasted the installation of an automatic chip dispenser in 1932. Fire Station Manager Sean Hennessy leads practice exercises on Central Pier and says about the difficulties: 'We have to take our own water and run hoses for up to 300 metres as there is no other access. We can't use the seawater as it is too far away for our pumps.'

We wait outside the Central Pier for a reporter from the local paper to meet us. While waiting, Midge seems to resolve something in his head and says:

'Guys?'

'Yeah?' we say.

'If they take your picture for the paper, can I be in it?'

It seems such a little thing (the issue, not Midge) and as both me and Jon are far too shy to throw our weight around as far as who gets to be in the pictures, we don't say no.

'We'll see what happens,' I say, immediately nervous about the added pressure of getting Midge in. I ask Jon: 'So this reporter, did she sound all right?'

'Yeah,' says Jon in what only I recognise as his best Sid James. 'She sounds a right sort.'

It's funny because it's the exact opposite of what Jon would say, and we enjoy a mental liberal high-five at being above that sort of thing.

Blackpool isn't what I wanted it to be. Screaming 'FUN' from every surface, it looks anything but. On the grey of a cloudy afternoon in September people wander around in shell shock, waiting to be told how to enjoy themselves next. A homeless guy sits in a doorway reading. He looks like the most cultured person for miles.

Opposite the pier is a row of seven or eight gift shops selling exactly the same stuff. A large sign on one reads 'BLACKPOOL ROCK, NOVELTY GIFTS, TOYS, LIQUID GOLD', seeing no tension or irony in selling buckets and spades next to amyl nitrate.

Blackpool doesn't know what it wants to be. It seems torn apart by its two personas, as the family destination of the north on the one hand, with its illuminations, funfair and award-winning beaches, and as Brighton's poorer, darker, older brother on the other, a sort of stag and hen party Gomorrah. The pubs that advertise as 'family friendly' also have faded patches of vomit on the driveway and only serve in plastic glasses in case two parties of stags meet. The veneer of FUN! FUN! FUN! is cracking, the signs are getting dirty and worn, and the 'cheap and cheerful' attitude is slowly losing the 'cheerful'.

———————

There are two more piers to go here, but first – with our backs to the greying waves and the rusting railing – we have to have our photos taken. It's for the local paper. We crush together and try to look human. The reporter is blonde and young. She has questions and enthusiasm. She smells incredible. She's alive.

———————

The reporter seems to recognise us immediately, probably because we look like we've been dragged around three-quarters of the country. Maybe it's the near-hysterical unreality of my weary brain, or it could be the complete lack of female company for nine or so days, or perhaps it's just the sight of a friendly face in such a grim, brash environment built entirely on facade, but she is stunning. I know that it must be mostly my mind fucking with me, because real people are not surrounded by a halo of light.

The interview flies by, and she's smart enough to know which bits she can cull from the press release and skilful enough to get us to say the quotes she can use.

'What do you think of Blackpool?' she asks.

I panic, knowing anything I say will have to be a lie.

'We've only just got here,' says Jon smoothly, 'but we can see it's going to be a big part of the book.'

The photographer arrives and we pose by the pier. Midge just walks with us as we go to where the photographer tells us and nobody questions us.

'Great,' says the reporter. 'Can I just get your names for the caption?'

Me and Jon tell her. She turns to Midge.

'Midge,' he says.

'What's your full name?' she asks.

'Just Midge,' says Midge and she looks at him hesitantly.

'We don't publish pictures without people's full names.'

'People call me Midge,' says Midge.

I'm not sure if he's making a point or worried about the DSS finding out he's on this trip.

She gets on the phone, and when she comes back she says, 'The editor says it's a legal thing. We can't put the picture in without your full name.'

'Midge IS my name,' says Midge.

I see her pretend to write 'Midge' down. We say our awkward goodbyes and then she leaves.

'I bet she wouldn't ask Madonna for a second name, or Cher.'

I leave Midge to think of himself in the same pantheon of multigenerational pop-diva legends and go onto the pier.

At the bottom of the urinal is a collection of wads of chewing gum. This is the most colourful thing in the faded and tatty arcade. The machines haven't been current for five or so years. In one of the 2p 'waterfall' machines, as an extra incentive, a £2 coin has been Sellotaped to a lottery ticket. The Central Pier is the second-oldest pier in Blackpool, originally known as South Pier until South Pier was built and a simple matter of logic earned it its new name. Central Pier was built as a more family-orientated pier, as opposed to the simpler North Pier. Today the giant Ferris wheel can be seen from both the other piers and most of the promenade.

As you leave the arcade the weather hits you almost immediately, the wind harsh and cold as the aggressive barkers shout at you to try their rigged, tatty games. I'm used to turning down even the most pushy chuggers and marketers on the high street, but I'm not at all ready for these guys. Maybe the end of season has sent them into a feeding frenzy, each competing for the sickest deer at the edge of the pack. Strangely, they all seemed to have London accents. I linger around the funfair at the edge of the pier, waiting for the barrage of pleas and very audible under-the-breath insults when I walk past.

Up the road, in muted colours and a criss-crossing of cables, the Tower is boarded around the entrance. Which is muting interest. It's also way too expensive: I'd had this plan that we'd do interesting things along the way, but we've had to skip Battle, only played one round of crazy golf and, if we're to make the Pleasure Beach, we can't afford the tower.

We hit the North Pier: sprouting tannoys pipe Badfinger. We hit a dead end: the man in the change cubicle sees us walk past but doesn't tell us that we can't exit at the back of the amusements.

BLACKPOOL North

Opened: 1863 (Architect: Eugenius Birch)

Length at start: 1,410 ft (430 m)

Length now: 1,318 ft (402 m)

Burn baby burn? Hit by boats in 1867, 1892 and 1897. The pavilion burnt down in 1921, and then again in 1938. To top it off, the pier suffered severe storm damage in 1997.

One of the earliest Sooty puppets used by Harry Corbett is on display on the pier. Corbett bought the original (yellow) Sooty on North Pier for his young son, later darkening the ears and nose with soot so they would show up on black-and-white TV.

The pier theatre has played host to Frankie Vaughan, Bernard Delfont (who coincidentally wrote a foreword to Bainbridge's *Pavilions on the Sea*), Morecambe and Wise, Paul Daniels, Russ Abbot, Bruce Forsyth and Hale and Pace.

It's the last surviving Eugenius Birch pier.

North Pier was built first, and was originally intended for a better class of tourist. It charged admission until very recently and its entertainment always used to be orchestral or a less bawdy comedian. It retains a sense of faded glory.

It has a small arcade, populated today by six or seven people standing around the push-penny machines as if in prayer.

———————

A tiny carousel spins idly in the doorway of the family bar, where there is no one stuck to the dark carpet but a gang of shaven-headed teenagers.

———————

I see Midge some way ahead of me, and next to him a group of three lads are swaggering around. Looking for distraction, interaction, anything I suppose, even violence, because anything is better than a numb, grey day in Britain's haunted fun house at that age. They're trying to pull some of the boards up from the floor when one spots Midge and they sway up close behind him. I look around for back-up. Jon's nowhere to be seen and the only other person is an elderly Chinese gentleman with a cagoule done up around his face like Kenny from *South Park*. Speeding up, I catch up to Midge. The boys are looking at me diagonally as I wait for him to take a picture of the carousel and we get out of there.

———————

I enthuse about how we can go to see the blue plaque that marks where Alan Bradley was killed by a tram. Alan Bradley was a very bad man, a very bad fictional man, in the eighties. Over 25 million people watched him take a glancing blow from a silent killer and, as *Coronation Street* viewers get pretty involved in the narrative, a lot of them probably gasped then cheered, as their PG Tips sloshed onto their plates of rich tea fingers. Generations of northern men have known not to interrupt while mum is watching her programme. They'd have sat reading the paper and possibly tucking into a Club biscuit.

Outside, a pair of homeless people are pouring cider out of its can and into discarded Lucozade bottles, so if the police stop them they don't look like they're drinking in the streets. They're merely refreshing themselves during the gaps in their cardio routines.

Jon wants to visit the spot where a character from *Coronation Street* died. It's apparently not far. I'm dubious, the rash on my legs really hurts and we are already in the sketchy part of town. It looks worse the further north you get. But Jon is adamant. It's only 200 yards away, Jon tells us, so we set off.

This end of town has obviously missed a couple of regeneration cycles, so crumbling plaster reveals dirty brick. The signs are damaged or not present any more, leaving only dirty ghosts where the vinyl letters have been. The windows are boarded or cracked and everything is faded like an old photograph. Jon tells us that it is just a little bit further. We walk nearer to a thousand yards than 200 before we get to a hotel. Jon walks out into the road waving his arms about, demonstrating where the tram hit this guy. I neither care nor know who Jon is talking about. But he thinks it's important.

The blue plaque is tucked behind a hanging basket, which is limply planted with anonymous and uncared-for flora. The hotel has the busy carpeting of all those we've seen, the stains not quite hidden. Fifty years of little accidents: spilt rum and coke and Mabel not quite making it. The carpet echoes the blotchiness of a frequently soiled inner thigh.

———————

I see a tram going back down the front and we all sprint to catch it. It kills my legs but it's better than walking back. Almost throwing ourselves on, I was expecting more. The outside is a bright wraparound advertisement for SpongeBob SquarePants, the relentlessly upbeat yellow sponge. But the tram is full of very old, unhappy people, coughing aggressively, or peering sadly out of the obscured windows.

———————

'Room for a little one on top,' gurns a young comedian-type as we board the tram.

There are drips down the curved stairs and a whiff of something that identifies this as municipal transport. A shuffling old guy swings his way to the door. I can smell the booze on his breath as he talks without much response about beer and pubs and trips away, fantastic pubs that are all gone now.

A funk descends on us. I'm not keen on funfairs and we're heading down to one of the largest. They're all sugar in the air, oil, hand jobs and stabbings. The grease in the hair of the speedway operator, the testosterone and overconfidence. I've not yet seen anyone in Blackpool smile, certainly not any of us.

South Pier turns out to be an expanse of costly rides too. I stare over the railings back up the tramline. Deserted, dirty stops, peeling paint and lamp posts only there to hold up grubby light boxes. The boxes are twisted and distorted in the autumn dullness, and we can see through the translucent facades to the workings behind. We've taken a pill and put on glasses that mean we can see the seaside as what it really is; a resting place for the desperate and hopeless.

The pavements laugh at us. 'Turned out nice, again,' they say. 'You get nothing for a pair.'

BLACKPOOL South

Opened: 1893 (Architect: T. P. Worthington)

Length at start: 492 ft (150 m)

Length now: 492 ft (150 m)

Burn baby burn? Fires in 1954, 1958 and 1964, each time destroying the grand pavilion.

Originally called the Victoria Pier, it was supposed to be more refined than the North and Central piers, and – we're told – 'at first provided little entertainment'. It now has rides advertised as an 'adrenaline zone', which seems in keeping with that tradition.

The South Pier has a big-top theme. Inside the arcade at the front the room seems massive and a mural of clowns make up a large portion of the space. I've never understood people's fear of clowns: I think it's sad that today we suspect the motives of any man that wants to wear a make-up disguise and hang around kids. John Wayne Gacy murdered little boys and buried them under his shed. Yes, he was a clown, but he was also an amateur painter and the majority of the population doesn't freak out when they see an easel. That said, the clowns painted on the walls of Blackpool's South Pier are the stuff of fuelled nightmares, waking dreams where proportion and scale are distorted beyond reason. Grinning demons of primary colours lurch out from the walls. I keep my head down and spot an eight-year-old child on a fruit machine, sitting on a stool so he can reach the slot.

Towards the back one of the booths has become a fish pedicure place, but the cushions are threadbare and half the fish lie dead, floating at the top of the tank.

The attractions at the Pleasure Beach are already closed for the night as we arrive. It's barely half five, and chains are draped over the barriers. The grease is heavy in the air – there's frying tonight. We beat an exit, as a horrific toothless guy calls 'show us yer rabbit' at a girl who may or may not have one, or want to show it if she has.

None of us suppresses our relief at the Pleasure Beach being closed and we take a slow walk back, past some of the worst-looking hotels and public houses to the car park. At least the walk starts slow, but then it turns into a brisk walk and soon descends into a straight-out retreat.

Building after building is rotting into itself. We step quickly, in case it's catching. A fun pub belts out thuds and neon. Outside, in a van, a machine drips Thatcher's cream. 'Coughin better toneet,' hacks a vested simpleton, strands of a fetid comb-over dangling into the red juice he drips. He hands the cone to a grateful child, who slurps it down while lashing at razor-beaked gulls. We've got to get away.

From an open window, grey flecks of net curtain mix with the smell of decay. 'Would you like it now or will you have it later?' A cackle.

The twisted mouth of a bloody tramp gargles at us as we reach the car park. Midge fumbling for the key, my hands grasping at the handle. The tramp points at his cardboard sign, written in brown: 'Me horse drowned.'

_____

Frankly we are shocked that we haven't been broken into as we arrive at the piermobile. We pile in the car, and Midge picks up the map. Jon takes the map off him. 'Just drive,' he says.

_____

Speeding away, tight to the coast, I feel something of a return to normality. The badness slips through the cracks still, like bacteria gathering in a broken shower tile. For the most part it's okay, but there's a festering. We can't spend too long anywhere.

_____

It's not hard to find St Annes Pier in Lytham St Annes. If you follow the coastline from Blackpool, probably driving a little quicker than strictly necessary, you'll find a charming village with wide streets, charity shops and Marks & Spencer outlets. Quicker than you can say 'blimey, it's a bit posh round here', you'll see the large mock-Tudor entrance. The village is sedately middle class, but with our hearts still beating from Blackpool it is a nice change. Part of my working-class-warrior roots winces when I admit this to myself.

ST ANNES

Opened: 1885 (Architect: A. Dowson. Mock-Tudor entrance in 1899 by J. D. Harker)

Length at start: 914 ft (279 m)

Length now: 600 ft (183 m)

Burn baby burn? The children's theatre burnt down in 1959, the Moorish Pavilion in 1974, and the Floral Hall in 1982.

The Ribble Navigation and Preston Dock Act (1883) and subsequent dredging of the river channels to improve access to Preston Dock meant that the pier was left on dry land, somewhat ruining the resort's steamer trade.

The pier has seen Gracie Fields, George Formby, Russ Conway and Bob Monkhouse perform, and in the seventies had a miniature zoo. In the ornamental gardens next to St Annes Pier is a statue of Les Dawson, who lived nearby.

Up close it looks like a grand cricket pavilion. I think I hear the thwack of willow, a ripple of applause, or is it sea breaking slowly onto the rough sand.

It's still bright, with the beginnings of the evening haze. We move druggedly towards the doors, on autopilot, silent. They're shut. The notice says 5:30 p.m. and, straining my eyes against the reflections from the clock on the frontage, I can see we're a minute or so past that. It's regular and ordered.

We take a quiet walk under the pier. Dusk isn't for another few hours, but the cloud cover is already making it dark. Jon disappears but, as tonight is his night to organise the place where we sleep, I presume it's something to do with that. On the beach somebody has been making sandcastles, but not plastic-bucket sandcastles. These are independent sand creations, hybrids of sand, stone, stick and feathers. Someone has drawn a stag in the sand with stones for eyes on its triangular head and sticks for antlers. They look closer to pagan fetish-worship objects than childhood doodle sculptures. If you scratch the polite surface of any Englishman you'll find an angry pagan waiting to rut, fight and howl at the moon. It's true, we love booze in this country purely so we can let ourselves go, wrap the wolf fur around us and run into the night. And the next day pretend we can't remember a thing.

The car park here is no doubt patrolled by regular men in regular hi-vis, men with an ordered way of ticketing. So I suggest that Midge should idle the engine on the double yellows outside, while Danny hops out on some unknown errand.

On our way out of town we pull into a NatWest, as Jon and Midge have to use the cash machine. I spy a cheap-pound-shop analogue across the junction. The rash on my legs at this point is so painful I decide, if I can catch it open, to buy some clean underwear, which might help.

'Wait here,' I say to Midge. He nods.

'Where you going?' asks Jon.

'Just over the road to try and catch that cheap shop open. Wait here, right?'

'Sure,' says Jon.

Bored with not being at the hub of activity, not knowing what Danny's up to, spotting rodent-like movement in the vacated back-seat nest, I make us pull round the corner so we can stock up on beer. I need something to kill the visions. I think I need to sleep.

I can see people in the shop near the door, so I sprint over the suddenly busy junction to try and catch it before it closes. The sharp pain of the rash stabs into my legs as I step out of the way of a car as it narrowly misses me. As I get to the door the security guard next to it is already shaking his head. Bollocks. I sprint across the junction a second time to catch them at the bank, even though it hurts. They're gone. I hear a beeping behind me, and see the car pulled up on the main road, where I was not 30 seconds ago. Seeing they're on a main road and that they shouldn't be stopping there, I sprint across the road a third time, just in time for them to pull off because a bus had pulled up behind them. My legs are burning at this point, something that could have been avoided if they'd stayed where they were like they agreed. A minute later they come walking round the corner.

'We're just going to get some cans for tonight. Do you want anything?' says Jon with no idea why my eyes are burning into him. I squint and shake my head.

'Where's the car?' I ask.

'Round the corner. You all right?'

I think 'NO I'M NOT FUCKING ALL RIGHT, I'M IN A LOT OF PAIN AND NEARLY KILLED MYSELF ON THAT FUCKING JUNCTION TWICE MORE THAN I NEEDED TO BECAUSE YOU COULDN'T STAY THE FUCK WHERE YOU WERE.'

'Fine,' I say pointedly.

I've booked tonight's campsite, or found it online anyway through the cracks of signal we could get as we raced away from hell. It looked fun: its site mentioned the Western-frontier-themed bar and boasted of musical visits by country legends. It'll be brilliant: we'll try line dancing. I'm reading out snippets of the promo:

'Great Birchwood Country Park. Fort San Antone is open every Friday & Saturday night, all day Sunday, with a fantastic carvery available... the biggest honky-tonk in Europe... acts such as Dr Hook... P. J. Proby...'

———————

I know that when I want to I can kill an atmosphere. I'm not proud of it and I rarely do it, but sometimes, when my head is stuck in that black cloud, I can give off the worst vibes imaginable. I seethe in the back while Jon and Midge navigate to the wild-west-themed campsite. It's interesting to see Jon trying to compensate for my bad mood, an extra note of bonhomie to his voice as he describes the saloon with pool tables and restaurant, the showers and the laundry room.

———————

Midge swings us off the main road, past a rotting shack and into a sea of mud. I get out reluctantly, sinking to the hems of my fetid jeans, and slip round discarded exhaust pipes and tricycles towards a door. There's no one home. The rusting metal flakes off the letter box as I rattle it.

Creaa-thump. Creaa-thump.

I call the number, but the answer machine squalls to a twisted-tape halt.

'No one about.'

'Let's just pitch the tent, we can sort it out later.'

So we do, the wheels of the car struggling to get purchase on the greasy surface as Midge pulls it near to a stretch of water. He and I try to get the tent up, and sort of succeed. I'm desperate for the toilet and search round the outside of a huge barn-like thing looking for the facilities.

———————

The field is near-flooded in places and basically gravel in others. With forced motivation Jon and Midge rush to help with the tent. They both decide to pitch it on one of the gravel bits. The palms on my hands still have bruises from the first night on hard ground, so I drag the whole thing to a place that isn't quite flooded. We'll be muddy, but the tent goes up.

———————

They are spartan, and mostly derelict, but eventually I see a chink of porcelain through a decaying wooden door. Dust and worse spawns into the air as I wrench it open, scraping the silted floor.

Shitting isn't pleasant. It hasn't been for the last week. I've sat trousers round ankles in cold, damp, dark and cobwebby rooms. I've been used to letting go quickly. The privacy it's given me hasn't outweighed the feeling of being vulnerable to everything from infection to missing something interesting. I squeeze, wipe and pull up with indecent haste and then attempt to wash my hands.

The taps whurp and gurgle, but nothing comes out. I step back to the tent – which has moved – wetting my hands on the soggy bushes it's now near. Midge sort of signals some sort of 'it's not worth asking' with his eyes. Danny has his reasons, obviously, and he's not in a good mood.

———————

Going back to the car to get my bag, I look at the window.

'Where's she gone?'

'Who?' asks Jon, knowing full well.

'Linda,' I say. Since I picked it up in Brighton I'd been keeping our pier count on the back of the postcard of eighties topless Page Three 'stunna' Linda Lusardi. I'd been enjoying the sideways looks and occasional smile from other cars, sometimes even the embarrassed fixed stare forward that the more prudish would exhibit.

'I've put it in the drivers door, just while we're at camps and parked and stuff. There's kids about,' says Jon, expecting a shouting match.

'How can tits offend kids?'

I see Midge wince at me shouting 'tits' loudly in the camp.

'They eat on them for the first year or so. It's one of the things I like about babies, we share an interest in tits.'

Jon just unlocks the door so I can put it back up in the window.

Not wanting to snap at them anymore, I take a look around. The saloon is closed this time of year, the laundrette is locked, and the showers look like somebody has hosed down an actual horse in them. The camp is obviously trying to retain a wild-west theme, but the only thing they have in common are a palpable mist of VD, the smell of shit and the unfriendliness of the locals that are hanging around this place. It would need two horses to reach the heights of a one-horse town. I return to the tent. They'll be drinking the cans that I have petulantly opted out of by now.

I suggest trying to find a drink somewhere. There's nothing here except scowling groups of men hanging round a sort of lodge area. They have large clean cars, polo shirts taut around broad backs and broader stomachs, and a boisterous danger sitting in the air around them. We have a few cans, but the idea of sitting in our own air – much less dangerous, but more brittle – is if anything less appealing than sharing theirs.

Midge doesn't want to drive, and Danny doesn't really want to go. So I volunteer. I haven't driven since Weston, and am sure that the residual alcohol in my blood makes this a fraught and illegal thing to do. I am in no way confident that everything I see is really there.

***

Jon doesn't like driving, much less in the dark on country roads, but he struggles through. The gesture is sweet and not unappreciated and I decide to stop being in a bad mood. It takes an effort and a few minutes but I screw in a smile. The pub we find is bland, but it's warm. I like being in civilisation again. We order some food, watch VH1 on the TV monitors, and I try and clear the mood. At the bar I watch the bartender take a call. He nods for a bit and then starts to cry. Neither Jon nor Midge notice, but my smile becomes genuine, and they do notice that.

***

We drink one, two maybe, or three or four. And climb back into the car. We arrive at the campsite without incident and leave the car where it sits. Light and noise creep from the barn. There's music – country, of course.

It's not the liveliest place. There are a few scruffy guys playing cards over in the corner but the sound is all coming from a jukebox in the centre of the wall. It's playing something that I dismiss as 'modern country': it's not Dolly or Kenny or Hank, it has a full sound without crackling, and I hate it. It's obviously a CD, the old-style-Wurlitzer look doesn't fool me for a second.

The place is cheap, Formica tables and rough, brown plastic seats. But a bar is a place I don't have to think: pint of lager, please.

The guy behind the bar has obviously been told to keep the western theme going. He's got the slicked hair, the apron and the slight crouch that the saloon tenders have in all of the films. The colour in his cheeks is almost sepia, but he doesn't slide the plastic glass on to the worktop.

Bored of talking, I decide to take a piss. It's a sort of defence mechanism in social situations. I'm fairly positive I don't go to the toilet much, unless I'm bored. It's something no one's ever going to comment on. You don't even have to announce it; you just stand and slip away. It'll give you chance to think of something to say, provide a break if there's a subject you want to change or an atmosphere you want to bust.

Scanning the edges of the room for a sign I don't really see anything, so I head down the only thing that may be a corridor, a space of sorts by the side of the bar against the back wall. It's the sort of decision I've made many times, too shy to ask where the bogs are. I often end up taking a turning for the dartboard. I front it out, of course, by inspecting the nap of the bristles. I check there's chalk, and I can tell you that 19 is exactly opposite 1.

For once I'm right. A thin panelled door is just ill-fitting enough to reveal urinals and a bucket in the corner. I go in and go through the motions.

Turning and zipping, I see there's a guy washing his hands at one of two sinks against the wall. As I approach he turns to the hand dryer. I see nothing much except the back of his head – shaggy, blondish – and that he's wearing a shirt, jeans and something I take to be a holster.

Thunk whuuuuuuuuuuuur.

'Have you seen the...' whuuuuuuuuuuuur '... dog?'

'No.' I haven't seen any dogs today.

'You will. You must. Tomorrow.'

He turns round and – while I can't be sure, of anything – it's the guy from the last campsite, now even more haunted-looking. I'm too polite and shy to do anything but attempt expressions that could be interpreted either as recognition or friendliness.

I head straight for the door. The bartender is crying.

CHAPTER TWELVE

SOUTHPORT IN A STORM

Today is our last English pier. Our last seven are in Wales. I am awoken by vultures, or some sort of bird anyway, and crawl out of the tent. It's about seven. I hold J. B. Priestley's *English Journey* tightly, wishing I could have finished reading it before leaving England behind later today. The book is protecting me. I'm by a pond, on a bench, in a muddy field. I've seen a lot of benches this past week or so, seats of all kinds, mostly with affixed plaques – resting places tied to the permanently rested. I think of some I knew. At the moment it's all cold and all real. And I'm not reading, but waiting.

Southport isn't far, but the mood hasn't quite shifted. We pack the car silently, fold in and get off. Without paying, without a goodbye, but not without Midge making a meal of putting the seat back into position for his little legs.

The fact we will be stopping the night in a nice warm chalet at Pontins tells me it's going to be a great day. We have marked the whole day and night to spend there, so Midge is relieved of any heavy driving duties today. The morning is what optimists call 'fresh', pessimists call 'bloody freezing' and I call 'uninhabitable for civilised human beings', but we pack the car under a lightly cloud-smattered sky. For the first time in quite a few days the whole car is getting excited, an atmosphere that increases when we make it to the village of Aintree, which is on the outskirts of Southport. We drive through and just before the road dips we can see Pontins over the other side, with a grey sea fighting the sun behind. The opening bass riff of a Led Zeppelin track kicks in over the stereo and we all sing along.

We get nodded through at the security gate and I have to swat away the thousands of memories that come flooding through. The booking still hasn't been properly confirmed, and I can't wander in like a misty-eyed moron gurgling about my childhood. The girl at the desk is wearing the uniform, and her make-up is thick. I smile and explain my situation. She smiles back and types something into her computer.

'Yeah, got the booking for Smith. But the chalet won't be ready till three.'

I look at the clock, it's 11. 'That's fine,' I say. 'Is it okay that we use some of the facilities on site until then?'

'Fine,' she says, 'although the pool's closed today.'

'That's okay, I just want to wash some clothes.'

'Oh, we don't have a laundrette, haven't had for years.' In my mind's eye I can see me biting the desk in two. 'There's one in the village.' My fingers are gripping the edge of the desk.

'Okay, we'll come back later.'

It's decided that we'll go into Southport – we're meeting a guy called Roy soon anyway. I'll go find a laundrette while Midge and Jon meet him and I'll catch up with them later.

Across the water I know is there, although there's none in plain sight, I can see Blackpool Tower. The Blackpool funk lifted this morning as we drove through the Pontins gates, Brett Anderson's 'Brittle Heart', the trip anthem, kicking in on the radio at exactly the right moment. We know then, in our clumsy harmony, that this is the third act, the validation.

Those of us who already have clean underwear (me) and those who either have or don't care (Midge) head back out into town to see the pier, which goes across a river, a road, a skatepark and a shopping centre before even reaching the beach. The beach is wide and the sea is so far toward the horizon that it's not easy to tell which bit is sky.

This pier is The Last of England and echoes a Ford Madox Brown painting of that name. Midge and I are huddled in a flimsy shelter against the wind. Though most of it is over land the pier is long, and the gale is harsh. If Dan were here we might go on, but I'm not that bothered to see the end. Seven more and then I need never see a pier again.

I kill time in the free hall of mirrors at the side entrance to Funland, which is an amusement arcade around the entrance to the pier. I sidle up to the ones that make me look thin and squint at the others. I hate mirrors. I've developed a way of coming at them sideways and defocusing my eyes when shaving or doing my hair. Anything not to look. But I've a thought about how the seaside is a fun-house mirror to its homeland. These resorts are holding up a distorted view of our island to itself. Sometimes you'll be able to laugh at what you look like, but sometimes not.

———

Southport is the one-time home of Chewits sweets, *Confessions* actor Robin Asquith, Red Rum and Louis-Napoléon Bonaparte who, according to local liars, got the idea for his massive redevelopment programme of Paris from the main promenade in Southport. But not one bloody laundrette can I find. I have a pocketful of change and a tenner to last the journey, and not one item of clean clothes to wear. Tonight is going to get messy, the last big blowout of the trip, but I will be in dirty clothes. I lug my washing back to the car.

The Asda we're parked in is one of the more massive superstores. I go in to buy some chewing gum so at least we have a receipt in case someone cares that we've parked there. The store has a massive clothing section, so I go and pick up a three-pack of the cheapest boxer shorts, some socks and a plain black pair of trousers. I also pick up two bottles of very cheap fizzy wine. This is the one time I'm grateful for self-service checkouts. I figure if my card gets refused I'll just ditch the stuff right there and walk out. 'DO YOU WANT CASHBACK?' flashes on the screen. In for a penny, I click '£20'. The machine thinks for a while, and I plan the route out of the shop where I'd have the least amount of eye contact. The transaction goes through. I snatch my card and the stuff before it has a chance to change its mind.

After a quick change in the toilets I stride out feeling like a god in clean trousers and pants, like some sort of movie-star millionaire.

Southport's pier is over a kilometre long, the second longest in Britain, but for me it has one essential advantage over the longest at Southend: it hasn't had a portion of itself turned into matchsticks by a drifting boat. As I arrive to catch the tram that runs along its length, it is already filling up with old people, bent grey people lapping horrible ice creams into toothless holes. One of the guys that gets on looks like a builder and turns out to be the driver. He climbs into the cab cheerily. One of his cassette tapes falls off the dashboard. It's *The Best of Aztec Camera*. It's probably not a very long tape.

The sea is right out, and even at a kilometre away from the front here it is just about discernible in the distance. The only thing to do when I get to the end is to go into the pavilion, which is half cafe, half classic penny arcade. The juxtaposition between the old and the new is sharp, but seeing as I had no need for a 'Tango Ice Blast' or a 'Shmoo Milkshake', I spend my time in the arcade. The tram leaves to go back to the front in ten minutes and I can see that I will have to stretch that out. Most of the penny machines offer no more entertainment than the miniature dioramas where the presented figurines mechanically wiggle about for a bit. One man in a cap and with his beer belly poking out slightly between his T-shirt and his bumbag stops me:

'Do you remember the one with the elephant in the cave?'

I know of no way of answering that without inviting further conversation.

'No.'

'Well, it had this cave, and when you put money in the elephant would...'

Tuning him out, I notice that the tram is filling up for the return journey

'That's great.' I smile, cutting him off as I walk back.

SOUTHPORT

Opened: 1860 (Architect: James Brunlees)

Length at start: 3,600 ft (1,097 m)

Length now: 3,633 ft (1,107 m)

Burn baby burn? Extended to 4,380 feet in 1868, but fires and storms (1933 and 1957) shortened it to its current length.

The second-longest pier in the UK and the oldest iron pier in the country. Unusually, it wasn't sectioned during World War Two but it was closed to the public so that searchlights could be installed to protect the industrial towns nearby.

A high-diver calling himself 'Professor' Bert Powsey often dived off the pier, a brave feat not so much because of the height but more for the lack of much water in the sea.

In the old-fashioned, penny-arcade amusements at the end of the pier is an automated doll labelled 'Have a laugh with Jolly Jack', which has been described as 'by far one of the creepiest things I've ever encountered' by one visitor.

Just outside there is yet another street named after Queen Victoria. She and her intimately pierced Prince Consort are huge presences in our coastal towns. Is that because the idea of the seaside as a resort blossomed – like the trains – under her reign? Was she truly inspirational, or just in the right place at the right time?

I'm waiting to meet Roy, a guy who made contact when we started talking about this whole thing on the Internet. He's a writer, psychogeographer and photographer with an interest in piers. And he offered to show us around the town. I don't know what he looks like, but – sitting at the table outside in the cold, fiddling with my phone in the hope of solace or entertainment – I'm sure I will recognise him.

———

Having texted Jon on the journey back, I meet him, Midge and Roy at the front of the pier.

'Did you see the penny arcade at the end?' I ask Jon.

'Nah, we only got halfway up and got bored.'

———

Meeting people from the Internet is weird, but less so – you may think – than being thrown together by accident of work or birth. It's certainly hard to start with, though, as you have common interests but no common experiences. Overcoming a lack of common experience is what the platitudes are for.

Roy says: 'Do you fancy going to the smallest pub in England?' Of course we do.

We walk along the seafront with Roy. Along with the pier, it's recently gone through a £23m redevelopment, so it's all white stone and smooth concrete. Roy tells us that he works for the student liaison office at Edge Hill University near Liverpool. Because of a record amount of students starting that September, Roy arranged for the excess students without accommodation to be put up in a couple of chalet blocks at Pontins. We tell him that we are to stay there that night and he promises to put something up on their Facebook group page.

The Lakeside Inn is 22 feet by 16 feet and is licensed to hold up to 50 people. For a weekday afternoon the wooden-boathouse or cricket-pavilion type place is pretty full – 50 people would be a standing-room-only party. There are about four or five groups dotted around and none are obviously tourists. It's good to talk to someone who isn't us, even if right now it is about piers.

England's smallest pub is quite small. Midge looks it up and down.

'I've seen smaller,' he says dismissively, probably forgetting that normal-sized humans are probably not allowed in the

Borrower pubs he normally frequents. We sit in the corner. Wherever you sit in the Lakeside Inn you're actually in a corner. We sit patiently waiting for the barmaids to notice us, which in a pub this size shouldn't be long at all.

'Well, we can go to Asda and do a big shop if you... Oh, hello lads, what'll it be?' asks the older lady with frizzy, hennaed hair. Roy orders a bitter. He's a man who's difficult to age really. His hair has a little grey, his glasses are Jasper Conrad, and the day we meet him he is wearing a navy-blue windbreaker with red tartan lining.

We go off to another bar – via me buying a new black notebook (soft cover, faint lines) in Waterstones. Roy knew the importance of my noting equipment, and knew just where to get what I needed. In certain circles – ours – the notebook becomes like a drug ritual or a magic spell. I celebrate by attempting to sharpen my pencil in the toilet of the bar. The Inn Beer Shop is set in a row of shops hooded by a pavilion-style canopy. It has a shopping-arcade concept and a sort of mock-Tudor vibe. It's a tight alley of bottles, an off-licence. But there are small tables and as you approach the counter, a couple of beer pumps rather than a selection of chocolate bars. It's bright, but decorated in a style that fades. The clientele are exactly those you'd expect to be drinking in an off-licence at about noon, most plumping for the scrumpy that is served from a plastic keg balanced behind the bar. We're like that too. We've got the air of itinerants, of day-drinkers, of a furry-yeasty fug replacing a layer of aloofness. We'll talk and drink, as we've nothing else to do.

The next place is an 'outdoor', a word unique to people from the Midlands. It means 'off-licence' and comes from the door in a pub where they used to sell beer for taking away. Anyway, this is a specialist-beer off-licence, mostly European bottled beer, but out the back are a few small tables and a couple of taps.

I pick a strong lager from the fridge and settle in the corner under a – slightly askew – picture of young Elvis. He tells me not to give up.

Blue Hawaii Elvis grins down from a vintage-advertisement display. Jon at this point only has to gesture at it for me to know its significance. Hawaiian Elvis is my favourite Elvis, while white-jumpsuit Elvis is Jon's. As we acknowledge its presence, 'Blue Suede Shoes' fizzes from the buzzing meshed speaker overhead.

We venture off again to a hotel basement. It's dark and full of bodies in the early afternoon. Red carpet swirls, coats of arms and suits of armour. Fortified against attack and holding out against despair. I go to the bar, then swerve and spill the sticky beer – some local, strong concoction, our guide reveals – towards the back of the room, scooping three pint glasses in my fingers and holding them out front like an unstable flag to my vintage motorcar. I reach them in an alcove, Roy on a wooden seat with decorative flourishes, which is raised higher than Danny's more usual pub chair. After distributing the drinks, I pull out a padded stool and step over to sit. The older man is talking and Danny is listening.

We toast with sweet pints in handled glasses. And then we leave, squinting into the hazy afternoon sun and not quite at right angles to reality.

———————

I know we go to two more pubs because their names are in my notebook. I don't remember them or saying goodbye to Roy. But I bet there were hugs involved.

———————

Midge is parked in the Clio on double-yellow lines outside. He drives us disapprovingly, but swiftly, into the camp, where we're waved in without question by the guys posted at the gatehouse.

The layout is imprinted on our minds like it is part of a former life. We know where to leave our carriage, how to announce our arrival and how to navigate to our rooms. A huge draughty place, it has never felt in the best of repair, but something about how it looks exactly the same as it always has suddenly makes it darker. A holiday camp is cut off from the outside world as surely as a valley with its own microclimate is safe from evolution or nuclear fallout. It's a Pimlico or Grand Fenwick, a bubble-preserved enclave of the sixties and seventies, and it now therefore seems even further adrift in time.

———————

Fred Pontin started building his resorts in 1946, ten years or so after Billy Butlin started building his. I don't know if his intention was to cater for the lower working class that couldn't quite afford Butlin's camps but that's what happened. My whole family would go to Pontins. We would book out two or three chalet blocks and everyone related to my nan or even in her orbit would go to Southport for two weeks in the summer. Even my uncle would pile four or five of his mates into a room (a practice strictly forbidden by Pontins) and drink for two weeks straight. It was awkward for me. I wasn't quite old enough to drink, something that the adults did almost to the exclusion of all else. I was too teenage to enjoy the family-orientated games, and decidedly too old to be part of the children's games.

The children were partly looked after by a group of bluecoats, the bluecoats being the performers/entertainment staff that were not at all a rip-off of Billy Butlin's redcoats. They ran games, treasure hunts and activities. And every night around nine they would be joined in dance and song by Captain Crocodile himself, before leading the kids out of the main ballroom to 'The Crocodile March'. A great way of delineating the night between children and adult time. Most of the babies and kids would be put to bed by one of the adults and left on their own. Every half an hour a bluecoat would walk around the aisles and if they heard crying from your chalet they would put your block and chalet number on a board to the right of the stage. The first few times I went to a proper church and saw the hymn order to the side of the pulpit I wondered why nobody was going to sort out those kids.

My brother loved the Crocodile Club and to this day can sing 'The Crocodile March'. Me, not so much. I would spend my holidays being snuck into the adult events sipping beer and watching the darts exhibition matches (according to family lore, my nan beat Bobby George once), or reading comics.

There were three or four Pontins sites our family tended to visit, but the one we went to the most was Southport. I can see the playground now where I spent the majority of my time, and most of the landmarks are in the same places. In fact the only concession to time that I can see are a series of branded characters. To complement Captain Crocodile, there's a sassy zebra, some sort of bird, and a man with upbeat hair. The thing is, they haven't removed a lot of the old branding or signage and even though the font colours and style of illustration are similar, it isn't exactly the same. Pontins went into administration just a few months ago and it seems it has no idea who it is or where it's going any more.

———————

Rows of boxy two-tier rooms, each identically pebble-dashed and greyingly whitewashed, surround squares of grass all facing inwards. The grass is just too long to be anything but permanently damp and the paths in front of each row are religiously stuck to. When you stay in a holiday camp you spend a lot of time in confusion: come round the corner into a square and you're convinced it's yours, and you walk round the edges looking at numbers which have no real pattern. You have to get out of the squares to get a bearing, then dive between the corner gaps of the next 'right one'. We're on the top row, in one corner. There's hardly a soul here.

———————

We grab what we need from the car and pile into chalet 104. I bagsy the shower first and flick the hot-water switch while Jon puts up a huge Cuban flag in the window. I throw the styrofoam head I have acquired from a skip at Midge and proceed to wield one of the wardrobe rails as a sword while I open the first bottle of champagne. We turn the TV on. As kids, both me and Jon remember PTV, a station for the camp which shows the schedule for that day, what to look forward to in the week and, as the technology developed, highlights of yesterday's activities. Switching around the channels we find it, slightly off tune, and looping the same 15 minutes over and over again. It lacks the tacky warmth we remember, looking now more like an emergency broadcast by a cheerful dystopian cult after a nuclear detonation.

———————

We spread out in our chalet, turning the telly and the hot water on. Along with the simple pleasures of having switches that do more than unlock car doors, it's a joy to have even the most basic of home comforts. We're happy and boisterous. Dan's running around with his shirt off talking loudly and constantly. Even Midge seems to have one of his happier-looking bemused smiles on.

The carpet is worn to a shine in places and the fresh double glazing is only on the front of the huts, but it's a comforting home. Bathroom, kitchen area and one bedroom with twin beds. There's a festive atmosphere too, forced through the closed-circuit fuzz of Pontins Television. It announces that we're already missing bingo.

But suddenly there's water everywhere, and a dark mood descends.

––––––––––

'Err, guys, we may have a problem,' I shout. Midge and Jon come in and see the water coming from a missing section of pipe in the cupboard behind the sink.

'Shit,' says Jon going back to the living room.

'Well, standing there laughing isn't helping. Do something,' says Midge, seemingly quite worried.

'Like what? I'm not a plumber.'

'I'm not a gynaecologist,' shouts Jon automatically from the living room.

'But I'll have a look,' we finish in unison.

'Stick your finger in it,' says Midge.

'That's the spirit,' shouts Jon.

'No, the pipe, to stop the water.'

'Balls to that, you stick your finger in,' I say. Midge sighs and sticks his finger in the hole. I shout to Jon to take the flag down while I go find someone.

I grab one of the building supervisors who is walking around talking into a radio. After he turns the water off he tells us he's going to find us another chalet. Twenty minutes later he comes back and tells us to go to 120. It's the next block over so we grab what stuff we can and go over to 120. I see movement through the large single pane of glass. I knock and a small Welshman answers.

'Hello?' He sees me, half-pissed and grinning at the insanity of the situation, clutching a bottle of Asda's own champagne, and then he looks at Midge, smiling but worried behind me, carrying his sleeping bag.

'Hi, our chalet had a leak so we've been sent to this one as a replacement,' I say smiling. He says nothing for a while.

'Oh,' he says.

'But it looks like you're using this one – I don't suppose you want us sharing? We're very nice.'

'No, we're all right, thank you,' says the man.

'Okay, we're going to sort it out now. Goodbye.'

'Goodbye,' says the Welshman.

Luckily another guy with a walkie-talkie is passing by. He looks at us standing there with our gear around our feet. He rolls his eyes. He takes us to 140 but this time I make him wait there while I check it's a) not occupied and b) has hot water. It does meet these very meagre requirements so I grab the guys and the rest of the stuff. Once settled, I open the second bottle by way of celebration.

'I wanted this to be good.'

Dan is frustrated.

Wind hums through the bathroom window like a hospital harmonica.

There has been a guy on a plastic school chair smoking outside chalet 106 since we first got here this morning. He's still going, puffing and staring in his shirtsleeves, as we head out for an evening's entertainment.

The chalets were sparse 30 years ago when they were new, but now they're positively threadbare. All the paintwork needs repainting, the carpets have bald patches and the furniture is mismatched. Although everything is very clean, it feels broken, like the set of an Eastern European film about cat AIDS. But these are the back blocks; the ones nearer the front, including the ones the students are using, have apparently been renovated – new furniture, double glazing, and new bathrooms fitted. To us, though, it was high luxury, like having a tent you can stand up in, or not needing to walk across a field to shower.

We arrive in the main ballroom for the evening's entertainment, to find it completely decked out in Christmas decorations: lights, tinsel and, on the stage, a plastic tree with fake gifts that all have tiny tears where the children have had a peek at what's inside. We choose a table in the middle. All the good tables, of course, will have been reserved with coats and bags when the room opened earlier in the day, and periodically checked up on by a series of people from within each group. I got paid 50p and a coke if I looked after the seats when I was a teenager. Seeing as I'd probably only be reading comics on the adventure playground or wandering around the arcade anyway, it was a bargain.

There is a Christmas quiz going on, as if a Christmas quiz is an actual thing that exists anywhere other than here. The room is half full or, as the new owners of Pontins would see it, half empty. All the families are hunched around the tables whispering about the answers, well the men are anyway, barely looking up to grab their pints, while the women sip at vodka and cokes, half-watching their kids running up and down and skidding on their knees on the polished floor.

Tinsel is draped flaccidly over the bar. It's summer. Apparently Morris dancers have decided that it should be Christmas every week – a pagan spell against the turning of time. Summer can't end if it's never summer and always Christmas. We celebrate with three pints of Carlsberg.

We perch at a table – square, brown-wood effect, wipe-clean. We survey the scene. The bar is partitioned off along one wall, at about waist height, and there are tables running alongside it. The main action is facing a huge stage at the opposite end to the sets of double doors, and row after row of four, six or eight-person tables face it and the polished dance floor before it. We're here to be entertained.

'Dan,' I say, 'do you think poor people are uglier?'

'No, they're not. It's your brain being conditioned by an idea of taste.'

But I'm not sure. When I was here before I was young and shy, but I felt that if I wanted to I could have connected with the people here. I'd envisaged talking to the people here now, finding out about what brought them to a place out of time for a week in September, but I can't think of a way in. I once had a rambling, drunken conversation with a guy that was convinced that grammar school had driven a divide between him and his family, such that he couldn't talk to them anymore. I didn't think that that had happened to me at the time, but there was something about going to university, about deciding I was 'creative' – or 'a creative', both sound shit, but there's no other word – and about living in an area far cut off from the pressures of the shop floor, which have all contributed to how I feel now. And what I feel now is a disconnect, not the usual disconnect of a few shandies or a haughty disdain for low culture, but a simple glass panel. I'm a time traveller from a more balsamic-vinegar age and I can only peer through the greenish glass. And feel sour. A green night.

I ask the bartender about the Christmas theme, wondering if it was a special theme week or something.

'It's Christmas every week,' with a slight shake of the head. 'I'm sick of it myself.' As if on cue, 'I Wish it Could Be Christmas Everyday' starts to play. The barman rolls his eyes, takes my money and goes for the walkie-talkie on the bar.

Jon has found a programme. Apparently it's time for a 'Christmas party'. Most of the Christmas parties I've been to normally involve telling your boss to fuck off and doing embarrassing things that it takes a few months to live down. This one is mainly a disco for the kids, the dances being led by one bluecoat on stage who demonstrates all the moves, and a couple more on the dance floor. The bluecoat is a mum-friendly, effeminate man who seems to turn around more often than is strictly necessary, revealing his bum held in place by his blue trousers. The couple on the dance floor are doing a good job of pretending to enjoy themselves and that they haven't done this 30 times this season, although from their body language I get the distinct impression that they don't particularly like each other.

———————

They go through the ritual songs that have filled holiday camps since the mid seventies. 'Tiger Feet', 'Wig Wam Bam', which is appropriate now – glam rock is Christmas, after all – but it's appropriate like a stopped clock. Glam is good family music: it stomps in drinking time for the dads; it has glitter and glamour for the mums; and it's a fantasy for the kids. And now, divorced from context, it's safe. In our context, as the regular thump makes it too loud to talk or even to think, it makes it drinking time. The bluecoats are trying to sell glittery and glowing tat, all available from the kiosk outside.

———————

Just as I'm beginning to be hypnotised by the fat swinging from the arms of one of the mothers who has got up to dance with her kids, it's time for the kids to go to bed. Me and Jon make eye contact and smile, as we both had been singing 'The Crocodile March' while getting ready earlier, and Jon thought if he bought me enough drinks he could get me to join in the march.

'Okay, everybody!' says the man over the microphone. 'Get ready for...' The kids look round to see him. '...The Slush Puppie!'

What?

The song 'Cold As Ice' comes on. No, not the original by Foreigner, the remixed version by M.O.P. A giant furry Slush Puppie mascot comes in. Jon's mouth is hanging open, and I'm scowling. Already guessing what's happened, which is that that thing, that precious special memory from my childhood, has been co-opted by a brand. Now, I love ice flavoured with sugar and chemicals as much as the next person, probably more, but this is sacrilege. I may have never done 'The Crocodile March' as a kid, but I still have fond memories of it. It indicated when the entertainment got good and I could stay up later than my siblings 'if I sat still and out of the way'. I really dread to think what my brother would have done had he been here to witness this. I suspect the police would have had to write a report about a large, crying man attacking a furry mascot.

As the kids are being led out to have their picture taken with the Slush Puppie (on sale in reception the next morning for £4.50), I notice it's soured the mood somewhat. The lights come up and the speakers say, 'We're having a break for a bit, don't forget your drinks at the bar for this evening's entertainment.'

'We should try and find some of these students,' says Jon.

'I could go back and check the Facebook group, see if there's any news about tonight,' I say, forgetting that the chalets don't have Wi-Fi.

'Or we could just go over and ask those guys over there,' says Jon, nodding his head to the table of obvious students looking bored.

'Excuse me, are you Edge Hill students by any chance?'

'Yeah,' says one of the girls, pretty in a casual way that only students manage.

'Are you the writers doing a book about piers?' says another. 'Sit down, guys.'

The students have just moved in but, like the barman, they're already sick of Christmas.

'We're really waiting for Jason,' says one of the guys cryptically. They all laugh. We ask about the camp and, as with anything new, the teething problems were annoying them more. They were promised Wi-Fi for the rooms. It's still being sorted out. Some of the rooms still had furniture that had to be replaced, and the buses that ferried them to the uni went at odd times, which meant they were missing lectures.

But it seems to have bonded them together quickly. They start buying shots. So do we. Me and Jon are drinkers, and session ones at that, but these super-sweet, cola-flavoured shots dropped into pints of lager look dangerous and definitely put us and the students on a level playing field. As the bluecoat show starts, we all clap and cheer a little louder than the families out that night. One by one the bluecoats are introduced onto stage. When Jason is called the students give an extra-loud cheer. He marches to the stage, resolutely not looking in our direction.

'Why Jason?' I ask the kid next to me who, like me, has joined the others in a standing ovation for Jason's walk to stage. He smiles and shrugs. You can see the force of will it is taking Jason not to look over, even though whenever it is his turn to sing or dance he is getting a thunderous reception. I guess by November Jason will have had a nervous breakdown.

The night goes quickly with shot after shot and conversation about their lives and plans. The bluecoats are replaced by a singer, competent in a crooner/big-band kind of way. He's delighted and confused as we all pile on to the dance floor to the opening notes of his taped backing track of 'Brown Eyed Girl'.

Just the ten of us dancing like nobody else was there, smiling and moving to a singer who probably hasn't had people dancing for five or so years. While a confused audience of working-class dads and mums watch on.

Sitting around a large round table, just aside from the main central area, is a group of the young, fresh and vibrant. They're a million times more alive than anything in the tableau facing the stage. They invite us to join them, at least one space round the table being empty. Something about a chap going to Alderley Edge, but I don't listen. Roy has sent word of us ahead.

In a grey lace dress and flushed cheeks, fringe heavy over deep brown eyes, and surrounded by about seven lads, is a stunning vision. I start to feel worried for her. It's not that I want her, I don't – she's young and has everything going for her, despite being at university in a Pontins camp. I have nothing to offer. What would we ever talk about? But I would die if she were hurt. England depends on her. Sometimes you just see a vision. I want to reach back into the past to stop any possibility of anything that's ever made her upset.

Not that she looks upset. She looks serene.

Two of the lads, Lance and Percy, are holding court. They're telling us how the place isn't how it's meant to be, that the bluecoats don't like them. They were meant to have their own bar – Pontins usually has two, one in the main ballroom and a smaller one where 'adult' comedians can prowl from about 10 p.m. – but that hasn't been sorted out. They too are in a permanent purgatorial state of festivity, cut off from the town, cut off from campus. They are bound together by circumstances and a code – a code which seems to be more against a force than for anything in particular. They drink like freshers, and it would be rude not to join them.

A giant white dog enters, stage right, and the commoners are transfixed. It seems normal to them, and so I take it as normal too. He's introduced and applauded. It begins to move with a swooping rhythm, hypnotic in all of its six-foot height. Its ears sway. The chant is about buying, wanting, drinking. The temperature drops. It becomes winter.

'... you're willing to sacrifice our love... ' they sing.

I freeze. Are we the sacrifice?

'You want paradise.'

'Someday you'll pay the price.'

The crowd sway, clap, eyes are to the front.

I can't be sure, but on the projector at the side of the stage I'm sure I see a tall green figure chained to a wall. The sacrifice. Snap, snap. Wheels turn pulleys and the – crocodile? – is splayed further. The dog howls.

The heavy green curtains part. A tall man takes the stage, well kept, blond, handsome if ageing. He tosses his dinner jacket onto the stand after he picks up the microphone. I can see God in the ruffles of his shirt.

'Hello, Southport, I'm Arthur Wakeman. Let's keep the party going. I'm going to sing you a song.'

And he does. Strings and horns swell out of nowhere, his voice is powerful and rich. The song is new to me, but I've always known it. My mouth is moving, mouthing chewily the words that I don't know but understand as soon as I hear. He's singing of everything that holds us together. It's the truth. It's not Elvis but right now this man is the king.

The dog is swaying still, but now to the swing sounds, disco-ball glitter spinning into his huge eyes. The music, the song is Arthur's. The place is Arthur's. He's at home, it's his castle.

As the last chorus climbs to its height, Arthur reaches for the mic stand. He swings it up, Freddie Mercury. I rise, get closer, the bluecoats are moving to grab him. The one they called Jason is nearest, I have to stop him. He's reaching the stage and I can do nothing but thrust out a leg. It doesn't stop him but it throws him off balance and he careers into the bingo machine.

The mic stand hits the spotlight and gleams like nothing I've ever seen. It has a golden handle and the side is the sharpest thing – with a thud it hits the dog just above its blue T-shirt. A head rolls and smoke fills the stage.

'Goodnight. God bless.'

He's gone as soon as he arrived, the music back to coming from the PA. The dog is slinking off, picking up his head for tomorrow. Captain Croc is leading the kids out of the room, back to chalets and to sleep.

There is only one way to beat the future and it's to dance to the tune of the past. I dance with the brown-eyed girl, and the rest. We all pour shots of thick red into our mugs and down them. 'You can do anything you want,' she whispers. If I knew what that was, I would.

I feel like I'm underwater: sounds are looming in and out. I keep having unexpected changes in perspective, in height, in angle.

Goodnight, campers.

CHAPTER THIRTEEN

WALES OF THE UNEXPECTED

I wake up the next day tasting bare mattress, which is preferential to the film on the inside of my mouth, which tastes like the floor of a New Orleans taxi cab. Midge is already up and in the shower. I stumble into the living room, where the great lump of Jon is still sleeping. I crawl onto the bed and give him a cuddle. He barely wakes and soon I have to fight dozing off myself.

———————

I wake on the double sofa – for privacy's sake, I'd called the only bed in its own room. Of course I made a play of magnanimity, taking the put-you-up rather than the actual beds – but really I wanted to sleep alone. Well, not alone, but not next to the unshowered. I wake with the bounce that, even without opening my eyes, I know signifies Danny jumping in next to me. That's okay, it's not as if I was slumbering with a semi and half a mind to take that further or anything. The grumble he gets isn't all hangover.

———————

'How do you feel?' I ask Jon.
  'Orrible,' he grunts, 'How's your head?'
  'I feel like a microwavable dog-shit sandwich bought in a petrol station and dropped on the forecourt.'

At that point Midge walks in from the shower, towel around his waist. 'What are you guys doing?'

'Spooning,' I say.

'Jump on,' Jon adds, 'room for a little 'un.'

'I wonder about you two sometimes,' says Midge as he goes into the bedroom.

We've a kitchen, but nothing to cook in it. I make myself a cup of hot water, more through desire for ritual than anything.

Midge looks into the rear-view mirror.

'I've worked it out,' he says, catching my eye.

'What? The satnav? Took your time,' I say.

'No, why people find you so charming, how you do it.'

'Really, how do I do it?'

'You talk really loud and really quick, so people don't get a chance to not like you. You're already shouting at them anyway,' he says.

'Oh,' I say. 'I thought I did it by trying not to be a prick, as that's pretty rare nowadays.'

'No,' he says. 'It's definitely the shouting thing.'

The mood is light and up, only a little tender and caffeine-fuzzy. We have often been unable to keep the number of piers there are left in our heads, but it's easy now: there are seven in Wales, five today and two tomorrow. It's Friday, I think, and we're going to make it back easily on time. We've all but done it and something has changed in my head. I think I've broken a link with the past. I think I understand my place at the seaside.

Midge puts his foot down and we almost hit the speed limit on the dual carriageway into our new country. We enter a tunnel, a cave blasted out of solid rock. The outside noise is muffled and the radio plays 'Tunnel of Love' by Fun Boy Three. I smile at it and the reception stays on all the way through.

A mining conveyor belt sticks out over the road and into the sea. It's not the pier; more like a dark-universe twin of one. The outcrop of a coke-blacked hell. But we're past the hump and I can see industry and commerce for what they are, things to be controlled but not afraid of. We drive under, focusing on the deep colours of the sea and the magical mist around the horizon.

———————

After a short while we get to Colwyn Bay. The road that follows the coast is a lot higher than the beach. We park and around the corner we see the pier. Standing high in the distance, even from here I can see it's dilapidated, but it suits the place, like Sleeping Beauty's castle. As we get closer we can see the signs telling us it's closed.

'Well, if we can't go on it, we're going to have to go under it,' says Jon. The hangover being in its third upward swing, I just nod slightly and head down the stairs to the beach. The pier is closed after a bankruptcy order brought against the owner Steve Hunt. He claims it was spurious and malicious. The council say it was for unpaid business rates. Before that, it was owned by a maritime engineer who, after trying to renovate and repair it himself, admitted defeat and tried to sell it on eBay.

Two hundred yards away from the pier a single metal chain fences around it. A sign warns that it's dangerous to go under the pier without a safety helmet. I look at Jon. He just shrugs and we step over it.

'Oi!' We look around and see an angry small man with a big guy who looks like somebody called central casting and asked for an 'English builder'. The smaller guy is waving his clipboard, although the builder is communicating quite effectively that he could give neither a fuck nor a shit.

'Can't you read?' he shouts. 'Did you not see the fence?' We had obviously seen the fence as it was quite tricky to step over, but even hung-over I can spot a rhetorical question when I hear it.

'Seriously!?' I shout back. 'It looks all right.' The hangover knives are killing every English instinct I have to just apologise and walk away.

'It's dangerous,' he shouts back. Something in his body language seems to say 'pesky kids'. I look at Jon. Again he just shrugs, so we turn back and head to the car. As we pull off and take a closer look at the pier, we see the angry clipboard man and the builder walking under it. Neither one is wearing a helmet.

COLWYN BAY Victoria

Opened: 1900 (Architect: Maynall and Littlewoods)

Length at start: 316 ft (96 m)

Length now: 750 ft (229 m)

Burn baby burn? The pavilion theatre burnt down in 1922, was rebuilt the year after, then burnt down again in 1933. In 1991 vandals broke in, smashed it up, and set it alight again.

During the seventies, the Dixieland Showbar hosted gigs by Motorhead, The Damned, Siouxsie and the Banshees, Elvis Costello, Slade, The Specials, Madness, and Cockney Rejects.

Battles of ownership and restoration have involved groups called Pier Pressure and Shore Thing. Hopefully the locals' sense of humour will continue longer than the pier, which now seems unlikely to avoid demolition. The Heritage Lottery Fund has rejected bids due to lack of council support.

The town looks tired and closed. The pier itself is returning to nature, with a tree growing from its mid section. We press on.

———————

When it was first built as a jetty in 1858, the pier at Llandudno was tiny, a mere 242 feet long. It was pretty much a cash-in on the rail connections that had just been opened in the town and a fuck you to the plans of a large-scale port redevelopment that was then in the works. In 1859 it was hit by the major storm that took 223 boats and as many as 800 lives that year in British coastal waters. The pier was repaired but essentially useless, as big steamers couldn't dock because it was too close to shore. Eighteen years later it was practically rebuilt and extended to its current length. And seven years later still, in 1884, it was extended again, but this time as an offshoot back towards the shore, so that it ended up having two entrances.

The car is parked halfway up the pier at its original entrance. Getting closer, the sounds of an old Irish crooner drift towards us and get louder as we approach. It's coming from a stall that seems to specialise in music that I, specifically, don't like: folk classics next to Irish ballads and obscure music-hall performers. No doubt Jon knows and stubbornly likes at least half of them. I think back to the first night on the tour bus in amicable John's garden, when he played the singing milkman or something. It stuns me for a second, because it seems so long ago, lumped together with memories of things long past.

LLANDUDNO

Opened: 1877 (Architect: James Brunlees)

Length at start: 1,234 ft (376 m)

Length now: 2,295 ft (700 m)

Burn baby burn? The pavilion was destroyed by fire in 1994 and never rebuilt.

The pavilion theatre often hosted political rallies and conferences within its vast auditorium. David Lloyd George, Oswald Mosley, Neville Chamberlain, Clement Attlee and Winston Churchill all spoke there. It's said that at the Conservative Party's conference there in 1948, a woman decided to abandon her previous career plans and enter politics. Her name: Margaret Thatcher.

Llandudno Pier is often used for filming Victorian and Edwardian seaside locations, including the 2002 update of *The Forsyte Saga* TV series.

I've been to Llandudno before, many years ago on a family day trip. About 20 of us trailed round the streets, the adults looking for a bar, unaware that pubs in Wales didn't open on Sundays.

The pier is strikingly traditional. Small shops at the entrance push those British holiday staples: country-music CDs and off-brand football tat. They should mix them up and have Kenny Rogers in a Newcastle shirt pissing over Willie Nelson. The only thing here that doesn't reek of bargain-market commerce is a bench and its plaque: 'Dave and Cath, together again.'

A small boy wants to go on a ride. 'It's closed, look,' his gran says. 'The man hasn't come, he only seems to come at weekends. Perhaps he has another job.'

'Why?'

'Better money.'

We make a detour through the arcade. I rest my hands and soon my face on an air-hockey table. The cool puff of air soothes my cracked skin.

———

'I just want to look in the town for a second,' says Midge. We've done the pier and before we make our obligatory shuffle around the town without really going into it Midge pipes up with an opinion.

'What?' says Jon, more out of surprise than irritation. Midge doesn't look up from his phone.

'I just want to go up there a bit,' he says, pointing towards the centre of town. Me and Jon shrug at each other and follow Midge as he power-walks away, head tilted more towards the phone than the busy roads or obstacles – like the numerous old people doddering around in that hunched shuffle they all seem to have.

'What are you looking for?' I ask as we follow him blindly up another street. So far Midge has been happy to go with the flow and not really have much of an opinion on anything that's decided.

'I want to check in on the Internet at the Job Centre – I've been doing it whenever we've passed one,' Midge says, trying to make sense out of the map on his phone. Behind his back, me and Jon make eye contact and squint at each other, but slowly we both realise this whole trip is just as pointless and born of the same innate male drive for completion that Midge is displaying now.

Midge finally finds it and we walk back to the car. I stop for chips despite it being only midday, knowing that I am at the point in the hangover where something needs to be in my stomach. Jon goes green when he sees them and Midge shakes his head.

'Are you not sick of chips by now?' he says.

I think for a second. 'I am, I really am.'

Then and there in my head I resolve never to eat chips again, and it lasts. For the rest of the journey.

Midge and the dole office are reminding us that we have to get him back by Monday, but we're relaxed: five piers, one more night. This is the home stretch.

The quickest way to the next pier is driving along the Marine Drive toll road. It costs £2.50 but to be on schedule for The List it's worth it. But rather than take in the five miles of glorious vistas overlooking Anglesey and Snowdonia, Midge takes it as a challenge to his driving skills. For the entire trip he's been at least ten mph behind the speed limit, much to Jon's frustration. You see Jon's foot often flooring the accelerator that isn't on the passenger side. But for some reason, when faced with a cliff-side road with sharp bends and others driving slowly to take in its famous views, Midge has decided that the only way to approach it is rally-car style along the crumbling Victorian-built road.

Around the top of the causeway, it feels like we're flying. Speed and height combined get us to Bangor in no time. Everything's going well, my head is clearing and we are able to park on the road right by the gates to the pier. The pier floats away from an Edwardian square of terraces, tall and dark stone, reassuring if not homely. We're going to have a lovely time.

There's a charge to walk the boards of Bangor Pier, but we're close to broke and we have to cheat the honesty box. It's hard to feel guilty in the warming sun, and we stretch out along the planks, which are comfortable and glowing.

Dotted, one left then one right and so on, along the pier are small huts. Painted in a dark green but mostly glass, little lost conservatories or translucent sheds. Some are closed, with posters in the windows. Some sell ice cream, and some have their doors thrown open and are inviting us in. There are people to talk to, and we know that is what we've wanted to do all along, to get chatting to the people who live the piers. The next hut we come to has a lady sitting outside. Sixty-plus but lively and dressed to impress, she engages us in conversation as we pass. She's on the Pier Committee.

'Yes, this is the Bangor that Fiddler's Dram sang about.' She shows me a clipping from a local newspaper. It has the band's singer Cathy Lesurf visiting again quite recently.

'They were making something for Radio Four.'

It's hard to overstate the folk-memory shadow that Fiddler's Dram casts over Bangor. I challenge almost anyone over the age of 30 to come here without the song playing in their head the moment they see a sign. It's a plodding folk tune from the seventies, and I can see the single now: a magnolia label with the artist and title in a very apt Cooper Black. As a tune it seems to wheeze along like the coaches that would have taken us on day trips, the accordion winding up and then down again. It's a perfect day out: community singing, flirting, the seaside, and all reasonably priced – the original sun, sea, sand and cider. It was played at every family party I went to for all of the eighties and nineties, when it prompted reeling around the living-room carpet, everybody linking arms and smiling. Rumour has it that it was really written about a trip to Rhyl, but that wouldn't scan. I love it and promise to listen to the programme next week.

BANGOR Garth

Opened: 1896 (Architect: J. J. Webster)

Length at start: 1,550 ft (472 m)

Length now: 1,500 ft (457 m)

Burn baby burn? A cargo steamer hit it in 1914.

It's the oldest surviving pier in Wales and used to be home to a one-legged high-dive act. The City Council bought the pier for 1p in 1974, but remain short of the necessary funds to restore it.

By the time we get to Bangor Pier the hangover is changing levels, from 'shock and awe' to 'tactical targeting'. The headache carpets the concentration and emotion centres in my head and makes everything seem like a massive effort that ultimately wasn't worth doing once it is done. As we get near the gate two kids walk through past the 'voluntary contributions' stand as an older couple leave. They notice the two lads haven't voluntarily contributed so catch them up and give them what I immediately recognise as a stern talking to. So far we've passed these stands with varying degrees of seriousness, more often than not Jon paying the full amount for us, more I suspect out of karmic superstition than obligation. The wind is brisk on the pier, which stretches out straight ahead with small pagoda huts dotted along the sides. The first of these houses an information office. Midge, eager to talk to people who are not us, walks in and starts a conversation. Jon wobbles in, hand on notebook. I ask my brain for permission to go in and join in speaking to the lady. My brain looks in the hut and sees the lady holding up a tea towel to Jon and Midge. Permission denied, soldier: stand in the cold.

Not soon enough Midge comes bounding out followed by a shuffling Jon. The wind chill is making it uncomfortable to stand around and I just want to be in my nest in the back of the piermobile snoozing along country roads. The next hut contains a gift shop, which sells fridge magnets, tea towels and interesting shells glued together. I follow them in to get out of the cold. *Please don't say anything, please don't say anything, please don't say anything*. The functioning part of my brain is pushing this thought at Midge.

'What are you lads doing here?' asks the lady behind the counter.

My brain drowns out Midge's explanation because it's screaming swear words at him, trying to psychically cause him to have an aneurysm. But then I realise this is just me being a grumpy bastard. The couple are genuinely warm and interested. The bits where I drift into the conversation they are finishing each other's sentences in the way only old couples do and telling Midge and Jon about their son. I feel a bit of a prick, actually, for being so grumpy, but the older gent can see I'm being left out so comes over and talks to me directly. His face is close to mine and he touches my arm occasionally, which makes me wonder about the last time I touched another human being, apart from the blonde bear and pixie punk I share a tent with.

'You see them.' He points to a basket on the floor, kid height, filled with plastic army soldiers with a folded parachute on their back.

'Oh, I used to have one of them, you throw them and they float to the ground, right?'

The old man nods patiently and I see him smile. His face is close to mine and I can see the red capillaries across his nose and cheeks.

'We sell them for 25p, but I have to drive a couple of towns away to get them,' he says.

'You can't make much profit on that,' I reason, 'what with the drive.'

He shakes his head with pride. 'No profit at all, but sometimes we get families and you can see they're struggling. It's nice to have something they can afford to treat the kids with.' You can see he's proud and he has every right to be.

For that moment, I do not fear getting old. If I can find a wife to sit in my hut and share toys with kids on the thin end of the plank then my future has no terror. All the things you supposedly give up and lose when you age I would gladly trade for a small quarter of my own and the wisdom to truly know wealth comes from what you give.

We reach the end, where there is a bench and a shelter. Even the hoodies sitting listlessly staring across the water are smiling.

I smile too. We can see our next pier, Beaumaris, across the bay on Anglesey. Four to go. Danny opens a bottle of cider. The wheels go round.

We're about to leave the mainland for the second time. Anglesey is an island that feels old. The bridge across to it is narrow and even though it's just a hop across from Bangor it suddenly seems further away once we get there. There's something wet and leafy about the place, and the buildings are greyer and more imposing. It has a vibe that suggests autumn, suggests wet Sundays in autumn in particular.

The Isle of Anglesey is a wild old place, and one of the first Welsh names for it was Ynys Dywyll ('Dark Isle'). Once the last holdout against the invading Romans, in the right mood you can still see hooded Druids in the trees eyeing you as you drive past. You can see the stones where they worshipped and glimpse the old ways still evident in the scratches and runes in rocks that are now covered in litter and grime.

Of course the pier is closed. A renovation by the local council who now own it, which includes a widening of the original width and a small visitors centre, has turned it into a small concrete jetty. As we walk up to the metal fences a fine rain starts.

'Hey Jon – look at this,' I shout.

'What?' he shouts back.

'This seagull has caught a massive fish,' I say, gesturing down to the beach. Jon comes over.

'That's not a fish,' he says. I look over again. 'It's a flattened, plastic pop bottle.'

'Really?' I look hard.

'Yep, fish are not rock hard, flat and light blue.' Sure enough the seagull finally finds purchase on the bottle and lifts it up. It is kind of fish-shaped though.

BEAUMARIS

Opened: 1846 (Architect: Frederick Foster)

Length at start: 570 ft (174 m)

Length now: 570 ft (174 m)

Burn baby burn? The T-shaped head was destroyed in the sixties due to deterioration – as well as a drop in pleasure-boat dockings due to the popularity of 'motor buses'.

It was the docking station for *Blue Peter II*, a lifeboat funded by the 1976 BBC Blue Peter Appeal. For some, the addition of a 'grotesque' floating pontoon has spoiled the pier.

Men in hi-vis move things back and forward behind a red plastic fence. We walk up as far as we can go, and then back. I dawdle, looking at a dog trotting down the pavement. As I reach the road I nod to a guy I think I know. He says he has a place to go to nearby at Rhosneigr and he strides off, a man with the tired contentment of a job done. He deserves a rest. We're all soon to have one, as there are only three stops left and then we'll have done it. As we get back into the car, I turn to Dan in the back seat.

'Piece of piss, this was, wasn't it?'

'Yeah, but we won't tell people that.'

Midge starts to drive off, but the car doesn't. It whirrs and wheezes but doesn't catch. Fuck. He tries again. Nothing.

———————

The car makes a sound. It's a familiar sound, but it's not a welcome one. We freeze for a second, none of us quite believing it. Willing it not to make that sound again. Midge turns the key again. It's the same sound. We all sit there. The engine turns over a couple more times as Midge guns at the key.

'Midge, leave it for a minute or you'll flood it,' I say, beating Jon pretty much word for word by seconds. We sit still for a couple more beats.

'Bollocks,' says Midge.

Jon just sits there in the first stages of a panic attack. We get out of the car and Jon gets in the driving seat, his mistrust of Midge's driving skills finally manifesting itself by checking it wasn't anything Midge was doing that was causing the car not to start. He turns it over a couple more times and pops the bonnet.

Looking at the engine, Jon reaches in and twists a couple of things. Midge is standing to one side, clearly hoping it isn't something he's done.

'Do you know what you're looking for?' I ask Jon.

'Not really, was kind of hoping it was obvious,' he says.

I pause.

'Well, it's a problem with the ignition – are the spark plugs loose?'

He fiddles with something. 'No,' he says.

'Distributor cap on?'

'Yeah, how do you know so much?' he asks. I shrug. Truth is, although I couldn't point to the individual parts I'm naming, I do have a fair idea how an engine works. Having a family of people who used to build cars must have rubbed off somehow.

'It's probably just a flat battery. We've been charging our phones with the radio and a satnav on. The alternator's probably not charging it up properly between piers.'

Jon nods.

'We'll see if we can bump-start it – if we don't have the radio on or anything charging from the cigarette lighter, it'll then give the battery a chance to charge.'

'What if it doesn't?' says Jon, clearly going to the worst place in his head.

'Look mate, it's either a problem with the alternator or the battery not holding the charge.' Jon looks concerned. I wouldn't trust me either.

We could phone the AA, but we're in possibly one of the most remote places in the UK with no money and gathering clouds. Do we fancy a few hours on this featureless patch of earth only to be told that it's something terminal? I doubt the policy includes stop-offs at three piers around the coast of Wales before taking us back to Birmingham.

Midge shouts 'Ready!' out of the window, so me and Jon give the back a heave. I'm always surprised how easy it is to push a car. We push it while Midge negotiates the parking space. On the flat he guns it too early and the jerk hurts our arms.

'Not yet,' shouts Jon.

We heave once more.

'NOW!' shouts Jon, and Midge turns the engine over – it jerks, but the engine catches. All three of us cheer and quickly, so as not to break the spell, me and Jon jump into the car.

'Go, go, go,' says Jon, before our doors close.

I feel pretty inadequate suddenly. Dan and Midge knew what to do, and it was all I could do not to let myself panic. I'm not grown-up enough for this.

It's radio silence in the car. We're scared of running the battery down and scared to talk. It's a long time now since we've had anything to say to each other. Somewhere along the line I've discovered that Victoria Wood's brother has visited every pier in England and Wales, and written a book about it. I look it up on my phone: he got to 66 including Wigan. Failure piles upon failure. I curse that we didn't look this up before we left and give the whole thing up as something that had already been done.

Dark clouds loom after the Snowdonian hills and I fill with foreboding about our next stop. It will have to be before we get to Aberystwyth as we need petrol – to be paid for on my credit card. I try to beg Midge to make that stop in a built-up area, but he drags it out along tight roads. The petrol warning light is on for some time before we finally pull into an unmarked garage in the middle of nowhere.

'Do you think it'll start now?' asks Jon.

We've stopped for petrol in the green hills west of nowhere. The petrol station isn't branded and we could be pouring moonshine and sheep's piss into the engine for all we know.

'Probably, it's had an hour or so to charge,' I say.

Jon nods. I can see he's worried so I'm trying to puff up the little car knowledge I do have to reassuring levels to alleviate his fretting nature. We get in and hold our breath as Midge turns the key. The engine starts. There is no cheer.

'Do you think we should find a garage? There's got to be one close by.' It's clear Jon is worried about lasting damage to the car. Midge stares straight ahead, pretending not to be part of the decision-making process.

'We could do, mate, if you think it's worth it.' The unspoken part being 'if you think you can afford it'. Jon must be eating into his own money by now and going to the garage could cost time as well. I have no way of contributing. I'm being slightly cruel here: I know Jon isn't asking for an opinion, that he's really asking for tacit permission. It's what he wants to do, but the awkwardness of the money situation plus the guilt if there is something seriously wrong bears down on me.

'It'll be all right. It started, didn't it?' I say.

Nobody answers. Jon taps at his phone for a while.

'There's a Kwik-Fit a few miles from here, what do you think?' says Jon, showing me a map I can't see from the back. Midge says nothing. I shrug. Jon pauses for a beat and deflates...

Aberystwyth is another hour away, and nobody has said anything for the last 20 minutes. Jon unfolds his arms, reaches over and turns the stereo on. Radio 6 once again fills the car.

'That means it's not the alternator, so it's probably the battery not holding a charge,' I say lightly. Jon folds his arms and looks out the window.

The sun comes out almost on cue and it continues to cut through the canopy of trees as we drive around the top of a flooded valley. There's a sign to King Arthur's Labyrinth. It would be nice to go there, although I didn't know he'd moved this far from Glastonbury and it's bound to be just a tourist trap.

We get into Aberystwyth late, it's dark and we've yet to find the campsite. Midge, with pointed non-assistance from Jon, elects to park in an area of student houses. Occasionally bin bags have been left where someone has got the wrong day and in a couple of places you have to step around different patches of unusually coloured sick. Every September the town swells by 50 per cent as the students arrive, and like any university town it takes a while for them to settle into the allotted gaps, like sand in a jar of stones. As Midge is deciding exactly where to park, Jon offers one piece of advice:

'Park on a hill in case we have to jump it.'

Midge turns a corner into a street with an almost vertical incline and struggles into a gap three-quarters of the way up. Without any trace of irony, Midge says, 'That all right?' I catch Jon's eye, and we both smile.

Getting a little bit lost we wander the streets of 'Aber'. It could be a Friday or Saturday night, because it seems that everybody is out at the pub. It's easy to tell the locals from the students, not just by affluence or the stubborn use of Welsh, but by attitude. It's clear the students are louder, more uncomfortable, not quite used to the personalities they decided upon on the journey here in the back of their dad's car. The locals are more tribal, stick together in groups and wince at every cheer and student whoop.

We have to reach the end of the pier via a snooker club, where you can watch football and get free hot dogs at half time. We step out of the fire door on to crosshatched metal, probably little more than a smoking area with pub-beer-garden tables. Sitting out the back by the air vents, a couple huddle as the wind rips across. They say nothing to each other and I don't think we feel right breaking the silence. A glance at the sea, and then back at the building which looks like a tatty mobile home. I jerk my head and we turn back inside.

ABERYSTWYTH Royal

Opened: 1865 (Architect: Eugenius Birch)

Length at start: 700 ft (213 m)

Length now: 300 ft (91 m)

Burn baby burn? Major storm damage, in 1872 and again in 1938 and in 2015.

Opened on Good Friday 1865, the same day as the town's railway station, it was the first pier to open in Wales. The pavilion still has plenty of amenities: a nightclub (Pier Pressure), a takeaway pizza shop, an ice-cream parlour, a snooker club and the Inn on the Pier. The inn advertises itself as 'the only 24-hour pub in Ceredigion', and on Thursday nights offers 'ALL BEERS, BOTTLES AND SPIRITS ONLY £1.50!'

The town of Aberystwyth is lit by long orange streetlamps along its front. The tide, which is fairly close to the barriers, picks up the orange and mixes it with the blacks and blues of dusk. I can pick out some people, a surf school, wringing the last drops of fun out of the end of the day's breaking waves. I imagine the satisfying, cold, wet exhaustion they must be feeling, along with the satisfaction of being part of a landscape older than language and communing with a power greater than law.

We put our coins in a Love Test machine. There's something thrilling about the way these pieces of crap haven't even had the most cursory update: they're stuck in the belief that electricity can just tell what we're like and there's been no concession to modernity, no allusions to DNA or even pH. I'm 'Wild', Danny is 'Cold', the machine is 'Wrong', and Midge 'Doesn't want a go'.

The piermobile shudders to life as we freewheel down a hill, a car coming up the road thankfully giving way. We nearly have to push the damn thing back up the other side. I'm tired and I want to go to bed.

Bed is at the Aberystwyth Holiday Village, a tarmacked, ordered kind of place just off a track from damp suburbia. All of human life is here, but really we just retreat to the warmth and electricity of the on-site social – the Asteroid Club.

At the campsite the car park is empty, but the only hill is slight and to park at the top of it our bumper needs to hang over the path to the reception building. Nobody is about so Midge writes a note explaining our situation and underlining how early we would be away in the morning. I'm dancing from foot to foot. I want to put the tent up and get into the bar that I can see is still open. Midge puts the note into the window and the very second we take a step away from the car we hear shouting:

'Oi! You can't park that there!' the thick Welsh accent softening the barked direction somewhat, but still sounding very stern.

'The battery's gone,' Midge calls up to the barmaid hanging out of the door of the club. 'We'll need to jump it tomorrow.'

'Well, you can't put it there – there's a funeral here in the morning!' she shouts before going back into the warm, as if funerals at campsites are standard practice. Too tired to argue, we push it down the hill and camp next to it.

'What are you doing?' I'm calling to Jon in the tent.

'Putting a fresh T-shirt on,' he shouts back.

'You've got fresh clothes left?'

'Yeah, one of the shirts I bought at Primark,' he says as he comes out of the tent pulling the T-shirt down.

'Mate,' I say.

'What?'

'It's the same,' I point.

'What's the same?'

'The tent on the T-shirt is exactly the same make and model as the one we've been using for two weeks.' I look again, and yes, okay the one we've been using is a bit creased around the edges from not being packed away properly, and leaning awkwardly from not being pitched with any real enthusiasm, but the tents are exactly the same. It doesn't seem much looking back, but at the time it seems almost magical. Like fate. To be perfectly honest, I think if any one of us at any point today had said 'let's just go home', we would have done. Two piers to the end or not, we would have happily sulked back onto the motorway. But, at this moment, that simple coincidence makes everything seem worth it.

A cat is incredibly curious as to what we're doing for a short while, until it realises we're putting up a tent. For a cat that lives on a campsite that surely must be a commonplace event, so he sods off into the club, throwing us a look to make sure we know where it is once we're finished.

Later, as we are retiring to bed, it joins us in the tent and looks like it's ready to spend the night until we clear it out in case it eats Midge.

———

The next morning, I try to count up the number of piers we've visited with the guys in the car on the way. We've seen a few extra – bonus piers – on the way, so it's probably approaching 60.

'Just two more to step on,' I say, to fill space.

'Well, just one if you read The List,' Danny tells us. I haven't really read The List for some time. 'Mumbles is closed for refurbishment.'

———

As I slam the boot down to trap in our kit that by now isn't packed with any sort of Tetris-style precision, more like ugly force and stubborn laziness, Jon looks over.

'Well, it's the last time we're going to have to do that,' he says.

'We?' I mumble. It's early, but with today being the last day you can tell we all want to get it over with. And we want to get out of here before the funeral arrives. Nobody needs to see that, bad juju all round, sceptic or not. Me and Jon push the thing to a jumping start and jump in the car without it having to slow down with the easy precision of a bobsled team. The car is dirty but comfortable, like sleeping in a friend's unmade bed.

Yesterday, you can tell, has exhausted us all. Jon has stopped reaching over to turn the indicators off for Midge, and Midge can't even summon the effort to mumble swear words about the other drivers. Enough piers, enough of this car, enough. But I have postcards to write.

———

Despite being closer to the end, in a way the drive to Swansea and then to Cardiff suddenly seems long. Long and depressing. The List, however, is king.

We're heading to Mumbles, near Swansea. Mumbles could have got its name from several things: the water against the rocks sounding like people mumbling, the Old Norse for 'snout' or, my favourite, in reference to a round-shaped hill, the Latin for 'breast' – although most hills are breast-shaped really, when you think about it. There's a rhyme about Mumbles which goes:

> *Mumbles is a funny place,*
> *A church without a steeple,*
> *Houses made of old ships wrecked*
> *And most peculiar people.*

When we get there, there is no real sign of any peculiar people, and the houses all actually seem to be exclusive, boringly designed apartment buildings that line the marina. Mumbles Pier was opened in 1898 and is the only pier on the whole trip we never see. The entrance is closed by massive gates for building work, and the angle of the coastline means it isn't accessible any other way. In the bathroom of an arcade near the entrance, a dad in shorts is standing at the only child's urinal, squatting his legs sideways so as not to cover his bare legs in piss. I use one of the other urinals, all of which are unoccupied. Peculiar people indeed.

MUMBLES

Opened: 1898 (Architect: W. Sutcliffe Marsh)

Length at start: 835 ft (255 m)

Length now: 835 ft (255 m)

> **Burn baby burn?** A small fire in 2012 damaged some of the decking.
>
> It was the terminus for the Swansea and Mumbles Railway, opened in 1807 as the world's first passenger railway.

I strain to look down the decking through a builders' fence, but see nothing.

A member of staff, in a sweat-stained, light-blue shirt that once matched the paint job, is bending over and resetting the Rock 'n' Roll 2p falls. It's gaping open, and the temptation is to nudge him so it all collapses, or to grab a fist full of coins – anything to make something happen here.

Nothing does, so we execute a pushed three-point turn (not for the first time, happy that Midge is small and light) and head for pier number 55.

It seems that a typical pier will go through a number of disasters, so it's kind of fitting that our last pier has weathered more than most. Penarth Pier nearly never got built in the first place when the builder went into liquidation just after construction had started. After it was finally opened in 1895, it enjoyed a period of prosperity, being included in an Arthur Atkins painting and benefiting from the building of a beautiful art-deco pavilion at its entrance. Then in 1931 a fire broke out in the pavilion, with 800 people on the pier, some of them trapped at the wrong end. A massive rescue mission was launched with local yachtsmen enlisted to help ferry the people to safety. No one was killed, but it took three days for the fire to die out.

We plod up from where we've parked the car in a state of reverie. We walk past a restaurant called The Fig Tree. I'm hit by the smell of garlic and pasta. A reminder of civilisation, home. Where food isn't just something to stop you getting light-headed when you get out of the car. Where sleep isn't something to do while we can't drive, and conversation isn't something just to interrupt the silence.

The pier comes into view and I'm surprised not to be disappointed. The art-deco pavilion is lovely even in its run-down state, perhaps because of its run-down state. My taste has always run to the somewhat gothic. We stand looking for a while. When we have reached each pier it has never been a group activity. Midge would normally have wandered off; me, enticed by the amusements, would already be looking around; and by the time I reached the deck I would normally have found Jon looking out to sea making notes. But this time is different. All three of us stand there, almost scared to go on.

PENARTH

Opened: 1895 (Architect: James and Arthur Mayoh, along with local engineer H. F. Edwards)

Length at start: 658 ft (201 m)

Length now: 658 ft (201 m)

Burn baby burn? In 1931 fire destroyed the wooden pavilion and much of the pier. In 1947 a large section was destroyed by a ship. In 1966, the paddle steamer *Bristol Queen* collided with the pier in fog, causing serious damage.

Since 2007, the pier has appeared in an ident between programmes on TV channel S4C and it was in a 2008 episode of

Doctor Who spin-off _Torchwood_. Gareth Bale was filmed playing football on the pier in 2014 for an advert.

2014 also saw the reintroduction of regular cruises around Flat Holm Island on a motorboat christened _Dame Shirley_ (as in Shirley Bassey).

The pier has a link with the RAF's 617 Squadron – the World War Two 'Dambusters' Squadron – as their squadron leader had strong family ties to the town. The pavilion observatory has been renamed the 617 Room and the 2013 reopening featured a celebratory fly-past by an RAF 'Dambusters' Tornado.

In the souvenir shop, you can buy pieces of rotting wood replaced in the 1994 restoration.

Penarth Pier has a glorious verdigris copper roof. The pavilion is about to be restored. I know this because I can see it from across the road, where we are now standing, delaying the moment when we've nothing else to aim for. I learn more about the restoration when we head into the exhibition that faces it over the prom.

The exhibition in the pier shop is nothing like that in Hastings, nor really the one at Herne Bay. This one has an Arts-Council-style, oral-history display that my eyes slide off, a model of the coming refurbishment that I don't look at, and a woman behind the counter who is resolutely not interested in the slightest that we've been to every pier in England and Wales.

Mumbles closed, Beaumaris just a wall, Penarth under threat of artless regeneration, it seems, Aberystwyth tacky in a dark way, and Bangor cute and loved. The last few piers we've been to are almost a microcosm of the whole lot. I'm sure I now look at each one through the prism of all of the others, but there are definite types: old, commercial and fading into the past; glossy and soulless; falling down; or loved and owned by the people who live and work near them. I like the last two types the most and the glossy ones not at all. If you're not going to let the weeds grow through and show life as lived then you aren't reflecting the place where you're living. If the seaside is a reflection of the country and ourselves, then it's the bits we see that aren't perfect that will feel right.

———————

We walk up and down the pier, very much numbed by the grammar of piers to really take in much detail. I get the feeling I want to do something, anything. The numbness is overwhelming and I need to shock myself into the present. Then I realise something. I've been to the seaside 50 or so times on this trip but never in the actual sea once.

———————

I stare across the water. I can see Weston – where we started an age ago – in the fuzzy way that you can see other countries over water. There's a plaque at the entrance to the pier here that commemorates someone swimming over the Bristol Channel to Weston and it feels like we should do that, or should do something more spectacular even. Overhearing a conversation on the prom about a lost dog makes me want to suggest that we should immediately drop everything to find it, and then go find all the lost dogs in the country. I don't mention this right now. Give it a week or two.

———————

The beach consists of pebbles. Smooth, cold stones shock the soles of my feet as I struggle to keep my balance. I'm mentally steeling myself for how cold it's going to be, but even then, as the first wave hits my legs, I'm shocked. Quickly I wade in till my shoulders are submerged and I have trouble breathing for the first minute or two. And, despite not wanting to put it off, it still takes me a minute or so more to dunk my head completely under the water. I take a breath, then my world is cold and salt. I feel it all go, the stress, the planning, the awkwardness. It feels like an age but my head is probably only under the water a few seconds. It doesn't matter.

After 55 piers plus some we didn't intend, after 12 days and 11 nights, after tents and beds, after many pubs, but mostly after hour after hour of that bloody car and its smell, it's done. What now?

A kid on the beach sits with an acoustic guitar, bare back against the sea wall. I think I catch him singing: 'You can go your own way.'

We have but one way to go, and only one method to take. It starts with a push.

CHAPTER FOURTEEN

BRUMMING ON EMPTY

Polly Harvey asks us to take her back to beautiful England. The car is subdued, there's no place or opportunity to celebrate, just a two-hour schlep back in a vehicle that isn't fit to make scenic stops. I want a drink so badly, but can't as I'll have to drive once Midge has got us back. I'm already worrying about how to start it again if it stops. At the moment it's going at least, going through backwoods A-roads: 'more interesting,' says the driver.

We get onto the M5 eventually and straight away see a sign that tells us there are delays from Junction Seven to Junction Five. I calculate that this will bring us back into Birmingham in time for rush hour. That doesn't happen, as soon afterwards we hit traffic around Worcester. That's a metaphor for returning to civilisation if ever there was one: three lanes of static, with cars slowly drifting across lanes near any junction. Next to us, as I stare blankly out of the window, is a battered white minibus with a work gang in it. They aren't talking either, though I suspect that's through tiredness rather than this hollow feeling I'm consumed by.

I'm not sure what I'm going back to. We've proved it can be done – not that anyone really cared enough to doubt us.

The bit I'm looking forward to is that hour or so before sleep when food doesn't taste right at home, when you want comfort, but everything's just off. A broken-down car sits on the hard shoulder, and the family is now sitting in the sun on the embankment with their golden retriever. I point and we sing a song for the last time.

Eventually we get back, drop Midge off at the house he shares with his dad. He leaves the engine running as we swap seats, shifting equipment and Danny about for the next bit of the drive. We wave Midge off. He's a terrible driver, but a very good man. We love him. Twelve days with barely more than six feet between the three of us, there's a lasting bond created here. With tears and a hug I drop Danny off too – door open, car chugging, keys in the ignition – and I've probably never felt more alone.

Later, I lie alone in bed: too hot to move, sweat droplets forming on my widow's peak and I contemplate what I'm going to do next. I haven't a clue. I'm not sure how this ends.

I often think back to the trip. What was it? I mean it certainly wasn't a holiday, but, even though it was hard at times, it wasn't work either. It was something we needed to do. A pilgrimage. Something our souls wouldn't have forgiven us for if we hadn't done it.

So who or what in our pilgrimage was the God we were trying to get closer to? I once heard a theory that the reason that we evolved the way we did, relatively hairless, with chamber lungs and the ability to float from the moment of our birth, is because we are descendants of the monkeys that met the sea. That branch of the ancestral tree settling near water. Now, I'm sure there are a hundred reasons why this is total horse shit, but it does explain one thing that nothing else does: our deep and utter connection to the sea. It never got old, that excitement of seeing the sea after a short time driving inland. Despite following the coast we still would race to be the first to spot it. And, when we got to the piers, the majority of time was spent just looking out to the horizon.

Piers are nothing if not adaptable. The ones that survive are the ones that can anticipate the needs and whims of the public. Be it in the terrible lowest-common-denominator way of Blackpool or the simplicity of Boscombe. Personally, I think the only reason piers exist is so humans can go out and collect themselves and connect to the deep, unknowable entity that is the sea. Of all the things that they offer, the piers that endure are the ones that are about this connection. Pier fishing, deckchairs, bars and restaurants offer not much more than a chance to sit and commune with something bigger than ourselves.

Like all pilgrims, the clothes we wore were modest and imbued with meaning. We deprived ourselves of food and suffered on the crucifix of our own excesses. And at the end we're changed.

———————

A story isn't just what happens while it's happening. A book of a trip isn't a record of what you did in the time you were living it – it's a record of all the living you did up to that point and maybe even more so the life you lived while writing it. Everything changes.

I'm sitting on a boat on the Adriatic, the sun blazing red low in the sky. Contrails crack the hazy cloud cover like the scorched earth a little way inland. I'm looking over the intensely clear water for the promised dolphins. I'm on honeymoon, with my Guinevere, but I'm scribbling these notes into a notebook identical to the one I had on the trip. Not everything changes.

It's now getting on for two years since we first started planning Pier Review and my view of life is very different. I've moved to the countryside, Danny moved to the coast. Midge remained in Birmingham, which is good for the city as we were worried that, like the ravens at the Tower of London, the kingdom would fall without him. Not everything changes.

So what has changed? I'm not telling you right now, except that the Clio destroyed itself as I sped down the M40 about a year ago.

But England, Wales, Britain, whatever, that does change: it evolves. And bound up in that are the echoes of how we see it. The edges of culture are important, and the edges of the landmass are too. Where we touch something we can't understand, the sea, where we can look out and away, in the spaces where we get space to think – that's where the evolution happens.

Our country, like a story, doesn't exist without its future as well as its past.

ACKNOWLEDGEMENTS

Danny and Jon would like to thank all those who have expressed belief in this adventure and the resulting book. That includes Harry Vale, Margaret and Richard Moorhouse, Pete Ashton (who also refused to come along to take photos), Ben Whitehouse, Laura McDermott, Brian Simpson, Julia Higginbottom, Louise Carrier and Mark Hill, all of whom backed the original crowdfunding bid, getting us on the road.

Our gratitude also goes to everyone who read early drafts and offered advice, puns, or spotted huge embarrassing mistakes, especially Julia Gilbert, Gavin Wray, Jon Hickman and Mat Atkins. We didn't notice missing an entire pier out on the south coast or that we doubled back on ourselves to get it. We didn't notice doing it, nor after when writing about it, nor even when editing: in fact if it wasn't for our agent Joanna Swainson we'd still be thinking 'Blimey, all these roads around Herne Bay look the same.' For that, and every other bit of valuable advice and help, and for believing that this was worth it, Joanna, thank you.

Jon would like to thank Libby, Poppy and Fritz for all things, including company, advice on Danny's feminism, helping us find out which bits just didn't work, warming the settee and not sitting on the keyboard quite as much as you would have liked.

Danny would like to thank his Mom, Dad, Craig and Caroline for their kind support, and anyone who has had to put up with him banging on about the book. He would like to dedicate this book to his Nan, who will never get to read it, but is proud of him anyway.

And of course we both would like to thank Midge, without whom, if we'd made the trip at all, we'd have probably done it at higher speed. You're a lovely man.

Have you enjoyed this book?
If so, why not write a review on your favourite website?

If you're interested in finding out more about our books,
find us on Facebook at **Summersdale Publishers** and follow us
on Twitter at **@Summersdale**.

Thanks very much for buying this Summersdale book.

www.summersdale.com